Unraveling the Wrongful Conviction

This book lays out the author's proven approach to investigating and assessing a defendant's claim of innocence whether pre-trial or post-conviction. The author weaves his 35 years of experience into a simple step-by-step process, showing the reader how to objectively investigate a wrongful conviction. He uses his case histories to describe an alternative to the "trial and error" methods so often used. As a result, this book offers a methodical and repeatable approach to assessing and investigating a defendant's claim of innocence. The book refers to the actual investigations, which led to dozens of exonerations, prison releases, acquittals, and dismissed charges in Murder I cases.

Claims of innocence may be common, but knowledge of an objective way to assess those claims is hardly universal. This book was written for the classroom and the field. It is essential reading for the student, the Innocence Project volunteer, practitioner, or anyone interested in correcting a wrongful conviction or avoiding the next false conviction.

Daniel Grothaus is a former journalist and investigative reporter, who became a criminal defense investigator, working mainly on capital murder cases. He helped develop innocence claims resulting in 15 exonerations/ prison releases; six acquittals at trial; and the dismissal of nine capital murder charges pre-trial. Grothaus previously worked as a reporter with the *Houston Chronicle* and the *Houston Post*, after earning his Bachelor of Journalism degree from the University of Missouri. While still working in print, Grothaus wrote and produced an hour-long documentary on pedophiles, *Child At Risk*, for the Houston PBS Station, KUHT. That documentary was awarded a National Emmy in 1986.

"Dan Grothaus is the investigator who convinced me that trained journalists make the best criminal case investigators. I have worked with him in several exoneration cases, and he brings an investigative reporter's curiosity, research, interview skills, and human compassion to the work. I still use his "Murder Memo" approach when I teach law students how to organize data in a criminal case file. The excerpts of his book that I read are well written and reminiscent of my experiences working with Dan. I teach a law school course on Fundamentals of Investigation, and I teach law school clinics. This book will be a valuable resource for clinical instructors whose work involves investigation of any kind, including civil, criminal, or family law clinics."

Sean D. O'Brien, *Curator's Distinguished Professor, UMKC School of Law*

"The author, Dan Grothaus, is unquestionably one of the nation's leading post-conviction investigators of wrongful convictions. I know this first-hand because I have worked with Dan on a few such projects. He is equally adept at spotting a convicted innocent person through a thorough evaluation of the case's usually voluminous historical record; then constructing an investigative plan from scratch from that record; and finally putting into action that plan by conducting a successful investigation that in the end produces the desired result—the unearthing of new evidence that will be instrumental in freeing the falsely imprisoned inmate. His book, *Unravelling the Wrongful Conviction*, which spells out step-by-step how to undo the Gordian knot of a false conviction is a ground-breaking classic which should be at the ready by all those investigators, lay or professional, and lawyers alike, who are engaged in such a noble enterprise."

Jim McCloskey, *Founder and Director of Centurion Ministries (responsible for 70+ prison releases)/Co-Author of When Truth is All You Have and Co-Author (with John Grisham) of Framed.*

"As a journalist investigating wrongful convictions, and as founder of the Midwest Innocence Project, I learned that the painstaking process unfolds better when lawyers collaborate with trained reporters who have become licensed private investigators. Dan Grothaus long ago set the standard for those skilled journalists with PI licenses. This book will become invaluable."

Steve Weinberg, *Professor Emeritus, University of Missouri School of Journalism http://www.steveweinbergauthor.com*

"We've learned so much about wrongful convictions in recent decades. But the lessons Dan Grothaus imparts strike me as particularly valuable because he shows the simple yet essential skills every cop, prosecutor, and defense lawyer should use to guard against the next wrongful conviction. With a journalist's eye for a compelling story and a nose for detail, Grothaus leaves us with a haunting realization: that if such basic oversights can be found with intensive scrutiny, how many unjust convictions—especially those outside of the most heinous homicides, which get the most attention—remain hidden in plain sight?"

Mark Obbie, *Member/director of the Criminal Justice Journalists, former Associate Professor at Syracuse University, and current freelance journalist. Originally a lowly cop shop reporter in Houston with author Dan Grothaus.*

"Dan Grothaus not only took my call from prison, but he knew what to do when I called. He knew what questions to ask, he knew what actions to take, and he knew the order it had to be done. This book shows there are no short-cuts to establishing actual innocence, and if the wrong approach is taken, an individual may unnecessarily spend more years in prison. Throughout my actual experience and after reading this book, I've learned to trust Dan Grothaus' process. If you are reading this book, I feel confident that you will too!"

Ricky Kidd, *2019 Exoneree*

"This is a must-read book for anyone involved in the criminal justice system – or who just wants to know more about it –, written in the no nonsense, "street" language of a veteran private investigator whose stories sound right out of a "Dateline" episode. Dan and I started our careers together as police reporters in early 1980s Houston, when the city was experiencing an all-time high in homicides and we were racing from one bloody crime scene to another. Dan went on to a career defending the innocent and in this book sets out how he proved the innocence of so many wrongfully convicted – and how other investigators, if they follow his tips, can do so too."

Jim Carlton, *Current staff writer with the Wall Street Journal and author of Apple, who started out as a lowly cop shop reporter in Houston with author Dan Grothaus.*

"Thirty years ago, I joined the Capital Trial office in Kansas City. It was in this same time frame I met Dan Grothaus. In a capital case the core team includes capital counsel, the mitigation specialist and a fact investigator. In my experience, Dan was the BEST fact investigator in a capital case. He understood the mission and was a good partner. What I remember most about those years was Dan's advocacy for our clients. His advocacy was to the team, and he sometimes found that he was the lone voice for the innocent client. Dan was often the one who identified the red flags in our cases, and he pushed us to work harder and smarter. In the US, 1 out every 9 people condemned to death row is innocent. Therefore, it was critical to have Dan in the mix, because he followed the facts and then he looked under those facts. Capital teams were better with Dan on the team. He saved many of our clients by working diligently and asking the hard questions, listening to the client and tracking down every lead. This book should be read by anyone working in the criminal justice system, especially those doing capital work."

Cyndy Short, *Former Missouri Public Defender, recipient of numerous awards in criminal defense work, longtime faculty member at the Trial Lawyers College, currently a Mitigation Specialist, Sentencing Advocate and Trial Attorney in Kansas City.*

Unraveling the Wrongful Conviction

A Guide for Analyzing Innocence Claims

Daniel Grothaus

Routledge
Taylor & Francis Group
NEW YORK AND LONDON

Designed cover image: Getty Images

First published 2026
by Routledge
605 Third Avenue, New York, NY 10158

and by Routledge
4 Park Square, Milton Park, Abingdon, Oxon, OX14 4RN

Routledge is an imprint of the Taylor & Francis Group, an informa business

Library of Congress Cataloging-in-Publication Data
Names: Grothaus, Daniel author
Title: Unraveling the wrongful conviction : a guide for analyzing innocence claims / Daniel Grothaus.
Description: Abingdon, Oxon [UK] ; New York, NY : Routledge, 2025. | Includes bibliographical references and index.
Identifiers: LCCN 2025011082 (print) | LCCN 2025011083 (ebook) | ISBN 9781032895321 hardback | ISBN 9781032895314 paperback | ISBN 9781003543299 ebook
Subjects: LCSH: Judicial error | Murder--Investigation | Presumption of innocence | False imprisonment--Law and legislation | Writ of error coram nobis | Criminal justice, Administration of
Classification: LCC K5560 .G76 2025 (print) | LCC K5560 (ebook) | DDC 345.764/02523--dc23/eng/20250313
LC record available at https://lccn.loc.gov/2025011082
LC ebook record available at https://lccn.loc.gov/2025011083

ISBN: 9781032895321 (hbk)
ISBN: 9781032895314 (pbk)
ISBN: 9781003543299 (ebk)

DOI: 10.4324/9781003543299

Typeset in Sabon
by KnowledgeWorks Global Ltd.

This book is dedicated to my brother, Robert John Grothaus II, KIA May 14, 1968, in South Vietnam. Rob was posthumously awarded the Bronze Star with the "V" for valor. Through his life and his death, Rob showed me how to be fearless.

And a special thank you to Dorothy P.

Contents

Disclaimer

In this book, I discuss several actual cases of criminal convictions and proven wrongful convictions. This is not a "tell-all" book. This book is intended to be an instructional guide to understanding how innocent people have been convicted and how I have learned to recognize a wrongful conviction and, if possible, prove innocence.

Each of these cases was newsworthy at the time, as were the legal challenges and appeals to these convictions. My discussions contain some work product from some cases, used with permission, and some fictionalized work product from other cases in which I had first-hand involvement. Often, my investigative work became part of the public records filed with the courts. Affidavits used in this book were first filed with the courts.

While providing the reader with a realistic look at these cases and my approach, I have made every effort to avoid infringing on any privacy, or ethical or legal privilege concerns.

DJG

Preface: Why I Do This

This frail woman opened her front door timidly. She was about 70 years old, very pale with long dirty, yellow hair. She was barefoot and wore only a thin, sleeveless, sheer nightgown at three in the afternoon. Glancing past her, I saw piles of newspapers stacked on the floor, filling the front room. Beyond the stacks of faded paper, I saw in the back room a large German Shepherd dog lying on a bed, his tail flapping wildly. Then the stench hit me.

Twelve years earlier, a woman named Wilma Amos had testified in the capital murder trial of *Texas v. Gary Graham*. The defendant – now convicted shooter, Gary Graham – had been charged in the 1981 robbery-homicide of Bobby Lambert in the parking lot outside a Safeway grocery store alongside the Gulf Freeway in north Houston.

Wilma had been a state's witness, supposedly an eyewitness to the shooting. But, curiously, she had not been asked at trial to identify the shooter, or if the shooter was even in the courtroom. Neither the state nor the defense asked her that question.

Court papers had identified the state's witness, Wilma Amos, with her age and address – from 1981. Police reports were not available. I could not find "Wilma Amos" in any public records or any court records in Harris County. The state had scheduled Gary Graham's execution for April 29, 1993, about three weeks away.

Before web-based databases existed, before the Internet had matured, only a few options existed when looking for a witness in a criminal case. Beyond the phone book and a source for non-published, landline phone numbers, there were voters' registration cards, marriage records, and court records. Sometimes, all you could do was visit the last known address, searching for someone in the neighborhood who knew your missing witness.

Wilma Amos was that witness.

This frail woman was that neighbor.

Wilma's old Houston neighborhood on the north side was a middle-class cul-de-sac of one-story, three-bedroom bungalows in decline. Each house had a cracked brick façade, a carport protecting clutter, and an attached garage. These were the once prosperous blue-collar neighborhoods from the previous oil boom, which had gone bust in 1984. This neighborhood could no longer be described as "neat and tidy."

Not surprisingly, the residential address used by Wilma Amos in 1981 was a vacant house, at the closed end of a cul-de-sac. Facing Wilma's former residence, a vacant house sat next door to the right and a vacant lot sat to the left. Directly across the street from Wilma's old address was the home of the frail woman and her German Shepherd.

Ignoring the stench, I introduced myself. I had reason to believe the witness, Wilma Amos, was a Black woman. Racially mixed neighborhoods were not common in Houston in the early 1980s. Wondering if I was even on the right street, I began to ask her about a former neighbor – Wilma Amos. In mid-sentence, I noticed a large black cockroach crawling up this woman's leg. I asked if she possibly knew, or remembered, a woman who might have lived across the street, by the name of Wilma Amos. "I think she might have been a black woman." Realizing my use of past tense, I corrected myself, saying, "I think she IS a black woman."

This frail woman maintained eye contact with a hollow stare. As she pondered, while holding her front door open with her raised left hand, I could see the cockroach moving beneath her flimsy nightgown, reaching her hip, still traveling north.

"Do you mean Wilma Cox?" she asked. This woman then smiled, showing good teeth. I felt good giving this poor woman any reason to smile. The cockroach continued up and out the opening of her nightgown, crawled onto the flabby bottom side of her extended left arm, then jumped to the door and disappeared around the corner into the stench.

This woman had been a friend of Wilma, only, she knew her as Wilma Cox. When she lived across the street, Wilma often went to the store for this frail woman. Wilma still visits this woman to help her out. This woman asked me if I would like Wilma's phone number. Almost speechless, I smiled, "Yes ma'am. Please."

She turned and walked into a room to the right, apparently her kitchen. She did not invite me inside but left her front door standing open. I stood frozen on her front porch. I noticed her concrete porch was cracked and had fallen away from the foundation slab. I stared at the German Shepherd lying in the back room as the dog stared back at me past the mounds of old newspaper. I noticed small piles of feces on stained papers covering the floor around the bed.

I tried to imagine what this woman's kitchen looked like and wondered how she would be able to find Wilma's phone number. In a short time, this woman returned with a thin piece of cardboard. It had a phone number written on the gray inner side of a Capt'n Crunch cereal box. I asked her if she still had Wilma's number written down somewhere in her kitchen. I made her promise me that Wilma's phone number remained somewhere in her kitchen. She said the number was on her refrigerator door. I asked her if she had family. Yes. She has two sons, one lives in Houston, the other lives in Chicago. I asked if her sons ever visit her. Oh yes, she smiled, all the time.

I drove away from this frail woman's house, realizing I never asked her name. I got what I wanted, but wondered if I should call the health department. Would that embarrass her? Would that shame her sons? I wasn't a social worker. I began thinking about Wilma Cox.

A few years earlier, I had left the *Houston Post* and my job as an investigative reporter for a brief career as a documentary producer with the local PBS station. That move led to a period of unemployment, followed by a short, stopgap career as a private investigator. This was the fifth year of that stopgap career. After turning down a job offer from the *Fort Worth Star Telegram*, I stopped looking for newspaper jobs.

The Texas Resource Center had called a few weeks earlier, asking for help on Gary Graham's case. The Center's lawyers wanted to make one last effort trying to prove Graham's innocence before he was executed on April 29. The lead attorney, Tony Haughton, a bright young attorney, had a few ideas and suggested some specific areas for me to explore. He had read the trial transcript and understood what might be done. I was still new to this business. Normally, back then, the attorney reviewed the case and gave me a list of assignments. This work was a lot like my work on the newspaper's City Desk.

Essentially, I was still following directions, interviewing witnesses, taking notes and filing reports – a general assignments reporter with a different kind of deadline.

Tony asked me to find Wilma Amos and interview her about this 1981 robbery/murder she supposedly witnessed.

I drove to the nearest Denny's on the Gulf Freeway to regroup. Sitting at the counter, I ordered apple pie and a cup of coffee. I looked at Wilma's phone number written on the back of the torn Capt'n Crunch cereal box. I wrote down her number in my notepad; then walked to the payphone next to the Men's room.

DG: May I speak to Wilma Cox?
WC: This is she.
DG: Ma'am, did you used to go by the name, Wilma Amos?
WC: Yes [laughing]. That was my married name. I don't use that name anymore. Wilma Cox is my original name.
DG: Ma'am do you remember ... is it possible ... did you testify at a murder trial many, many years ago?

WC: *Oh my, yes. Yes, I did. Oh, that gives me the chills just thinking about it.*

DG: *So, do you remember testifying in a murder trial against a man named, Gary Graham?*

WC: *I don't remember his name. But I remember testifying. I was so scared. Whatever happened to that young man they had in the courtroom?*

DG: *Well, ma'am, he was convicted.*

WC: *Oh my. Well, they had the wrong man sitting there. That was not the person who shot and killed that man at the grocery store.*

DG: *Ms. Cox, the State of Texas wants to execute that young man you saw in court. I sure would like to come over and talk to you about that.*

WC: *Oh, my dear lord....*

DG: *Would it be possible for me to come by this afternoon and talk to you?*

WC: *Well, no, not today. I have hair appointments lined up from now 'till 8. But tomorrow would be OK.*

The next day, at about 11 in the morning, I knocked on Wilma's screened porch door. Her boyfriend was asleep, sick she said, on the couch in the front room. Wilma said it was OK for us to talk in the living room, as long as we didn't get too loud. We sat on cushioned chairs across from her sleeping boyfriend.

Wilma made a living cutting hair in the back of her house.

She was about 40 years old with very dark skin, large round eyes showing lots of white and a tense smile.

I explained again that "the man she saw in the courtroom" was going to be executed by the State of Texas. I did not tell her this execution was three weeks away. I sensed that Wilma did not handle stress well.

After some small talk, I asked Wilma if she could still remember that day at the grocery store from 1981, when a man was shot and killed outside. With that, Wilma started rattling off details, facts, and bits and pieces of memory in a somewhat fluid order. She recalled mostly relevant details of that traumatic incident, without hesitation. Turns out, she not only witnessed the shooting death of Bobby Lambert in the parking lot outside the Safeway store about 9:30, the night of May 13, but she saw the shooter inside the store, at least three times, close up, in good lighting. And that shooter – she was certain – was not the man she saw in the courtroom.

Wilma offered two good reasons why she never told anyone that the wrong person was on trial for Lambert's murder. First, no one ever asked. And second, she was incredibly intimidated by the court system, the judge, the men in suits, and the men with badges and guns. Almost all of these men, coincidently, were white.

On my legal pad that day, I wrote:

Wilma 4/8/93

You were shopping. You bumped into Lambert. Glove prices.

I was in next line next to him. He finished first and walked out. I forgot something. I left about three minutes later.

Outside boy shot him. Ran right by me and my van.

I heard the gunshot as I left the store. I saw shooter in the store earlier. He was wearing dark pants and white jacket and saw him a couple of times in the store.

He walked around with a loaf of bread.

I saw him three times. At register he just lay bread down. He was behind Lambert in line.

Kid walked out behind Lambert. Kid just walked around like he was watching somebody. He made me (nervous) ... suspicious looking.

Kid left right behind Lambert.

He Lambert told me at meat counter he was in process of moving to Houston and staying with his brother until he could find a place. At a motel but was going to move in with his brother.

Lambert nice person, friendly and outgoing.

Police came to my house next day.

I went cold blank on boy's face.

Police brought photos – several sets.

Took me to a lineup. Didn't pick out.

At time never really saw Graham.

I asked police to show me suspect's pix. They said no. They showed me a set of pix said he was in there. But I didn't recognize him.

I wrote my report that night and faxed it to Tony Haughton. Two days later, Tony and I drove out to Wilma's house. We went over her recollection of the shooting and her testimony. Her version of events remained consistent. She impressed us both as being genuine and sincere.

Before his original trial, Gary Graham's defense team never contacted Wilma. (Gary Graham's defense team consisted of defense attorney Ron Mock and a part-time investigator. Ron Mock was a popular court-appointment for capital murder cases in Houston because he never contested the state's case. His work ethic practically guaranteed any capital murder trial, in which he was the appointed defense counsel, would never run over a week. Judges liked that. Ron Mock kept their court dockets running smoothly.)

During my third visit, Tony Haughton and I obtained Wilma's signature on an *affidavit*. She declared in simple language that she had witnessed the shooting of Bobby Lambert, she had seen the shooter earlier, inside the store, in good light, and Gary Graham was not the person she saw shoot and kill Bobby Lambert.

I later put this Page 1 news clip in my Gary Graham file:

[Published April 29, 1993, in the Dallas Morning News]

Austin (AP) – Gov Ann Richards on Wednesday granted a 30-day Stay of Execution for convicted killer Gary Graham seven hours before he was scheduled to die by injection.

Mr. Graham's attorneys praised the decision, saying it will give them the opportunity to present compelling evidence of Mr. Graham's innocence to the Texas Board of Pardons and Paroles.

Meanwhile, prosecutors said it was just another small delay in the tedious, 12-year journey for justice.

The case has gained nationwide attention, including a petition for clemency signed by 15,000 Californians. It has sparked almost daily ... See CONDEMNED on page 30A.

Of course, there was additional investigation done on Graham's case. Graham's alibi was formally documented. Other witnesses from the grocery store were contacted. Additional witness interviews corroborated Wilma's recall. Eventually, the Houston Police Lab confirmed that the bullet used to kill Bobby Lambert could not have come from the gun police found when they arrested Gary Graham seven days after Lambert's murder.

The homeless, 17-year-old Gary Graham was arrested several days later following a mini-crime spree, robbing several people with the same .22 handgun. One of his victims had been shot, none had been killed. He confessed to ten armed robberies (all committed after the Lambert murder) but had always maintained his innocence in Bobby Lambert's robbery/murder.

All this investigative work and the subsequent legal challenges threw Gary Graham's case into some kind of twisted legal limbo. The Texas courts would only revisit a case such as Graham's if "New Evidence" had been developed. Wilma Amos/Cox was not "new evidence" since she testified at his initial trial.

Eventually the U.S. Court of Appeals for the Fifth Circuit granted Graham relief. They noted that "there is a large body of relevant evidence that has not been presented to the state court" and recommended that the state hold an evidentiary hearing. However, the State of Texas denied Graham's request for that evidentiary hearing. The State courts claimed none of this evidence, including the affidavit signed by Wilma Amos, constituted "new evidence."

On June 22, 2000, the State of Texas executed Gary Graham, without any state judge hearing Wilma Amos describe what really happened that night at the Safeway store. Reportedly, it required five prison guards to physically remove Gary Graham from his cell, place him in shackles, and carry him to the execution chamber where he was strapped onto a gurney and injected with a lethal dose of chemicals.

In the simplest of terms, I believe the best way to undo a wrongful conviction, or prove innocence, is to ask the right witness, the right question, the right way, and then listen carefully.

The trick is identifying the "right witness," and then knowing "the right questions" to ask.

This book describes the methods I use to evaluate a case, build an investigative strategy, identify the potential "right witnesses," locate those witnesses, and then approach those witnesses the right way, with the right questions. My way is not the only way. But my way, having evolved over 30 years, has been successful more times than not.

This work is tedious. This environment is not for the timid or the ultra-sensitive. I am not suggesting that this is a "macho" job. It is not. Quite the contrary, this work requires compassion and empathy and emotional strength and balance. There is no room for ego or an easily bruised sense of self.

One must maintain a sharp focus and learn to work intelligently, diligently, and relentlessly.

I hope this helps.

Chapter 1

How Do I Start? Where Do I Start?

> **Note to Reader**
>
> Throughout this book – whether you are an observer or a participant in this system – I am speaking to you as a fact investigator for the defense. I am never speaking to you as a lawyer. I am never offering legal advice or legal direction. All my suggestions are based on my experiences, over the past 35 years, investigating more than 100 complex murder cases for the defense.

The more serious and complex crimes have life-long consequences for both the victim and the suspect – if convicted. We may debate the appropriate punishment for these most serious crimes but not the need to punish those persons who commit these life-altering crimes. Aside from society's desire to punish, there is also the community's desire to isolate the dangerous person from the rest of us, for our own safety. Who disagrees with that?

And, certainly, we all agree that an innocent person should never be convicted and punished for any crime that person did not commit.

I disagree with the public official who celebrates an exoneration with the claim, "this shows how well our system works." This is said of the system, which imprisoned the wrong person for 10, 15, maybe 20+ years. That wrongful conviction was probably based on avoidable mistakes. Mistakes consistent to some degree with an inferior investigation (by both the police and the defense), a blindly zealous prosecution, some defense counsel incompetence or indifference, a judge's reticence to intervene, and some bad luck. All, mostly preventable, human error.

A good deal of energy is devoted to the prevention of crime itself. Preventing a rape or a murder or any violation of one person by another is a worthy exercise.

DOI: 10.4324/9781003543299-1

An even greater amount of energy is devoted to the prosecution of the accused. That too, is necessary.

However, the US system of justice devotes very little effort identifying wrongful convictions, mistaken or malicious prosecutions, or reckless investigations. The checks and balances for human error within the justice system are woefully inadequate. In fact, our justice systems, represented by the states' Attorney Generals, prosecutors, and state laws, often fight tooth and nail to maintain the status quo – the original conviction.

Maybe the only way our system might learn how to reduce wrongful convictions is for all of us to continue to find even more undeniable examples of those mistakes. Maybe more exonerations will force public officials to see that the system isn't working as well as they claim.

Exonerations are not proof that the system works. That's Orwellian doublespeak. Exonerations are glaring examples of our justice system's failures.

And let's not forget the larger number of "exonerations" discounted by semantics: Confronted with overwhelming evidence of a wrongful conviction, the state will offer this innocent person a chance to plead guilty to a lesser offense for "time served." Rather than remain locked up another three years, waiting for a drawn-out re-trial, on top of a successful habeas appeal which has already lasted five years – the wrongfully convicted pleads guilty to a reduced charge – to a crime he did not commit. That plea is accepted, in exchange for his immediate freedom.

That is a sick, twisted technique that allows the state to avoid the stigma of an "exoneration." Based on the mountain of *exculpatory evidence* (evidence of innocence) a habeas team must produce to gain any relief, (i.e., a new trial) – the odds of a conviction at a second trial are remote, but not impossible. So, the state holds on to that option to retry the case, as its final leverage in protecting the status quo.

I personally saw Lloyd E. Schlup Jr., from the ground-breaking 1995 *Schlup v. Delo* case, get up from the witness chair in open court and walk into the jury room to vomit into the trash can, before coming back out and pleading guilty, under oath, to second-degree murder. His plea was in exchange for a sentence of "time served," in a case in which his attorneys had already proven his innocence in his habeas case – the appeal which led to his new trial.

Testimony in his new trial was to begin in the Pulaski County Courthouse that morning on March 23, 1999. Schlup's plea allowed him to walk off of Death Row that day, even though he had an underlying sentence of life, still to serve. He was innocent of the prison stabbing which had placed him on death row. Yet, the possibility of the state still being able to convince a jury to return him to Death Row for that murder – a crime he did not commit – existed. So, after vomiting into the jury room's trash can, Schlup pled guilty to murder II. The state avoided the embarrassment of a Death Row inmate gaining an acquittal in a second trial. The state was also able to maintain the 1984 prison stabbing of Arthur Dade, as a *cleared case*.

Lemon White, in Kansas City – same thing. White was convicted in 1989 and sent to Missouri Death Row for a 1987 drug house robbery/murder in which three actors slashed the throats of three persons (two survived). Two others were convicted and sentenced, one to life without parole (LWOP) and one to 15 years. Evidence that I developed indicated White was *not* the third attacker.

We (the defense team) had identified and located whom we believed was the third attacker, residing in a federal prison cell in Michigan, convicted in a different case. The state was not interested.

A Federal Court overturned White's conviction, granting him a new trial. After a Federal Appeals Court affirmed that ruling, the state offered White a plea deal, to avoid a new trial. Rather than wait and chance a re-trial, White accepted the offer to walk off Death Row and walk out of prison, in exchange for his plea of "No Contest" to a Murder II charge on the same crime.

An exoneration of a Death Row inmate may have been front page news.

The *Kansas City Star*, on April 1, 2006, ran the headline, "Former death row inmate free after no-contest plea," on page 3 of the Metropolitan section (Section B). Exonerations are generally front page news stories. Such a plea deal makes for far less publicity, and a far less interesting news story.

More recently, Willard O'Neal, discussed later in this book, also chose a plea deal for time served.

On December 27, 2001, Willard O'Neal voluntarily met with Tulsa police and discussed the robbery/murder of Trapeze Lounge owner Bruce Chamberlain. O'Neal knew Bruce. O'Neal last visited the Trapeze Lounge on December 21, just one night before Bruce was killed, while walking to his car with the night's receipts, accompanied by the club's bouncer.

The bouncer survived the shooting and told police they had been ambushed and robbed by *two* black men wearing masks.

Ten months later, based on a third party's identification, police arrested Willard on October 30, 2002. Willard was charged, then convicted, then sent to prison, where he spent the next 17 years for a crime he did not commit.

In September of 2019, O'Neal, represented by lawyers with the Oklahoma Innocence Project, faced a protracted and risky legal battle. We had developed extensive evidence of O'Neal's innocence. The state understood its case against O'Neal was threatened with new evidence. So, the state prosecutors made what they considered a generous offer.

O'Neal, at age 52, traded his "No Contest" plea to Murder II for his immediate release and the chance to spend time with his ailing 87-year-old mother.

O'Neal was the *only assailant* charged and convicted of this crime. No co-defendant was ever identified or suspected by investigators. That is not uncommon in wrongful convictions, that the *number* of convicted assailants doesn't even match up with the *number* of assailants reported by eyewitnesses.

We developed, and were ready to present, strong evidence of O'Neal's innocence, including evidence of the two likely assailants. The state was not interested.

Undoing a wrongful conviction is difficult. It seems the law, the system, and legal reasoning work against proving innocence once a conviction is obtained.

But it can be done.

Like any problem needing a solution, the first thing to do is define the problem. Wrongful convictions are certainly problems in search of a solution. Fortunately, all criminal cases and convictions are described (i.e., defined) in writing. Literally everything is done in writing.

So, I start with the paper.

All of my work in each of my Innocence cases began long after routine appeals had been filed and denied. By then, the paper generated by these efforts often filled several Bankers' Boxes.

In these habeas cases, I seldom found original defense files organized and orderly 20 years after the crime. In most cases, it looked like the defense files were dumped out on the floor, then shoveled back into their boxes for storage.

(For the sake of clarity, I'll refer to all post-conviction casework as *habeas work*. These cases are most commonly described as "habeas cases.")

This is where I begin.

Understand, I am talking about the defendant's legal file. When a defendant is charged with a crime (Murder I, in my examples), a defense lawyer is appointed or hired.

(Depending on the state and that state's system, a Public Defender may automatically step in to represent the defendant, or a private attorney may be appointed by the court if the defendant cannot or does not hire their own counsel. Federal Court also uses a Public Defender system, supplemented by attorneys who sign up to be appointed in conflict cases, known as CJA appointments.)

As that lawyer begins representing her new client, she begins funneling paper into the client's legal file. It is expected that the entire case (from the defendant's perspective) will be represented in that file, all the way through the trial, the jury verdict, and the final judgment.

This legal file may remain in the lawyer's possession, or with the Public Defender's Office, or be placed in storage. Or it may be turned over to the defendant, or the defendant's family. I am not aware of any inmate, convicted, and sentenced to Life or Death whose legal file has ever disappeared, or been purposely destroyed. However, in the world of Wrongful Convictions, I would not be surprised to hear it has happened.

Note to Reader

Even a missing file can be overcome. Read on.

From my experience, the defendant's legal file contains: all the original charging documents, indictments, Probable Cause statements, Discovery including police and lab reports, miscellaneous investigative material obtained through motions, pre-trial motions, responses, court judgments, defense attorney notes, defense team memos, defense team investigative reports (if any were done), media news clips (sometimes), prosecutor's filings and notifications, trial witness lists, trial prep notes, jury notes, witness files, court records, trial court exhibits, and witness depositions (in some states). All of that, before any appeals are filed. (The relevance of most of these documents will be discussed later.)

An exhaustive amount of material to be sure.

In terms of sheer volume, I have seen Discovery alone, in a complex federal capital murder case, exceed 5,000 pages. The more complex the case, the more complex the investigation, and the greater volume of legal activity, all documented on paper.

In contrast, I have seen state Murder I cases with fewer than 100 pages of investigative reports (i.e., Discovery).

Discovery is legal shorthand for investigative material the prosecutor (state or federal) must turn over to the defense, early in the pre-trial phase. In layman's terms, the prosecutor must share with the defendant the investigation of the crime, and the evidence developed by that investigation which led to the criminal charge or indictment against the defendant. It is the Discovery, these investigative reports, which I hope to find somewhere inside the boxes of legal briefs and trial transcripts.

When beginning a new case, I was often invited to review the entire legal file to become familiar with the case. I lifted the box lids never knowing what I would find. Some boxes were organized. Some only appeared to be organized, and some were clearly in disarray. Truthfully, I seldom found a wrongful conviction case file I could describe as "well-organized." One reason may be due to a case file going through so many hands, as various lawyers arrange material for pre-trial prep, then trial, then standard appeals, with each set of hands and eyes, looking for different things.

Note to Reader

If you have a case, but you don't have the legal file, or you don't have Discovery, or you don't have anything but a bad feeling about someone's conviction, please read on. Later in this chapter I'll describe what to do with that scenario.

So, Again – Where Do We Start?

Good question. But, first, the better question: what are we looking for?

Note to Reader

For now, I will discuss this mess of a legal file as if it were a paper file, or a scanned equivalent in digital format. My organizing methods remain the same no matter what the media. See "Digital Discovery" at the end of this section.

This quantity of information and materials can overwhelm, whether I am looking at several boxes, or the equivalent contained on compact discs (CDs) or a thumb drive, or several gigabytes shared in the Cloud as digital – and poorly labeled – folders containing PDFs.

The material in this legal file – paper or digital – will likely include the pre-trial material mentioned earlier, plus appellate briefs, trial transcripts, more court judgments, and maybe some records or files, which don't immediately make sense. I may even find court papers from other cases which may eventually become relevant, or I later find they were simply misfiled.

Note to Reader

Before you panic, or your eyes glaze over – relax.

What you do with this material depends on your role.

As the fact investigator, you are looking specifically for Discovery – the police reports, lab reports, crime scene photos, and the Autopsy – any and all investigative reports dealing with the crime and the gathered evidence leading to the criminal charge.

You can set all legal material aside.

The more appeals filed in this case, the greater chance of duplicate Discovery items. You may find a second or third copy of police reports which may or may not be complete. In fact, each set of police reports you locate may contain different sets of reports. Some reports may be missing, compared with the other sets in the file. You will want to identify ALL of the police reports, and all lab reports found throughout the file and gather them into one folder.

If you are the attorney, you are looking for specific issues and legal claims. You have learned elsewhere (law school, I hope) what you need and where to look for your issues and claims – because you will not find any legal advice in this book.

So, if you are the fact investigator, or a lawyer or a student or individual attempting to investigate a case of innocence, you are in the right place.

I have been fortunate to work with some excellent criminal defense attorneys based in St. Louis, Kansas City, Houston, Nashville, Chicago, Little Rock, New York, and elsewhere. The best attorneys respect a good factfinder. Most of these attorneys would have also made good fact investigators. A good factfinder has that burning desire (and ability … and patience) to find out *what happened.*

Whenever I explore the possibility of innocence, I find I have two roles: investigate the crime – and – investigate the investigation. I investigate the crime, using the original police investigative reports. My focus then moves to the investigation conducted by police which led them to their suspect – now, my client. And my investigation includes the defense team's pre-trial investigation. In wrongful convictions, I generally find defense team investigations lacking, often non-existent.

These two tasks are simple, albeit tedious. Investigating the crime begins with the original police Reports. Eventually, if necessary, I learned how to expand on the original police investigation, even 20 … 30 years later. After reviewing the original police investigation of the crime, I carefully track the investigation as police "built" a case against the defendant.

With more experience, I began recognizing anomalies in an investigation, anomalies which could develop into legal defense issues. While carefully reviewing the original police investigation, I might find a reckless disregard for a fact, or a possible Brady violation, or potential prosecutorial misconduct. If I identify one of those factors, I often find indications of all three. *(Those "factors" will be discussed later.)*

And any anomalies I find (or think I find) always lead to discussions with the lawyer. The lawyer's guidance was more critical earlier in my work. Over time, I understood on my own what to look for. But it took years of evaluating cases. And it still led to a discussion with the lawyer.

So ... Let's Begin Already ...

Here is my over-arching reason why I'm slow to explain *where to begin*. Conducting these investigations requires one absolute ingredient for success – "methodical organization." Most habeas cases, when I'm asked to investigate innocence, start with a legal file in disarray. Any haphazard, rushed, or impulsive approach to a disorganized legal file is not likely to identify the problem – if a wrongful conviction even exists.

In every case of innocence I developed, the solution started with a careful review of the Discovery found somewhere inside the legal file. The ultimate answer may be found elsewhere (maybe with a witness, maybe with an object), but I always found the problem with the case (i.e., the factor leading to a wrongful conviction) somewhere in the Discovery. The same Discovery material the prosecutor shared with the pre-trial attorney. The same Discovery material stored somewhere (hopefully) inside the legal file. The question was always, where?

I have seen many a talented criminal defense team (pre-trial and habeas) stumble or fail, for lack of organization. Besides pure luck, the only common denominator I have seen with successful defense teams is the ability to organize massive amounts of information so that every scintilla of evidence – literally all relevant facts – is retrievable at any given moment.

Based on my experience, the two most common legal prongs of attack in a wrongful conviction case, besides actual innocence, are a *Brady Claim* and/or an *Ineffective Assistance of Counsel (IAC) Claim*. (See "Contributing Factors," in Chapter 4.)

In plain language, Brady Material is evidence that state or federal investigators discovered that Prosecutors failed to share. This evidence must be *exculpatory* (i.e., helpful to your client's claim of innocence). And this evidence must be *substantive*.

Trust me, I have seen many legal hairs split over the dueling definitions of "discovered" "exculpatory," and "substantive."

"Withheld Evidence" won't be listed in any "index" found in the legal file. This entire book is an exercise in conducting a methodical investigation, which *might* help a fact investigator stumble upon Brady Material. Brady Material – withheld evidence – was, by definition, hidden from the original defense team. Common examples may include, but are certainly not limited to, "misplaced" lab reports, undisclosed "lab findings," undisclosed witnesses, undisclosed "deals" offered to state witnesses, or undisclosed witness statements (i.e., police interview reports).

A gray area also exists when defining a claim of *Ineffective Assistance of Counsel (IAC)*. The description of an attorney's "trial strategy" versus his incompetence, will always be a contested issue. However, when the defense attorney makes *no effort* to investigate the crime, or the alibi, or any claim made by the defendant, that gray area may tend toward black-and-white.

In habeas cases, both Brady and IAC claims fall clearly within the scope of post-conviction, legal strategy. My habeas investigations were almost always done under the direction of the habeas attorney. Even after 30 years' experience, I will have questions about Brady Material, and what constitutes an IAC claim. Here, I often find the twisted logic of the law clashing with my objective journalism background. I always follow the attorney's direction here. But as a general rule, I attempt to discover facts and gather evidence about anything *close* to a constitutional issue. Let the lawyers assess the fine points.

For all of those reasons, when invited to help on a habeas case, I know the lead attorney is responsible for the initial step made with unpacking the legal file. However, I also know my role, the first thing for me to do: isolate the original pre-trial defense investigation and whatever might be considered original Discovery material. This includes all the investigative police reports and lab reports. Every file I pull from the legal file, I designate as either *Investigative* or *Legal*. It was also important to determine, if necessary, that all Discovery found in the file was provided, *pre*-trial – to the original defense team.

Before the habeas attorney can consider Brady Material, she needs to know what the prosecutor disclosed. Depending on the age of the case, the original defense attorney may not be able to recall what was disclosed before trial. Or, two decades later, the attorney may no longer be with us. Or she may not wish to cooperate with a habeas team trying to prove she was incompetent or ineffective.

I encountered a different complication in *Oklahoma v. Karl Fontenot*, in which the case (and legal file) had changed hands several times over the years. Different appellate attorneys had obtained and added material to the boxes. Working with Attorney Tiffany Murphy at the Oklahoma Innocence Project, we determined that appellate attorneys had obtained investigative reports from the state which the original trial attorney never received. The appellate attorney did not realize she had received Brady Material (it happens). We were eventually able to identify what Discovery material was delivered to which attorney, at what phase in the case.

Part of our "investigation of the investigation" became: "what did each attorney receive and when did he or she receive it?" Also, "what Discovery was shared, with whom, and when?" (As an aside, we later learned that no one prior to our team had thoroughly read all of the police reports.)

So, where I start – what I do first, is attempt to locate and identify all of the original Discovery Material. I am not concerned with the legal twists and turns this case may have taken – beyond the conviction itself. My job is much simpler. My role is to "investigate the crime" and then "investigate the investigation."

For that reason alone, I no longer have panic attacks when confronted with a new case containing massive amounts of paper. I know exactly what I am looking for.

Now We Begin ... Organizing the Paper

Most of these boxes or digital folders will contain large legal documents, already numbered, by page. There will be trial transcripts, Appellate briefs, Depositions – all numbered and hopefully labeled. These files represent the legal aspect of the case.

I check to make sure each of these "legal" documents is accurately labeled. I can't assume a label matches the file. Now is the best time to place Document "A-B-C" in a folder, labeled "A-B-C." I do the same with digital folders and PDFs.

If I find boxes where the paper is not divided or labeled (or digital folders full of unidentified PDFs), I identify each document and place it in a separate file, or folder. It is sometimes easiest to first isolate the lawyers' and the courts' work-product. If necessary, I identify the document, I organize, and I label: *Transcripts* (by Volume) ... *Appeals* ... *Respondent's Answer* ... *Judgments* ... *Exhibits* ... *Correspondence*. For the most part, except for Court Exhibits and Depositions, I do not consider the legal work product to be of any interest in my initial investigation. But it still needs to be organized.

If a digital file is full of random PDFs, I create broad-topic folders and organize these PDFs in generic ways. If these random PDFs are part of the criminal investigation, I create specific folders for their organization (i.e., crime scene, police reports, lab reports, photo line-ups, etc.).

I may find odd things in these boxes, like a bankruptcy, or a divorce file, or banking records, or phone records. The divorce case or the bankruptcy might list parties I do not recognize (not yet anyway). In that case, I will put all those divorce documents into one folder and mark it "Divorce: *Smith v. Jones*." If, and only if, this divorce file became relevant to my investigation, I might break it down for closer review.

Meanwhile, it is helpful just knowing this divorce file exists, and knowing where it is, just in case this divorce, or these parties, become relevant to my investigation. It also means I can move on to the next stack of paper. I do the same with any miscellaneous materials and data, which do not immediately appear relevant. I use a descriptive subject label and move on, keeping the labeling simple, but accurate and alphabet friendly.

Label: "Phone Records 816-679-5252" – (I don't know who these cell records belong to.)
Label: "Jones, Melissa – Bank Records (1998 – 2001)"

I consider the alphabet to be a great tool. I carefully choose the first word of any file or folder as a generic subject (i.e., *Phone* Records ... *Bank* Records ... *Forensic* Report ...) or, if it is evident these records are part of an individual's background investigation, I use the *last name*, *first name* of the witness/person.

Label: Grothaus, Dan – Bank Records 2004
Label: Cotter, Ed – phone records
Label: Glynn, James – Criminal History

I call this *witness-centric* organization. I've found witness-centric files and witness-centric labels to be trial-friendly, lawyer-friendly, and investigation-friendly.

All of these examples of organization apply to PDFs and digital folders. To do this right, I must open each PDF document and then label each PDF consistently, creating an alpha organization by subject or by witness.

Tedious, yes, but none of this organizing is a waste of time.

By going through the box of loose paper, or the digital folder with random PDFs, oddly labeled, or mislabeled, I force myself to go page-by-page – literally – through the entire legal file.

Not being a clairvoyant, I cannot know what's in a folder or a stack of paper, or that 47-page PDF until I physically go through that file, page-by-page.

Sometimes, I have found a missing lab report, or a handwritten note about a witness, on the third page of a four-page police interview/report. I have found relevant Discovery mixed in with legal papers. All these items would remain lost forever, without this one-time, back-to-front, top-to-bottom, beginning-to-end inspection of the defendant's legal file.

This is the first of many tasks which are simple, yet tedious.

My organizational goal, hopefully the goal of every criminal defense team, is to be able to locate the relevant witness comment or specific crime scene description or reference to a physical item, on the numbered page of a specific document – on demand. When I can ask a colleague over the phone to pull a copy of Lab Report #12 found at Bates page 258 in the Master Investigation File – that case is organized. *(Later, I will discuss the magic of Bates stamp numbers.)*

I had spent the weekend in Nashville searching for a critical witness and re-interviewing two other witnesses prior to their scheduled testimony at trial. I had been working on a capital murder conspiracy case with multiple defendants. Trial was entering its second of six weeks in US District Court. The lawyer was experiencing information overload, not uncommon, even for experienced criminal defense lawyers.

That Monday, while driving back to St Louis, the attorney texted me, clearly stressed, during a ten-minute court recess. "What was the caliber of the ammo used in the murder of Andre?"

A simple question. The lawyer needed the answer ... immediately. I'm driving 70 miles an hour down the Interstate. (I know I should have pulled over, but I was anxious to get home.)

I reached into my briefcase on the front seat, pulled out the notebook I use for interviews and found my Murder Memo. I turned to page 2 of my Murder Memo and read:

Lab Reports: The two bullets removed from victim were .38 cal bullets from .38 cartridges. They do not match either gun found in RW's possession.

Above that line (still traveling at 70 mph) I saw this entry:

Physical Evidence: Police recovered two handguns from RW's bedroom. A .357 revolver and a 9 mm semi-auto handgun.

The government was suggesting through testimony that one of the handguns recovered from the defendant's bedroom might have been the murder weapon. Not true. They couldn't be related. The attorney wanted to be positive before calling out the government for misleading the jury.

The lawyer got his answer ... immediately.

Being organized is critical.

So, even if these boxes (or digital folders), at first glance, appear to be somewhat organized, I still go through each manila folder, to confirm the document matches the label. If the file appears full of random paper (or PDFs), I'll go page-by-page, until I know exactly what is in each manila folder and I know the contents match the file label. Going page by page is the only way I will stumble across the missing fingerprint card, or the missing photo of the alternate suspect, or the missing lab report, which becomes crucial – absolutely crucial – months later. Tedious but necessary.

If I need to break up a file of random documents into several files or move those documents into a more accurately named folder – I do it, right then.

Understand at this stage of my investigation (going through boxes), I may know little, if anything, about the crime. I sure don't know enough to recognize what is or is not relevant to a defendant's innocence claim, or the state's evidence.

There is a reason for my conviction to organization. Having worked on scores of habeas cases, related to complex Murder I convictions: I wonder how many innocent men and women remain incarcerated because a piece of paper was misfiled, or mishandled, or lost, by the defense team?

Organizing and labeling that paper in those Banker's Boxes is a useful exercise. The same applies to labeling and organizing PDF files. It is the only way I can know, with certainty, what occupies each box of paper, each folder of PDFs.

As mentioned, an organized file is not my sole objective.

As I go through the files, taking inventory and organizing, I segregate all "Legal" material and place that material to the side. Depending on quantity, I may put all the legal-related files in a "Legal" box, or all of the digital legal-related-files in a "Legal" folder. It's there and will remain there for anyone following behind me who wants to research a legal matter.

I am specifically looking for the Discovery – the complete set of investigative reports, photos, diagrams, notes, etc. The police analysis of the crime, followed by the investigation (and all evidence gathered), which led to criminal charges.

Organizing the entire legal file this way, beginning-to-end, I hope to locate all police reports, the autopsy, lab reports, forensic reports, witness interviews, crime scene reports, crime scene photos, and diagrams – all the good stuff (if it's still in the legal file).

From experience, I know I may find these investigative reports in one accurately labeled folder, or I may find this material spread throughout the legal file. The legal file may contain multiple sets of police reports. Each set of police reports may be slightly different. The reasons don't matter; maybe the previous legal teams were less concerned with organization. They were only thinking about their trial, or their appeal. They sure weren't thinking about my needs 20 years into the future. So, I am not surprised if I find the police investigation broken up and spread throughout this legal file. And I may find multiple sets of police reports – and they may not be identical sets of reports.

But, for now, I am simply gathering all these investigative police and lab reports into one folder. Any report or document related to the initial investigation of the crime and the crime scene, to me, constitutes what I describe as investigative *raw data*. These initial police reports represent the closest I will get to pure, unbiased descriptions of the crime and about *what happened* – all gathered at or near the time of the crime. For that reason, finding, or creating, a complete set of the initial reports is critical.

I will discuss the way I organize these reports later. For now, I'm just interested in identifying every piece of paper related to the police investigation.

Note to Reader

You will find that Investigative reports of a major crime are created and organized differently from one Law Enforcement jurisdiction to another, and between different agencies (Municipal Police Department, State Police, Highway Patrol, FBI, etc.). But those investigative reports – however they are formatted – will generally contain the same elements of raw data about the crime and their investigation.

I identify and set aside all of these investigative reports by police and government investigators. If the lawyer wants to maintain the integrity of these boxes as they arrived from wherever, I will copy all of this investigative raw data, and set aside my copies of those reports, to organize later. That way, the original legal file can remain intact – for whatever reason.

Other raw data which I hope to find in the legal file includes any investigative work conducted pre-trial by the defense team, or by any fact investigation done post-trial in other habeas work.

The original defense attorney may have interviewed some witnesses, maybe alibi witnesses, maybe fact witnesses. I have found this work-product often overlooked by subsequent habeas teams. I don't know why. I consider all witness interviews equal whether they are in a police report or a defendant's legal file. Any relevant information contained in those reports will need to be verified. But I definitely consider any defense team investigation to be part of the raw data.

I have seen, in the defendant's legal file, a collection of folders – one for each state witness. These witness folders contained all police reports, criminal history, all Discovery related to that witness. What I seldom found in those files were notes from a defense team member who may have interviewed that witness – suggesting they were never interviewed by the defense.

These original witness files may offer some insight into the original defense team's level of effort – or lack thereof.

In my cases where a wrongful conviction was confirmed, I seldom found investigative notes from the defense team. Sometimes, the defense file itself became evidence of the defense team conducting no investigation ... as in, none whatsoever.

In Mo v. Ricky Kidd, I started with no legal file or police reports. Eventually, I obtained a complete police report (discussed below) but did not obtain Kidd's legal file until several months later.

Kidd's legal file contained several witness folders, including one for Ricky's alibi witness, Monica G. On the day of the crime, Monica had spent that entire day with Ricky, from morning through late afternoon. The two ran errands and visited several third-party witnesses throughout the day.

When I pulled the defense attorney's witness file labeled: Monica [redacted]*, I found the two pages of the police report from her interview – nothing else. I found no defense team notes describing her full day of continuous, verifiable activities spent with Ricky before, during, and after the time of the double homicide. Monica later confirmed that the defense attorney never interviewed her prior to her trial testimony.*

Many of their activities that day were not contained in the police report from her police interview. Monica had told me what facts she had offered the police, which the police had left out of their report. Those missing facts corroborated Ricky's alibi. (I have found that police seldom spend time proving their primary suspect's innocence.)

So, the defense attorney relied on an inaccurate police report of Monica's full day with Ricky, in preparing for Monica's critical alibi testimony at trial. Maybe not surprisingly, Monica's testimony was not as compelling as it could be. Monica appeared nervous to the jury, since, prior to her testimony, she never discussed that day with Ricky's defense attorney.

That witness folder in Kidd's legal file – void of any attorney notes – was evidence that Kidd's attorney never spoke to her main alibi witness prior to trial.

As I continue looking through the defendant's legal file for investigative reports (i.e., Discovery), I also look for any witness depositions which may have occurred pre-trial. (At least eight states, including Missouri, allow witnesses in criminal cases to be deposed before trial. Several more states and Federal Courts may allow for a witness deposition under certain circumstances.)

A deposition is a formal interview of a prosecutor's fact witness, or an investigator, or an expert witness who will be testifying for the state. Both the state and the defendant are represented by counsel and allowed to question the witness. The witness is placed under oath and legally bound to be truthful (unlike a police interview). A court reporter records the spoken word, and a transcript is made creating an official record available prior to trial.

I consider a formal deposition, similar to police reports – as investigative raw data, but unique for several reasons.

Prior to this deposition, the investigation has been completed, and the defendant has been charged. The prosecutor may coach these witnesses before the defense attorney's deposition. The witness has had sufficient time to think about his or her narrative. Regardless, a deposition offers an accurate record of their narrative – which can be a big improvement over police reports.

More About Organization and Organizing ...

Regardless of the legal file's organization, or complete disarray, this file is not the crime scene. Any cluttered mess I find does not need to be preserved. If necessary, I'll take a photo of the dire disorder and get to work – starting at one end of the box going page by page, if necessary.

My job as the fact-investigator is to organize the Discovery I do find, so I can investigate the investigation and investigate the crime, not preserve the status quo. This chaotic mess may be what led to the wrongful conviction I've been asked to review.

If I find raw data from the original investigation scattered throughout the boxes (and PDF files), I methodically pull and gather all of the police reports, crime scene reports, and lab reports, and put them into their unique piles. (While doing this, I also attempt to identify duplicate copies of reports, which I am sure to find.)

My goal is first, find, then, second, assemble all paper (or PDF reports) related to the investigation, all police reports, lab reports, all forensic analysis, witness interviews, etc. into one folder.

Once I have isolated and assembled all investigative reports comprising the raw data, I separate these reports into their natural categories (i.e., Initial Police Reports, Crime Scene Investigation, Police Interviews (Reports), Autopsy Report, Crime Lab/Forensic Reports, Depositions, Witness Records (provided in Discovery)).

At this point, I have a choice. I can create my Master Copy of Discovery now, or I can complete the next and last step of organization described in Chapter 2. It will probably depend on the volume of material, and the patience of the defense team.

If now is the time, then, once I am sure I have found every scrap of paper (or random PDF) representing the available Discovery found in the legal file, I declare this to be my *Master Copy of Discovery*. I understand that the police reports – at this stage – don't need to be in a specific order. I may still have some duplicate reports in my Master Copy, but I have tried to identify and discard duplicate reports. And I believe, for now, I have only one set of the original police reports.

This Master Copy is ready to be "*Bates stamped.*" Bates-stamping a Master Copy of Discovery is simply jargon for using a numbering system to paginate this Master File. (A 'Bates stamp' is an automatic sequential numbering device used by courts and paralegals – in layman's terms, it creates page numbers.[1])

To me, this is a crucial step in organization – creating a Bates stamp of the Master File numbers 0001–???? – and then set that Master File on the shelf. Now, everyone involved in this case can obtain a copy (or PDF) of the Bates-numbered Master File, and break up this raw data, and organize it however they want, to do their job. Now, with this Bates-stamped Master File of Discovery, any attorney, or paralegal, or factfinder can ask a question about a witness interview, or a lab report, or a piece of physical evidence, by referring to "Bates #00395." That is the essence of "being on the same page."

If new Discovery is located, or later added to the existing Discovery, it can simply be added to the Master File, with Bates numbers continuing in sequence.

Now, please allow me to add one more caveat – based on my experience. I have opened more than one legal file to find the Discovery, the bulk of the investigative reports, or maybe just the police investigative file, already Bates-stamped. Great. Like finding a deck of cards at a lake house, how do I know all 52 cards are there?

I must go page-by-page, making sure no pages are missing. Sometimes, the missing pages (and I always found some) were located elsewhere in the legal file. If the missing pages were not located in the legal file, those pages became relevant to my "investigation of the investigation."

I believe most current copy machines, as well as scanners, will create Bates numbers on paper documents and scanned PDFs. Before that technology existed, I bought a manual Bates stamp to use on my Master Copy of Discovery in Ricky Kidd's case. That was the most expedient at the time. Another simple, yet tedious, task.

1 Thank the patent holder, Edwin G. Bates (c. 1890s), for the awkward legal jargon, "Bates stamp" (versus "Bate stamp") used to describe his manual stamping machine for sequential numbering.

This Master File of Discovery may include several easily defined categories (police reports, lab reports, depositions, cellphone records). When Bates-stamping, I have used the simple numbering system of "00001" to the end – maybe "00537." I have personalized my Bates stamp with my initials or initials for the organization who hired me: "DJG 0001" or "OIP 000732." I have used the alphabet, breaking large amounts of Discovery into smaller categories, using: "A 0001" then "B 0001," and so on. The latter method may help me distinguish between, and keep track of, 1,000 pages of police reports, 250 pages of lab reports, and 500 pages of depositions. Or, using Bates numbers 00001–01750, I accomplish the same thing. The volume shouldn't matter. After I have Bates-stamped a Master File of Discovery, anyone can find #649 – the forensic report describing the caliber of the murder weapon.

Missing Police Reports? No Legal File? No Worries ...

The Open Records Request

I understand that all wrongful conviction assessments don't start with a Banker's Box filled with legal case material and Discovery. Some cases just come with a bad feeling or a plea for help, like this one from a young man convicted of a brutal double homicide in Kansas City (Figure 1.1).

Ricky Kidd had provided me with a written summary of his case. He spelled out the reasons he believed were behind his wrongful conviction. He thought his summary would be enough of a road map for me to prove his innocence. Only it wasn't.

When I asked to review the police reports, Ricky sent me a few reports, explaining that he had discarded those he did not find relevant in proving his innocence.

Note to Reader

Years later, Ricky understood and appreciated why review of the complete police investigation was critical to learning what happened before, during, and after the double homicide – a crime Ricky was not involved in whatsoever. Once I obtained the entire police report, I was able to see clearly where the investigation stopped being fact-based and started being agenda driven.

Ricky Kidd 528343 6C-109
Southeast Correctional Center
300 E. Pedro Simmons Dr.
Charleston, MO 63834

February 17, 2005

Dan Grothaus
Grothaus Investigations
600 West 61st Street Terrace
Kansas City, MO 64069

RE: My Wrongful Conviction

Dear Dan:
I'm writing today regarding acquiring your services. As I'm sure you recall, we had made contact some time ago and a little work was done in preparation for my case. Phillip Gibson came aboard, we thought financial resources would come from elsewhere, unfortunately, that turned out not to be the case. My financial situation has been at its worse over the past year or so. A host of obstacles stood before me trying to get the smallest of work done. [redacted] Are objective is to touch bases with you, as to the direction we would like to go with my case. And of course, that would consist of talking services fees. While understanding you must be paid for your services, it's important for me to know specific amounts, as for me to focus in on exactly what need to be done to acquire the amounts. I would also need to know specifically what the service fees would get me.

[redacted]

Figure 1.1 Ricky Kidd's first letter to Dan Grothaus, requesting help proving he was wrongfully convicted *(Continued)* [redacted] Given that Phil is not my attorney anymore, positive results in contacting [redacted] would serve as an influence for another attorney to take on the case pro bono. So as you can see, locating and contacting [redacted] [redacted], with positive results, will prove very valuable for varies of reasons. Mr. [redacted] is also the only witness in my case who identified me. The break through of having him recant or admit he was giving a deal, or enlighten us to the surroundings of his identification would dramatically change the full scope of my case.

[redacted] Together we can fight for justice and make a difference. I look forward in working with you. Talk to you soon.

Sincerely,

Ricky Kidd

Figure 1.1 (Continued)

Ricky's case was not the only case I started without a legal file and only a few police reports.

Sometimes, if I'm lucky enough to start with a legal file, I can only hope to find the full set of Discovery sent to the initial trial lawyer. Looking at the condition of the file, I'll make a judgment call on whether it appears I have the original Discovery – or, if I'll need to be resourceful. I have started cases where the previous defense attorney misplaced the entire police report. I have looked through a legal file and seen that someone had taken the original Discovery apart. The file's condition left me wondering if all the police reports had been returned to the file.

(Understand the problem with incomplete or missing reports may be a dated issue. The cases I have worked c. 1980s and 1990s were all paper cases. Later on, maybe by 2000, Discovery was often delivered in digital formats, a PDF of the entire police report with lab reports etc. was not so easily misplaced, or broken apart.)

So, whatever the reason a defendant has no Discovery, or no legal file to share – just a compelling claim of innocence – no worries.

All states have some type of Open Records Law. Most (maybe all) of these state laws were patterned after the Federal law known as the Freedom of Information Act (FOIA). These state laws allow private citizens to make an Open Records request for government records, generally considered to be public records.

In general, an *open public record* is any record created by local, state, or federal public employees, with the use of public tax dollars. That was the theory anyway. Then our state legislators began adding exceptions and exemptions.

The police and lab reports describing the investigation of a crime, which led to a conviction in open court, are public records. Investigative reports pertaining to an "ongoing criminal investigation" are almost always excluded and considered an *exception* to the Open Records Laws (i.e., making those reports "Closed" Public Records).

However, once the investigation is completed – once a conviction is obtained in open court – the investigation is closed (i.e., no longer "ongoing"). Those police reports, pertaining to that crime, which was funded by citizens' tax dollars, generally become available as a Public Record.

Jurisdiction to Jurisdiction, Open Records requests may still be challenged – or simply ignored. Open Records requests for police investigations in closed cases are sometimes contested. (The Texas Attorney General once argued – successfully – that their investigation of a murder resulting in a conviction and the Death Penalty remained "ongoing" until the *final disposition*, meaning, the execution.)

I have read the Open Records statutes in several states. It's also necessary to read the "definitions" of these Open Records and understand what that state's law considers "exceptions." The state laws will spell out the necessary protocol for filing an Open Records request, what costs may be involved, and a process for appealing a rejected request. (I always start first with the Law Enforcement Agency itself, their records clerk, or their website, for information on how to request a police report or Open Record.)

Generally, these "public records" belong to the department or agency which created the records (i.e., the Municipal Police Department, the State Police Agency, the County Sheriff's Dept. the FBI, etc.). The records request must be addressed to the "Custodian of Records," or "Records Custodian" of that agency or department – the agency which initially created the record.

In a multi-agency investigation, sometimes the main department – say, the Kansas City Missouri (Mo) Police Dept. – will provide investigative reports (of the same crime) conducted by the Jackson County Sheriff's Dept. or the Missouri State Highway Patrol. Be aware that, sometimes, an Open Records request will need to be sent to each and every agency involved in the investigation of a single crime.

In some jurisdictions, I have had success sending my Open Records request for a criminal investigation to the state's prosecutor. Their office then provided me with the Police and lab reports they used to gain their conviction. Understand, the prosecutor's office will only send the police reports in their possession – the police reports the prosecutor received from the police.

In different cases, in different states, I have made Open Records requests to both the prosecutor and the investigating police agency. In those cases, I received two different sets of police reports from the prosecutor and the police agency, based on the same Open Records request.

I have found different jurisdictions within the same state (obviously looking at the same Open Records Law), holding two distinctly different opinions of their legal obligation as to what was, or was not, an Open Record.

As a journalist, I learned to be creative and obtain my Open Records any way I could – through the front door, the back door, the side window. I learned to ask, and be grateful whenever I got a positive response.

As both a journalist and a criminal defense investigator, I always took the time to identify the Records Custodian by name, and address my request to that person. That normally required one phone call. If my request was local, I also took the time to hand deliver my written Open Records request. The exception: if I am able to talk to the Records Custodian by phone and that person is expecting my written request by mail or email.

My goal was to always know who was receiving my request, and be assured that a paper trail would exist if I needed to follow-up on this request weeks later.

I realize that some, maybe many, law enforcement agencies now allow Open Records requests through their websites. I still confirm the name of the Records Custodian and determine a way to follow-up if necessary. I do that by asking two simple questions: "When should I expect a response? ... (and) ... May I call a week or two after that, if I haven't heard from you?"

I never found it helpful to pressure records clerks or suggest that they expedite my request over all others. I do believe it is professional to gain a reasonable expectation and request permission to follow-up if that expectation isn't met.

When writing a formal letter, I keep my Open Records request simple: "Pursuant to the Missouri Open Records Laws I am requesting access to, and a copy of the following police reports ..."

Figure 1.2 shows how I obtained the police and lab reports in Ricky Kidd's case.

Grothaus Investigations
301 E 63rd St.
Kansas City, MO 64113

Licensed Investigator - Missouri
Missouri Notary Public
dgrothau@swbell.net

Office 816-361-9191
Cell 816-679-5252
Fax 314-395-9214

20 April 2006

Mr Daniel J Haus
Legal Dept.
Kansas City Police Dept.
1125 Locust
Kansas City, Mo 64106

RE: Open Records Request

Dear Mr. Haus:

Pursuant to the Missouri Open Records Act (Rev Mo Statutes Chap 610), I am requesting access to and a copy of the following:

The complete investigative police file pertaining to the homicide of Oscar Bridges Jr and George A Bryant. Both men were apparently killed about 11:40 am on 2/6/96 by the same actor or actors, at Mr Bryant's residence, 7009 Monroe, Kansas City, Mo.

It is believed that your police department's investigative case file is known as KCMO PD Case Report# 96-013994.

As a result of this investigation, both defendants – Marcus D Merrill and Rickie L Kidd were convicted several years ago and sentenced to Life Without Parole.

This Open Records request includes, but is not limited to: access to, and copies of all written investigative reports, witness interviews, witness statements, lab reports, forensic reports, diagrams, audio recordings of all witness interviews and statements, video recordings of all witness interviews, witness statements, and physical lineups conducted for the purposes of witness/suspect ID, as well as (4-color) copies of all photographs used in photo line ups for the purposes of witness ID of suspects throughout the course of this investigation up to and through the final disposition of this case by way of the two criminal convictions obtained in Circuit Court.

I look forward to your response. Your time and consideration of this request is greatly appreciated. Best regards.

Sincerely,

Daniel J Grothaus

Figure 1.2 The Open Records request Dan Grothaus sent to Kansas City, Missouri, Police Dept. (KCMO PD), seeking the homicide investigation file in Kidd's case

At this point in Ricky's case, I knew a good deal about the crime and the investigation, including the KCMO PD Case#. To request any investigative report from a law enforcement agency, I will always need the basic information, so that the agency can search for and identify the correct records, before deciding whether or not they will release them as public records.

At times, I have searched newspaper archives to determine an exact date, time, and location of a homicide. I submit an Open Records request with all the identifying information I have. (Of course, I always have the name of the person convicted of the crime, so there should at least be an arrest record, which can be connected to the criminal investigation.) Exact time, date, and place (address) of the crime are important to the records clerk. Victims' names are helpful. If I think I have the correct Police Report# or CN (case number), I offer it as a possibility.

At this stage, I always assume the records clerk receiving my request will at least try to find the report, If I can just give that clerk enough information.

I also request every kind of report which may apply without getting too wordy. I never want to miss out on a record because I did not specifically request it. Nor do I want to ask for so much that the request gets ... *lost* ... (so to speak).

In response, KCMO PD provided me with 380 pages, a set of the police reports and (in-house) lab reports used to charge and later convict Ricky Kidd. I received the standard package. I never expect to get everything just because I asked for it – not the first time.

No Legal File? ...

A defendant's legal file may be easier to obtain than the police reports. Every convicted client I have worked with remembered their trial attorney's name. (Knowing anything is possible, the court docket from the inmate's conviction will also identify the trial attorney.) If that attorney is still in practice, the client needs to send a handwritten release to the attorney, asking his or her former attorney to release the defendant's entire file to whomever he indicates. The inmate may also – very prudently – ask his former attorney to instead *copy* his legal file and provide a copy to whomever. (That's what I would suggest.)

Copying a legal file may be expensive. But obtaining, then losing, a legal file is far more expensive. These legal files may contain evidence of a wrongful conviction, which is apparent only to the factfinder who agrees to "investigate the investigation."

I have never known a practicing attorney to balk at a former client's request to release or copy a client's legal file.

If the trial lawyer is retired, same approach. If the retired lawyer can be located, there is a good chance contacting the retired lawyer will lead to the defendant's legal file sitting in storage somewhere. Or the defendant's legal file may still be with the lawyers who took over the trial attorney's practice.

If a lawyer is no longer with us (deceased), I look for a former law partner, or some lawyer or legal secretary or paralegal, who may have worked with the retired/deceased lawyer. A former co-worker may know who currently controls the deceased lawyer's legal files.

If the trial lawyer was a State Public Defender, that state's Public Defender system may have a simple process to locate legal files which have been sent out for storage. Once the Public Defender's Office receives a written release, the entire legal file will be sent to whomever the defendant names.

If the trial attorney was appointed by the courts, or hired as a special public defender, that legal file may either remain with that attorney (being in private practice) or be retained by the Public Defender System. A phone call should resolve that question. I have placed written release samples on the following pages (see Figure 1.3 and 1.4).

It's my understanding that the legal ethics related to the attorney/client relationship include a *duty of care*, part of which is to maintain the client's legal file as long as it remains relevant. A life sentence, I believe, suggests a lifetime of relevance.

Note to Reader

Despite knowing the inmate's legal file may include Discovery (i.e., police and lab reports, the investigation's raw data) ... there is a chance it may not. I will always attempt to obtain both – the Public Records of the police investigation, as well as the inmate's legal file.

Digital Discovery

When I first wrote this chapter, all of my cases literally involved boxes of paper. As the 2000s marched on, technology turned our paper world into a digital world. In criminal cases, filed after 1999, the Discovery was generally delivered on a DVD, or a thumb drive.

Looking back, I now understand why habeas cases which went to trial between 1997 and 2007 may be a period of "anything goes." Some defense lawyers were slow to adapt. These lawyers refused to look at a case file on their computer and requested all Discovery and legal filings be printed out

PUBLIC DEFENDER

MISSOURI STATE PUBLIC DEFENDER SYSTEM
Director's Office
Woodrail Centre
1000 West Nifong, Building 7, Suite 100
Columbia, Missouri 65203
Telephone: 573-777-9977
Fax: 573-777-9976

AUTHORIZATION FOR RELEASE

I, ____________________, hereby authorize the Public Defender to release the following **original** Public Defender attorney discs and files to:

Name: ____

Street Address (no P.O. Box) ____

City: ____________________________ State: ______ Zip **Code:** ______________

Case Information:

Case Number: _____________________

____________ ____________________________
Date Client Signature

Subscribed and sworn to me this ____ day of _________________, 2024.

____
Notary Public

Commission Expires: ___________________

Figure 1.3 A copy of the Authorization for Release of records form, available on the Missouri Public Defender Website

AUTHORIZATION FOR RELEASE

I,______________________________, hereby authorize ____ (attorney, Law Firm, etc.) _____ to discuss my legal case with, and release a copy of my Legal files (and/or DVDs) from my legal case to:

Name: ______________________________

Street Address (no P.O. Box) ______________________________

City:______________________________ State: ______Zip **Code**: ___________

Case Information:

Case Number:_ ________________________

Other: _________________________

Date:__________ Client Signature____________________________________

Client Name and ID# ________________________________

Subscribed and sworn to me this_______day of________, 20___.

Notary Public

Commission Expires: _

Figure 1.4 A generic form which may be used as an Authorization for Release of records

on paper. As a result, some cases from that time period remained as paper files. Looking through the Legal File's box of paper from that time period, I sometimes found a DVD labeled: Discovery.

Also, during that time, Police agencies were adapting to the digital world, in different ways and at different speeds. The quality of digital Discovery (i.e., police reports) covered the spectrum. Some agencies were asked to scan their typed or handwritten reports into PDFs to provide as Discovery. This approach could result in 150 separate PDFs (representing 150 single reports and supplements). Sometimes, it appeared the person scanning police reports would take breaks, and the reports were randomly scanned. Some pages would be poorly scanned and unreadable. I found scanned copies of only the front of that police department's two-sided police reports. And of course, some digital Discovery included a lot of duplication.

Eventually, software evolved, and homicide investigators were able to write reports on their computers, creating a more coherent investigative file, which could be forwarded as one digital document.

I can't be definitive here, other than to say, Discovery in habeas cases from that time period (1997–2007) may come in just about any form available.

I personally have evolved from being a print journalist with a notepad, to an almost paperless Factfinder and Investigator. I'm not tied to paper – just organization.

Note to Reader

I will explain in the next chapter how I deal with digital Discovery versus paper Discovery.

Scanning Suggestions

Only a few wrongful conviction clients started out like Ricky Kidd, where I began with a plea for help, Ricky's ideas, and not much more. Most of my Innocence cases were conducted through a regional Innocence Project, or through defense attorneys who had gained Court funding on a habeas appeal, or with attorneys conducting a pro-bono appeal, funded by their law firm.

In cases where I started with minimal case material, I controlled the flow of Discovery material and the initial review of the legal file. I was able to organize the material from the beginning.

When asked to investigate a habeas case by an organization or a law firm, that team has already scanned the legal file with, shall we say, mixed results.

Some habeas teams may think it best to scan every page of the newly acquired defense files and then preserve the original paper files, so they can start working on the case. Unfortunately, they may copy and scan entire files in each box, without first looking at, or reviewing, or evaluating what they have. I've seen this done all too often with negative results. *(When a disorganized pile of paper is scanned blindly into a PDF, that becomes a digital copy of a disorganized pile of paper.)*

I suggest the teams hold off and not make scanning and copying their first move.

I believe, from experience, it is far better to pursue the more primitive task of sorting by hand, separating the legal paper files from the Discovery and all of the investigative raw data. The latter is what the fact investigator needs.

Ideally, the habeas team (law firm, organization, etc.) creates a Master Copy of the raw data (police reports, lab reports, etc.) and scans that Master Copy of raw data as a standalone file. Adding Bates stamp numbers would be ideal. Whether or not this Master Copy is organized in chronological order, it will serve the same purpose, having a Bates-numbered Master Copy accessible for future discussions.

Ideally, the habeas team places an emphasis on organization *prior* to printing/scanning/duplication. The goal is to create a useful file, logically categorized and easily searched, with a Master file of Discovery, ready to Bates stamp, then share with the team.

One last suggestion: there is value in taking the time to go through the police reports, lab reports, investigative reports, page-by-page. Sometimes, paper police reports are two-sided and need to be dealt with before scanning. It's also helpful to make sure all the pages are right-side-up, top-to-bottom.

Another big problem I've found after reviewing scanned Discovery in dozens of cases is duplication. I have reviewed a PDF containing 600 pages of police reports, which were actually three sets of the original 200-page report, each set slightly different.

I have seen 2,000 pages of police reports represented by about 100 separate PDFs, in which duplicate reports occasionally included a missing page, missing from the previous version of the same report.

A simple, yet tedious, solution to duplicate reports is to print the paper reports – all 2,000 pages if necessary. Then, like a deck of cards found at the lake house, start putting each page, each police report, in chronological order by date and time. Compare each new report (date and time) with the previous report on that same date and time. After confirming it is an exact duplicate, set it aside. It will take a few hours. But that is the only way to identify and eliminate all duplicate reports that have multiplied over the years, as more and more hands made more and more copies for their own use, and then preserved their copies in the same box.

That tedious exercise creates a 300-page police report in one PDF (versus 2,000 pages of random confusion) for all future eyes to review.

Chapter 2

Organizing the Raw Data

By the time I received the police and lab reports in Ricky Kidd's case, I had already learned, first-hand, that the state could get it wrong. By then, in 2006, I was approaching my twentieth year as a criminal defense investigator, first in Houston, then in Kansas City. Ricky Kidd's case would be my fifty-third capital murder investigation for the defense (pre-trial and habeas).

My first experience occurred in 1993, when I interviewed the eyewitness (Wilma Amos) in the Gary Graham case. Her witness affidavit (along with other corroborating eye-witness accounts) convinced Texas Governor Ann Richards and then a state Judge to stay Graham's scheduled execution. The court's refusal to hold an evidentiary hearing, and the subsequent decision to execute Graham in 2000, did not in my mind discount that evidence of innocence.

The next year, still in Houston, I interviewed a 15-year-old boy who described how police had taken him out of school one day and coerced him to walk into a Grand Jury and describe a fatal shooting in his neighborhood – a shooting he had heard about but had not witnessed. The boy's false testimony, fed to him by homicide detectives, incriminated an older teen (my client) under indictment for Capital Murder.

This 15-year-old witness led me to the actual eyewitness to the shooting, whom police had been looking for but had not found. Those two witnesses convincingly excluded my client from any involvement in the shooting. Capital Murder charges were dismissed against Leroy P.,[1] based on those two, timely, interviews.

In Kansas City, I gained invaluable experience working with attorneys in the state Public Defender's Capital Division, working as their *First Phase*, or *Fact* Investigator in Capital Murder and Murder I cases. (The *First Phase* of a Capital Murder trial determines guilt or innocence. The *Second Phase* of a Capital Murder Trial determines the appropriate punishment, Life Without Parole, or Death.)

1 A fictitious name.

DOI: 10.4324/9781003543299-2

Before Ricky Kidd contacted me, I had helped criminal defense teams in Kansas City gain four acquittals at trial, and four dismissed Murder I cases prior to trial. I had also helped other lawyers in Missouri and Tennessee gain five exonerations or prison releases in plea deals like Leamon White. I always looked at acquittals at trial, or Murder I charges dismissed, as Wrongful Convictions *avoided*.

During that same time period (1995–2005), I worked on defense teams in 28 Capital Cases which ended in convictions. Most of those convicted received life without parole (LWOP). A few were sentenced to death. I believe all but one of those defendants were guilty.

I mention these cases and results only to explain that I spent those years developing an understanding of how to investigate the crimes. In habeas cases, where innocence may be an issue, I learned why I needed to also "investigate the investigation."

So, with Ricky's case, I had an idea about what needed to be done, and how I wanted to do it. There were no attorneys involved at this stage. Just Ricky's persistent claim of innocence and my curiosity.

In response to my Open Records request, I received a stack of paper from KCMO PD with a letter confirming that these 380 pages represented the entire investigation into the double homicide of Oscar Bridges and George Bryant.

This was the raw data – the crime scene investigation, the lab reports, the witness interviews, evidence inventories, line-ups, 9-1-1 calls, the initial neighborhood canvas, anonymous calls to the police TIPS hotline, alibis, and suspect interviews. This was the state's entire investigation, in random order – 380 pages of ... what?

What I decided to do with those pages shaped my investigative approach to Wrongful Convictions (and all criminal defense work) moving forward – with good success.

I had noticed that many defense teams never bothered to Bates stamp the police reports, making it difficult to find and discuss issues with the lawyer. Instead, we would just copy the police report and share, and then discuss – repeatedly.

The first thing I did with Ricky's police reports was Bates stamp the 380 pages, so I at least had a Master Copy of Discovery, numbered 0001–0380, for future reference.

The next step was crucial.

It had struck me, from previous cases, that randomly pulling and reviewing specific police reports only gave me the information from that report, or that witness interview – without context. I may find, and then focus on, a specific police report which looked like a critical turning point in their investigation – without knowing what led the police to that witness, or that event.

Most of my work in earlier cases had been guided by the lead attorney, who provided me with the Discovery she thought I needed, to pursue what she thought I should pursue. Only rarely was I given the entire Discovery and asked to review an entire investigation. Whenever I did, I always learned much more about the case than the attorney was able to offer in our meetings.

Rather than try to read the Bridges and Bryant homicide investigation in the random order it arrived, I decided to first arrange the reports in chronological order.

When I finally put hands on paper, I learned that organizing the police reports in strict chronological sequence was not that time consuming. It took me less than three hours to pull and place all the police reports and lab reports (380 pages) in chronological order.

This method of organization is simple. (Again, tedious, but simple.) In every case I have worked on since 2006, I dismantle the Discovery (if allowed) and organize the police reports and witness interviews into chronological order – by the date and time of the witness interview, or the investigative event. I do the same with the lab reports, and all other forensic reports. I keep them separate from the police reports, but I still organize them in their chronological, or sequential, order – by date and time, or by lab report number.

I'm still waiting to see Discovery material (i.e., police reports) delivered in any logical order. I've found Discovery/police reports arranged in reverse order (last to first). I've seen Discovery/police reports which appeared to represent a conscious disregard for order. I have never seen police reports of a complex homicide delivered in chronological order, representing how the actual investigation unfolded. So, I do that myself.

Later, I'll discuss how this method worked in *Mo v. Ricky Kidd*. But, first, the unforeseen benefits of reviewing an investigation in strict chronological order. That method, I learned, serves three purposes: first, that order allows me to see how the initial investigation developed. Second, reviewing in chronological order allows me to see patterns, identify missing reports, and identify witnesses who were not interviewed. Third, reviewing in this order forces me to read each report, page-by-page.

Years after completing my Kidd investigation, this same simple method helped me develop an innocence claim in *Arkansas v. Laquanda Jacobs*. The defendant, a teenager, was wrongfully convicted of capital murder (Death had been waived) in a 1993 "trial" lasting one and a half days, including jury selection and jury deliberation. I laid out, and arranged in chronological order, the nearly 400 pages of police and lab reports, where

I found far more factual information than appeared in the 259 pages of trial transcript.

And this method helped me in *Oklahoma v. Karl Fontenot*. After a few alibi witness interviews and a cursory review of the prior attorney's notes, it became clear that no prior defense team had ever reviewed the original investigation, the police reports – the raw data – in this case. In response to our Open Records request, we obtained, and I printed out, 832 pages of micro-filmed police reports, and got started arranging them in chronological order.

It worked for me in *Mo v. Lamar Johnson* and *Mo v. Chris Dunn*, two St. Louis City cases, in which the police reports in each case totaled fewer than 100 pages. Following the chronological progression of the original police investigation proved critical in *assessing* their claims of innocence, and then *proving* their innocence.

In Chris Dunn's case, the chronological review identified an eyewitness, named by police, but never interviewed by police. In Lamar Johnson's case, the chronological review helped us identify police and prosecutorial misconduct.

This method has worked on every complex murder case I have investigated – and all other types of criminal cases I have been asked to review. This method helped resolve a wrongful conviction in a sexual assault case (*Mo v. Ted White*) and a wrongful conviction in Illinois for a series of armed robberies. A police investigation is a police investigation.

Understand that this step is not about reviewing reports, just organizing and arranging all police reports in a chronological sequence for later review.

If the original criminal investigation stretched out over years (as some do), I first take the interviews and reports received in random order, and break them down by years, then months, then days, etc. A more typical investigation spans several days, or weeks. I organize piles of reports by date, beginning on the day of the crime (which is normally, but not always, the first day of relevant investigation). Eventually, I sequence by hour (then by minute) until I have the exact order of witness interviews and the order in which facts were gathered (i.e., *investigative events*).

When I later start reading, and review the investigation in chronological sequence, that sequence provides context. Reviewing in chronological sequence shows me how each investigative step led to the next step in an investigation. Reviewing police and lab reports in sequence helps identify a missing lab report or relevant tests never conducted. Or I may find one police report refers to a previous witness contact, on a certain date. With the reports already in chronological order, I know that report, or that witness contact does not exist – at least not in my set of reports.

And when I say "Time and Date," I'm referring to the time and date police interviewed the witness, or the date the police recovered a record, or the date the police discovered some fact. Some police reports list a date the report is completed, or transcribed, or "distributed internally." Most reports show the date a supervisor "approved" the report. Some police department investigators create a *Summary Report* listing several witness interviews (summaries) and various police activities in one continuous report. That Summary Report is dated weeks after those interviews were conducted. I am not interested in when the report was written, or when the interview was transcribed. The significant date is the date and time that the police interviewed that witness or obtained that information. I may copy the Summary Report, creating a page for each witness interview, or investigative event. I place these witness interviews and police activities in their proper chronological order, based on the date each interview or event occurred.

Not just the date is important. Investigations will experience a flurry of activity on a particular day. Such a flurry of activity might occur early in the investigation, or months later, maybe based on an anonymous tip or discovery of a new, critical fact. Spread throughout hundreds of pages of reports, I will find several witness interviews conducted on the same day. I organize those witness interviews in their correct sequence. If the reports provide the exact time, I arrange the reports in sequence, by time.

Note to Reader

I have placed some sample police reports at the end of this chapter, showing where you may find the time/date of the actual interview or investigative event (Figures 2.1–2.6).

Some police reports may provide the date of the interview, but not the time. I'll look for anecdotal information within the interview reports and try to arrange these interviews in the order they were conducted. When I later review these interviews, I often see that one witness interview was conducted with the knowledge gained from a previous witness interview on that same day. That is helpful context in understanding the investigation.

When I reviewed the Tulsa Police reports in Willard O'Neal's wrongful conviction case, I found significant value in determining what information the police gained during an interview at 3:30 a.m., which was used in the witness interview conducted a few minutes later, at 3:45 a.m., which added to information they used during their 4:15 a.m. witness interview.

Knowing the exact sequence, and evaluating that sequence of fact-gathering, can enhance my understanding of the thought process steering an investigation. It can also show whether or not information was "fed" from one witness to another.

Note to Reader

When I refer to "police" and "investigators," I am also referring to federal agents, "Special Agents," "SA" who work for the FBI, the DEA, ATF, etc. And any reference to "police reports" and "investigative reports" includes the FBI's standard "302" form, as well as the DEA and ATF Investigative Reports.

The Autopsy

I place the Autopsy Report and any related investigative notes in a separate file. The Medical Examiner (ME) may use an in-house investigator. That investigator may visit a crime scene before the body is removed. These investigator's notes are separate from the police investigation but are certainly a part of my investigation. So, they need to be placed in chronological order.

An ME's investigator may make notes and take photos. This investigator may diagram body placement at the crime scene, or diagram wounds separate from the ME's official autopsy. I keep all autopsy-related reports and notes in one file. Usually, the autopsy, as a part of the investigation, is conducted within hours, or on the day after the crime scene is processed. All findings from the autopsy should be placed in that investigative sequence. Relevant findings might include cause of death, time of death, weapon(s) used (i.e., bullet caliber, etc.). Relevant findings could even include the potential number of assailants, or number of weapons, or number of wounds (i.e., gun-shot-wounds (GSW), stab wounds, or blunt force blows to the head or body). These are critically important facts, which should direct any fact-based investigation.

During a recent habeas investigation of an Alabama Capital Murder conviction which led to a Death Sentence, our investigation led to a review of a possibly related, still unsolved homicide nearby, in Georgia. Even though we gained access to a related legal file and most of the police reports/homicide investigation, certain facts remained unclear.

The victim's cause of death in police reports was euphemistically described as "death by firearm." Newspaper accounts suggested only that the victim had suffered a fatal gunshot wound. The Discovery we were able to obtain and review did not include the autopsy. From state to state, autopsy reports aren't necessarily included with homicide investigations or included in routine Discovery.

In the very back of one of the boxes I reviewed was a slim manilla folder, containing one piece of paper – the victim's Death Certificate.

The Death Certificate's cause of death: "At Least 12 GSWs."

This fact was relevant in our determining whether this unsolved homicide may have been a daytime robbery – or an execution. The cause of death suggested the latter.

When later reviewed, the autopsy, aka the Medical Examiner's report, may identify, or mention anecdotally, some physical evidence which could prove significant. Eventually, it may be necessary to cross-reference physical evidence noted at the autopsy (i.e., a recovered bullet, a piece of jewelry, an item found in a pocket, a latent print found on the body) with the evidence inventory found in police reports, or the inventory of items sent to the lab for testing. A piece of evidence at the autopsy could be mishandled, or somehow fall out of the stream of evidence collected at the crime scene, or collected, but never sent, to a lab for processing.

The timing of the autopsy relative to the crime may also impact the relevance of those findings. If the cause of death is not initially obvious, autopsy findings could influence witness interviews downstream.

In cases of a "Missing Person-presumed dead," a homicide investigation may begin before a body is recovered. This absence of evidence due to *no autopsy* can greatly impact this investigation. Even facts surrounding a body, recovered a few days after an investigation begins, can impact the investigation. In Karl Fontenot's case, the body of Denice Haraway was not discovered for nearly two years after her alleged abduction, and assumed kidnapping, rape, and homicide. In fact, the victim's body was discovered following Fontenot's jury trial and wrongful conviction.

In that 1984 case, Fontenot and Tommy Ward were convicted of kidnapping and murder in the disappearance and presumed abduction of Donna Denice Haraway – despite no recovered body and no physical evidence. Ms. Haraway disappeared one April evening, while working at a gas station and convenience store on the eastern outskirts of Ada, Okla.

Fontenot was convicted, based solely on his admissions from a coerced confession, in which he loosely described her kidnapping, rape, and murder by knife, at the hands of Tommy Ward, Odell Titsworth, and himself. In Fontenot's coerced confession, he claimed they disposed of her body inside or beneath an abandoned house west *of Ada.*

It mattered not to the prosecutor (or the jury) that his confession matched no facts discovered before the body was recovered. (Odell Titsworth had a rock-solid alibi and was never charged with any crime.) Nor did it matter to the state that Fontenot's confession was contradicted in full, by the autopsy conducted after Ms. Haraway's remains were discovered on January 21, 1986, in a rural area of Hughes County, several miles east *of Ada.*

Whenever a victim's body is recovered at the crime scene, the autopsy is generally conducted the next day. However, autopsy findings may not be immediately available to investigators in the field for days or weeks. Sometimes an autopsy will develop new, relevant facts – not evident at the crime scene. For that reason alone, I place the autopsy or ME reports in strict chronological sequence. When reviewed in sequence, those reports may offer context impacting the entire investigation.

Sometimes an autopsy will just confirm what investigators had already surmised at the crime scene (and what is contained in their police reports). Sometimes an autopsy will reveal a dramatically different set of possibilities. Maybe the bullet caliber doesn't match the presumed murder weapon. Maybe a subtle piece of evidence like a partial bloody fingerprint is ignored (... since an eyewitness has already identified a suspect).

Only when I review these findings in sequence, will I notice discrepancies between facts found in the field, versus facts discovered at the autopsy. By organizing the investigation in chronological order, my review may find some "facts" ignored or identify "facts" inconsistent with other "facts."

Arranging the reports in order, my review may determine when a *fact-driven investigation* starts to become an *agenda-driven investigation.* Only when reviewed in sequence, will I see the investigator's "hunch" start to carry more weight than evidence discovered during the autopsy, or elsewhere.

Forensic/Lab Reports

After organizing *crime scene reports*, the *area canvass*, and all *witness interviews* into their chronological sequence, I turn to my stack of lab and forensic reports. Depending on the case and the volume (or lack) of material, I divide those reports by category. There may be *ballistics reports* (firearms), *latent print processing reports*, *fingerprint cards*, *Gun Shot Residue* (GSR) tests conducted on immediate suspects, and *presumptive DNA tests* (i.e., testing for human blood and bodily fluids), conducted on recovered material. *DNA analysis* may be requested months later. Less common are forensic tests conducted to determine time of death or cause of death.

Other forensic reports I've seen include actual *polygraph exams* (raw data) and *voice stress analysis* (VSA) exams conducted on witnesses. I have also seen microscopic hair comparisons, and microscopic *fire pin comparison* of shell-casings. Some of these "tests," like the VSA or a visual hair comparison, have been scientifically discredited. Some tests may be accepted science, but only in some jurisdictions based on Federal Court rulings. I have found forensic reports with findings or conclusions using science not accepted by the court. That's an issue for attorneys. Whether the science is discredited or not, the lab report was part of the investigation. The test results were obtained and likely used to direct the investigation.

Like the Medical Examiner's report with notes, depending on the volume, I may keep a file of reports for each forensic category, and then copy the reports and place them in their chronological order with the police reports.

Every case and every jurisdiction follow unique protocols governing what is tested, when, and how. From case to case, I never know what to expect in terms of forensic reports. All I do at this stage is gather up all forensic reports, separate them by category, and put them in chronological order. Only after arranging the entire investigation in chronological sequence, will I realize a report is missing, or maybe a whole category of lab reports is missing. Or I may find an entire subset of evidence was never analyzed.

When organizing lab reports, I review the formatting used by that jurisdiction. I am looking for a way to sequence these reports, ideally by date, but sometimes by lab case number, sometimes by a simple lab report number. Some lab reports will be numbered in sequence for each unique crime – Lab Report: #1–#23. By organizing these reports in sequence, I may find #11 and #18 are missing. Sometimes I must use the lab report's date as the sole identifier and find another way to inventory lab reports to make sure I can account for all lab analysis conducted on this case.

Later, when reviewing witness interviews, I may see a police interview or an investigative memo refer to a lab test result, or a lab report, not included in my Discovery. I may also see a police investigator question a witness – and refer to the results of a forensic test not included in my set of reports. I must consider the investigator may have lied to the witness to gain information or lied to the suspect to gain a confession. Or the investigator may have been sharing results from an actual forensic test conducted – a forensic test not shared with the defense. Either way, it is significant.

That's a good and practical example of the relevant detail I may notice, by first organizing the entire file and all reports in chronological order.

Tracking Physical Evidence

Related to the lab reports is the important task of identifying all physical evidence gathered in a homicide investigation. I find it helpful to gather and organize all evidence inventories found throughout these police reports.

Inventories may be found in crime scene reports, in a separate report written by Crime Scene Investigators, in police reports related to the execution of search warrants, and even inside a witness interview report, where police gain a written release, on the spot, to search a specific area. Police are generally interested in weapons, cellphones, and items which might contain blood, hair, or latent prints – all *physical evidence.*

Often, the autopsy will produce its own list, or inventory of physical evidence. I make extra copies of those physical evidence inventories and place them in a separate file with the lab reports.

When I review the entire file in chronological order, I may track each item removed from the original crime scene (or autopsy, or suspect vehicle, etc.) through the entire lab process. Some items might go through several labs for processing. (An item might be processed for DNA, then tested two different ways for a latent print.) Sometimes, testing for one piece of evidence (a latent print) might prevent subsequent testing for another (potential DNA). So, the order and method of testing must be carefully considered by the police (and prosecutors) and evaluated by my investigation.

First, organizing these inventory lists in sequence will allow me to later identify what was seized, by whom, and then sent where. This process could help identify potential cross-contamination of the suspect's items with the victim's DNA, as well as the suspect's DNA "found" at the crime scene.

In any complex case with a long list of seized physical evidence, I expect to find that the police (crime technicians) use one numbering system to identify these items. Then the lab will use a different numbering system and a unique case number to ID these same items. Then again, the prosecutor will label each item differently as court exhibits at trial. One item seized at the crime scene, and identified as *A-12*, becomes *C2* at the lab, and then becomes *Exh 58* in court.

Only a methodical organization of these inventory lists at this stage allows me to keep track of these items throughout the investigation.

Depending on the evidence in this case, I may need to identify and track *each item* containing potential DNA or (fingerprint) latents, so I can later identify each item which was *not* tested (... but could still represent exculpatory evidence). Or, following my review, I may need to identify an item – presumably tested – but after review I realize there is no lab result found in Discovery. (In a worst-case scenario, an item might represent exculpatory evidence, so the written lab report was never delivered to the prosecutor or police, thus skirting disclosure rules.)

When reviewing the entire case (i.e., *investigating the investigation*), I will, at some point, need to compare the court exhibits presented by the state at trial with each of these other inventory lists to determine if all relevant items were used to convict – and identify what items were excluded.

I hope that explains the importance of organizing these police and lab reports in sequence, as well as the evidence inventories. Those forensic reports – once in sequence – become organizational tools for any investigation of the crime, and any investigation of the investigation. In habeas cases, this organization can become important building blocks in proving innocence.

I don't consider myself to be any kind of forensic expert. That's not necessary. Most lab reports are written in plain English, rarely clouded in scientific terms (DNA analysis is the obvious exception). All reports are dated, or time/date stamped. All reports relate to specific items of evidence collected from somewhere, related to this crime. A methodical review of all forensic reports will probably reveal what I need to know about the forensic investigation.

But it starts with my willingness and ability to organize the paper.

Why I Read Police Reports First ... (Or ... Why I Read Trial/Grand Jury Transcripts Last)

At first glance, those police reports might look confusing, maybe overwhelming, and difficult to review. One may look through a defendant's legal file and notice the trial transcripts and witness depositions are neatly bound, arranged in order, with pages numbered – a much easier read.

I don't see it that way. The good stuff – *the raw data* – will always be found in that stack of police and lab reports. Allow me to explain.

Through trial and error, I have seen how my simple method of organizing a police investigation allows me to properly *investigate the investigation.*

What's wrong with reading those trial transcripts first? Why not start with the easy read? Isn't the trial transcript an accurate presentation of both the state's case and the defendant's legal defense?

Yes ... and no.

Lawyers I have worked with in habeas cases generally like to start with the trial transcripts and legal briefs as a way of becoming familiar with a case.

It's relevant that habeas attorneys are looking for legal issues. Factfinders are looking for facts. As the fact investigator, trying that same approach (transcripts first) under the lawyer's direction, I found that sequence created problems of bias and perception.

I once experienced the pre-trial equivalent: reviewing Grand Jury transcripts before reading police reports. Grand Jury transcripts are sometimes available in some jurisdictions, shared with the defense as Discovery.

I was asked to work on a very complex federal conspiracy case, involving several murders in multiple states over a ten-year period. In preparing for trial, one of the defense attorneys tried to grasp this case by first reviewing all the Grand Jury transcripts. He then shared his notes with another attorney who came on board later. Both attorneys assumed the Grand Jury testimony by some government witnesses, and a federal agent who often testified on behalf of other fact witnesses, was truthful. The lawyers took all Grand Jury evidence at face value. The evidence presented in these transcripts convinced the attorneys that their client was guilty of all charges, and then some.

Yet, not only was the client's actual guilt in each of these crimes an issue, but so was the government's ability to prove that guilt with truthful testimony. And with so many murders on the table, gaining an acquittal in one or more murders could literally prove the difference between life and death.

Once I (as fact investigator) started reviewing the police reports and witness statements, I found multiple instances of federal agents speaking for witnesses to the Grand Jury, which contradicted the witness' police interviews. Compared with the initial crime scene investigations and witness statements, I found third-party testimony to the Grand Jury liberally sprinkled with embellishments and misstatements. The defense lawyers, having assumed these Grand Jury embellishments and fabrications were truthful testimony, were slow to develop theories of reasonable doubt once these contradictions began to surface.

This was also a case of time running out. Complex cases require lots of time to prepare and be prepared for unexpected twists and turns – like embellished Grand Jury testimony by state and federal agents.

Not surprisingly, all these witnesses whose statements were "embellished" before the Grand Jury were facing steep sentences, or generous sentence reductions, depending on their level of cooperation. I was told that the witness testimony eventually "matched up" with the special agents' Grand Jury testimony, even if the statements contradicted the initial police reports. By not reading the original police reports first, I think the defense team lacked helpful context for these Grand Jury embellishments.

Reading trial transcripts in a habeas case, to me, is no different from reviewing Grand Jury transcripts in pre-trial mode. The reader may learn the state's (i.e., prosecutor's) case, but the reader will also be looking at the crime and the investigation through the prosecutor's filter. Facts will be left out. Exaggerated claims may be offered as fact. Witness testimony at trial may differ slightly, or significantly, from what that witness told police at the time of the crime.

False testimony read in a trial transcript will not be labeled as such. False testimony will likely go unchallenged, especially if the case represents a wrongful conviction.

I've found that some habeas lawyers who read only the trial transcript can develop a bias favoring the government's position that their client is guilty. I've seen that "presumption of guilt" become hard to shake, when factual evidence of reasonable doubt, or evidence of actual innocence is developed, in piecemeal fashion. At that point, I have seen lawyers (some, not all) who have been looking for trial error or constitutional claims have a difficult time considering how to prove actual innocence.

Objectivity ...

And I have more reasons why – in habeas cases – I prefer organizing and reviewing the police reports first, in chronological order. In many cases, it was helpful to read both – police reports in order, and the trial transcript afterwards, to note all the discrepancies in witness statements.

If I had read the trial transcript first, or read only the trial transcript, I would have been exposed to but a fraction of the gathered evidence. And the trial transcript forces the reader to process a skewed and filtered picture of the crime and the defendant's actions, as presented by the prosecutor. The prosecutor's case is designed to be persuasive – not objective – in describing the crime and the defendant.

I understand the trial transcript is the lawyer's road map for appellate issues, giving her an inventory of options. But I believe evaluating a wrongful conviction claim, or preparing an innocence case, requires an "unfiltered" and "unbiased" look at the original investigation. Evaluating innocence requires a thorough and objective investigation of the crime and – along the way – an objective investigation of the investigation.

This is a good time to discuss objectivity. I consider objectivity a critical skill in assessing an innocence claim.

It is difficult to be objective. As a professional journalist, I saw how difficult it was to approach our work without conscious or subconscious bias. Being objective takes effort. It is far more natural to allow prejudice and bias and various hard-wired beliefs into our thought process. *Objectivity should be our goal.* Pursuing that goal requires effort.

Absent that effort, it serves no good purpose to approach these cases with a bias or an agenda. History and evidence suggest that most of those convicted of murder are guilty, and some of those convicted of murder are not guilty. My experience suggests that some, but not all, convicts who claim innocence may be innocent. (I have had many conversations with prison inmates who acknowledge their guilt and understand why they are sitting in prison. These admissions are gained only after a certain level of trust is developed. Interestingly, these inmates who acknowledge their guilt appear to be the most at peace with their status. I hesitate to use the word "content.")

I have worked with defense attorneys, pre-trial, who held no objective belief that their client could be innocent. Some may have bought into the social norm that the state would never charge someone with a crime who wasn't guilty. I found some defense lawyers, despite their liberal façade, were hard-wired with racial bias. Some may have been simply worn down by the steady stream of guilty clients.

I have seen habeas defense teams commit the same mistakes as the police – develop *a theory of innocence* on a *hunch*, or on *wishful thinking* – then try to prove that theory. This subjective reasoning leads them to look for someone who fits their hunch as an alternative suspect – instead of investigating the case. Setting out to *prove* someone is innocent is no different from the police starting to *build a case* against a suspect before completing the investigation. I prefer following the facts. I let the facts prove innocence – or sometimes guilt – when I'm asked to work on a wrongful conviction case.

Just because a convicted felon is lucky enough to gain the attention of a regional Innocence Project, or a competent habeas team, I don't feel any obligation to assume they are innocent.

That's the *very long* explanation for why I prefer reading the original investigative reports first. Reading these reports, in chronological order, shows me how those *facts* led police to their suspect. I can later see how those facts were presented to the court. I find it much easier to remain objective when reviewing the original fact-gathering in chronological order. That method is guided by logic and common sense. Using that method – in cases of a wrongful conviction – I'm confident an orderly review will reveal problems and mistakes in the state's theory of guilt. I'm far less confident that reading the trial transcript first will offer the same, or even similar, results.

Practicality ...

My conviction to this approach has only grown stronger over time. Initially, on habeas cases, I would meet with the attorney who described the case and the crime, based on his knowledge of the case. The attorney's knowledge of the case was almost always gained by reading the trial transcript and talking to the convicted client. The lawyer thought he knew the case. Then, after I read through the police reports, it sometimes felt like we weren't even discussing the same crime. The questions and theories I developed after reading police reports, witness statements, evidence inventories, and lab reports were often foreign to the lawyer who had only read the trial transcript and maybe a few significant police reports. He was only familiar with the facts the prosecutor wanted the jury to hear, or the facts the defendant wanted to emphasize.

The reason that a client's case became a wrongful conviction may be related to reasons why no one should use the trial transcript as their sole understanding of the case. At court (in the trial transcript) the defense lawyer may not have offered any push-back to the state's theory. The defense may not have offered an alternate theory. Maybe the court wouldn't allow significant facts or defense theories into evidence. The defense case may have suffered from weak cross-examinations and ineffective witness rebuttals. The trial transcript may not offer any defense witnesses at all. Remember, one of the reasons for a wrongful conviction is Ineffective Assistance of Counsel. That's not just a legal term.

I have seen such high levels of incompetence among some defense attorneys in first-degree murder cases, I think *criminally negligent* may be a better description than *ineffective*. I've seen alibi witnesses ignored; eyewitnesses never approached before the trial. The crime scene was never visited. The trial transcript suggested that the defense counsel never read, or only skimmed through, the police reports. I've seen Murder I cases where the defendant was never properly interviewed by his own attorney. The defendant's suggestions of what may have happened were ignored. The defense conducted virtually no investigation of the police investigation, or of the crime. The defense attorney lent no credence to his defendant's claim of innocence. I have seen the state's case offered to the court and the jury, unchallenged, with only perfunctory arguments. The cross-exam of state witnesses was no more than clever questions possibly based on observations made that day. The defense attorney understood little of the case, beyond the state's theory or what she read in the Probable Cause statement. The defense counsel appeared to be learning about this case, right along with the jury.

It is true that an innocent defendant may be convicted despite an aggressive and competent legal defense. However, when the defense gives the state's theory a free pass, the whole system suffers.

I believe a methodical, chronological, and competent review of the crime and the state's investigation will help make the trial transcript a much more effective road map for habeas claims.

As for Brady Material, there will be none found in the trial transcript. There will be no clues there. And Brady Material, by definition, won't be found in the police reports.

But a review of the police investigation in chronological order has helped me identify many Brady Material issues in several Innocence cases. I don't see how any other random approach would have been as helpful. Only by investigating the investigation in sequence, page-by-page and line-by-line, will the potential existence of Brady Material be discovered.

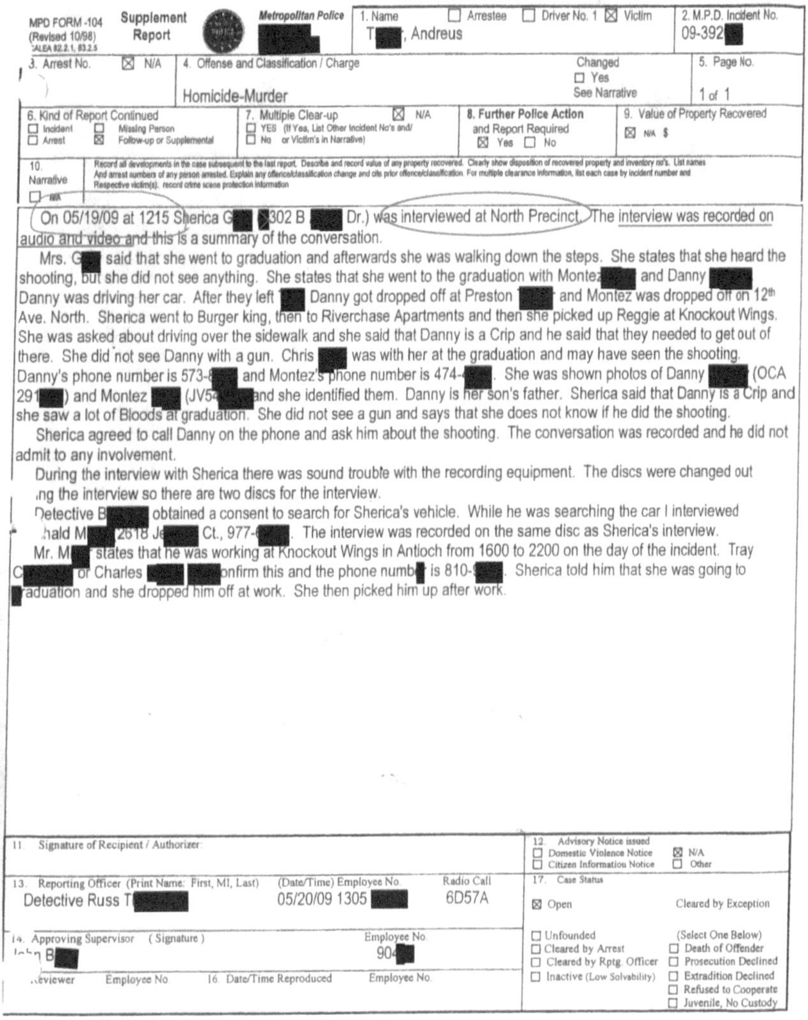

MPD FORM -104 (Revised 10/98) CALEA 82.2.1, 83.2.5 — Supplement Report — Metropolitan Police [redacted]

1. Name ☐ Arrestee ☐ Driver No. 1 ☒ Victim
T[redacted], Andreus

2. M.P.D. Incident No.
09-392[redacted]

3. Arrest No. ☒ N/A

4. Offense and Classification / Charge
Homicide-Murder
Changed ☐ Yes See Narrative

5. Page No.
1 of 1

6. Kind of Report Continued ☐ Incident ☐ Missing Person ☐ Arrest ☒ Follow-up or Supplemental

7. Multiple Clear-up ☒ N/A ☐ YES (If Yes, List Other Incident No's and/ ☐ No or Victim's in Narrative)

8. Further Police Action and Report Required ☒ Yes ☐ No

9. Value of Property Recovered ☒ N/A $

10. Narrative ☐ N/A
Record all developments in the case subsequent to the last report. Describe and record value of any property recovered. Clearly show disposition of recovered property and inventory no's. List names And arrest numbers of any person arrested. Explain any offence/classification change and cite prior offence/classification. For multiple clearance information, list each case by incident number and Respective victim(s). record crime scene protection information

On 05/19/09 at 1215 Sherica G[redacted] [redacted]302 B[redacted] Dr.) was interviewed at North Precinct. The interview was recorded on audio and video and this is a summary of the conversation.

Mrs. G[redacted] said that she went to graduation and afterwards she was walking down the steps. She states that she heard the shooting, but she did not see anything. She states that she went to the graduation with Montez[redacted] and Danny [redacted]. Danny was driving her car. After they left [redacted] Danny got dropped off at Preston [redacted] and Montez was dropped off on 12th Ave. North. Sherica went to Burger king, then to Riverchase Apartments and then she picked up Reggie at Knockout Wings. She was asked about driving over the sidewalk and she said that Danny is a Crip and he said that they needed to get out of there. She did not see Danny with a gun. Chris [redacted] was with her at the graduation and may have seen the shooting. Danny's phone number is 573-[redacted] and Montez's phone number is 474-[redacted]. She was shown photos of Danny [redacted] (OCA 291[redacted]) and Montez [redacted] (JV5[redacted] and she identified them. Danny is her son's father. Sherica said that Danny is a Crip and she saw a lot of Bloods at graduation. She did not see a gun and says that she does not know if he did the shooting.

Sherica agreed to call Danny on the phone and ask him about the shooting. The conversation was recorded and he did not admit to any involvement.

During the interview with Sherica there was sound trouble with the recording equipment. The discs were changed out ,ng the interview so there are two discs for the interview.

Detective B[redacted] obtained a consent to search for Sherica's vehicle. While he was searching the car I interviewed hald M[redacted] 2618 J[redacted] Ct., 977-[redacted]. The interview was recorded on the same disc as Sherica's interview.

Mr. M[redacted] states that he was working at Knockout Wings in Antioch from 1600 to 2200 on the day of the incident. Tray C[redacted] or Charles [redacted]onfirm this and the phone numb[redacted] is 810-[redacted]. Sherica told him that she was going to [redacted]aduation and she dropped him off at work. She then picked him up after work.

11. Signature of Recipient / Authorizer

12. Advisory Notice issued ☐ Domestic Violence Notice ☒ N/A ☐ Citizen Information Notice ☐ Other

13. Reporting Officer (Print Name: First, MI, Last) Detective Russ T[redacted] — (Date/Time) Employee No. 05/20/09 1305 [redacted] — Radio Call 6D57A

17. Case Status ☒ Open — Cleared by Exception

14. Approving Supervisor (Signature) Iohn B[redacted] — Employee No. 90[redacted]

Reviewer — Employee No — 16. Date/Time Reproduced — Employee No.

☐ Unfounded ☐ Cleared by Arrest ☐ Cleared by Rptg. Officer ☐ Inactive (Low Solvability)

(Select One Below) ☐ Death of Offender ☐ Prosecution Declined ☐ Extradition Declined ☐ Refused to Cooperate ☐ Juvenile, No Custody

Figure 2.1 A random (redacted) police investigative report of a homicide witness interview

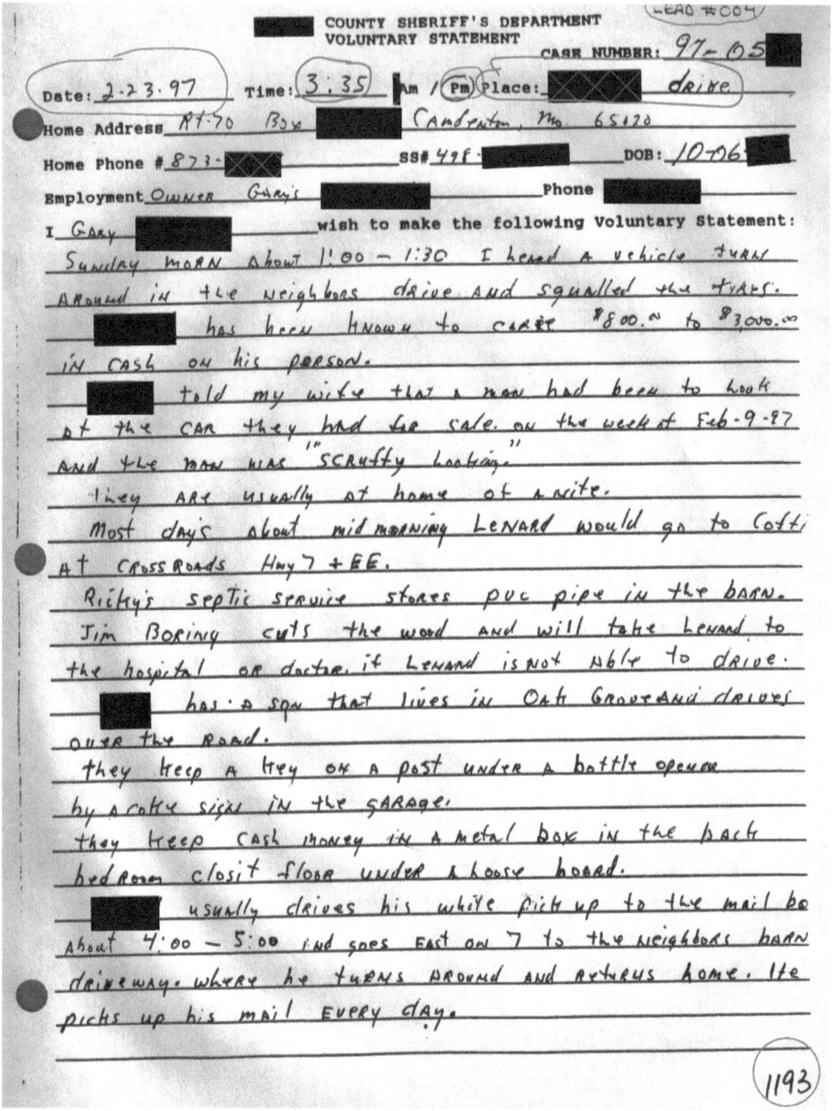
LEAD #004

[redacted] COUNTY SHERIFF'S DEPARTMENT
VOLUNTARY STATEMENT

CASE NUMBER: 97-05[redacted]

Date: 2-23-97 Time: 3:35 Am / Pm Place: [redacted] drive

Home Address Rt 70 Box [redacted] Camdenton, Mo. 65020

Home Phone # 873-[redacted] SS# 498-[redacted] DOB: 10-06-[redacted]

Employment Owner Gary's [redacted] Phone [redacted]

I Gary [redacted] wish to make the following Voluntary Statement:

Sunday morn about 1:00 – 1:30 I heard a vehicle turn
around in the neighbors drive and squalled the tires.
[redacted] has been known to carry $800.00 to $3000.00
in cash on his person.
[redacted] told my wife that a man had been to look
at the car they had for sale on the week of Feb-9-97
and the man was "scruffy looking."
They are usually at home at nite.
Most days about mid morning Lenard would go to Coffe
at Cross Roads Hwy 7 + EE.
Ricky's septic service stores pvc pipe in the barn.
Jim Boring cuts the wood and will take Lenard to
the hospital or doctor. if Lenard is not able to drive.
[redacted] has a son that lives in Oak Grove and drives
over the road.
they keep a key on a post under a bottle opener
by a coke sign in the garage.
they keep cash money in a metal box in the back
bedroom closit floor under a loose board.
[redacted] usually drives his white pick up to the mail box
about 4:00 – 5:00 and goes East on 7 to the neighbors barn
driveway. where he turns around and returns home. He
picks up his mail every day.

1193

Figure 2.2 A random (redacted) witness statement taken in a homicide investigation

City of Tulsa
TULSA POLICE DEPARTMENT
Supplement Report

INCIDENT NUMBER: 2001093117

VICTIM: Bruce Leroy Chamberlain
Address: [redacted]E. Newton ST Tulsa, OK 74115
Phones: 838-8[redacted]

Crime Type: Homicide
Location: 3101 S. 101st E. AV
Date/Time: 12/23/01 (0245-0305)
Original TRACIS by: Officer C.L. Kellerhals
This Report By: Michael[redacted] Z-3[redacted]
Date of Report: 03/06/02@1:57 PM

Crime stopper Report on pg 207

On 03/06/02 at 0930 hours, Charity[redacted]TPD #1602[redacted]was located and arrested at[redacted]E. 71st PL #1610 for outstanding Felony warrants. Miss[redacted]was transported the Detective Division where I interviewed her in reference to the homicide of Bruce Chamberlain.

Early on in the investigation, Miss[redacted]was mentioned as possibly being involved in the 11/14/01 robbery of the Trapeze Lounge. Because of this allegation, individuals advised me that Miss[redacted] might also have been involved in the homicide.

The interview of *Charity[redacted], W/F, TPD #160[redacted] DOB: 08/0[redacted]SSN: 448[redacted]home address: [redacted]E. 71st PL #1610 Tulsa, OK 74136* was recorded on an audio cassette-tape. For details, see the transcribed statement. The following is a synopsis of the interview:

- She was a bartender at the Trapeze Lounge at the time of the 11/14/01 robbery.
- She denied involvement or direct knowledge in the robbery.
- She quit working at the bar shortly after the robbery, citing a conflict with Chamberlain as the reason for terminating her employment.
- She denied involvement or direct knowledge in the homicide.
- She was at her apartment located at 7331 E. 48th ST on the night of the homicide.
- She had heard that[redacted]and[redacted] might have been responsible for the homicide.
- She also heard that [redacted] might have been one of the persons involved in the homicide.
- She stated that the Trapeze Lounge was "overrun" with drug dealers, many of whom were associated with the dancers.
- She stated that Chamberlain had many enemies.

[redacted]was identified as being[redacted] I/M, TPD #173[redacted] DOB: 11/2[redacted] SSN: 08[redacted] home address: [redacted]E. Ute ST Tulsa, OK 74106.

Investigation to continue...

Page 1 of 1, 10/29/02 1:57 PM

MLZ
B. CHAMBERLAIN III supplemental.doc

2001093117

202

Figure 2.3 A (redacted) police report of a witness interview in the Bruce Chamberlain homicide investigation

KANSAS CITY, MISSOURI POLICE DEPARTMENT

INVESTIGATIVE REPORT [CASE DOCUMENT]

SUPP CASE #96-013994

TITLE OF INVESTIGATION	SUBJECT OF REPORT
HOMICIDE	INTERVIEW OF:
1. George Bryant, B/M, 4/27/63 2. Oscar Bridges, B/M, 12/11/57	Barry [redacted], W/M, 6/[redacted]/59 9103 E. [redacted], KCMO Ph. #737-47[redacted]

REPORT BY:	ASSIGNMENT:	DATE:	PAGE 1 OF 4 PAGES
Det. Kent M[redacted]	Homicide Unit	3/13/96	

On 3/12/96, at 1800 hours, the reporting detective responded to the Adam's Mark Hotel, 9103 E. 39th Street, with the purpose of serving an investigative subpoena to obtain any records related to M[redacted] M[redacted], who reportedly had been staying at the hotel.

The reporting detective contacted Barry [redacted], W/M, 6[redacted]/59, Security Supervisor at Adam's Mark, and served him with the subpoena.

On 3/13/96, at 1930 hours, Mr. H[redacted] responded to Police Headquarters and gave the reporting detective the records from the hotel pertaining to M[redacted] M[redacted]

Mr. H[redacted] stated when he obtained the records and observed the $39.00 room rate, which is the employee discount rate, he recalled M[redacted] staying at the Adam's Mark. Mr. H[redacted] advised while he was staying at the hotel, M[redacted] lost an AC adapter in room 1410 which was returned to him. M[redacted] also lost a pager with the number 523-7410. A copy of the lost and found records were placed in the file.

Upon reviewing hotel records, two rooms were rented to Marcus M[redacted] on 2/2/96, Rooms 1406 and 1410. Mr. M[redacted] shows an address of 4402 Askew. A third room 710 was also rented on 2/4/96 for one day. M[redacted] departed rooms 1410 and 1406 on 2/6/95. Upon reviewing the Adam's Mark Hotel billing records for each room, the following telephone calls from the room were recorded.

ROOM #1410

DATE	TIME	TELEPHONE NUMBER CALLED
2/2/96	23:15	923-3226
2/2/96	23:26	756-1720
2/3/96	08:33	356-0358

Supervisor: Sgt. David B[redacted]
js/ibh
Form 107 P.D.(10-80)

File Page #
A00327[illegible]

Figure 2.4 A (redacted) police report describing an investigative event and witness interview in the Bryant/Bridges homicide investigation

Report of Findings
Regional Criminalistics Laboratory
1525 Holmes
Kansas City, MO 64108
(816)234-5036 Fax #(816)234-5570

VICTIM: GEORGE A. BRYANT
JUNIOR O. BRIDGE
SUSPECT: UNK UNK
OFFENSE: HOMICIDE

CASE # 96013994
REPORT # 11
DATE: 03/13/97
REPORTED BY:
WILLIAM L. N[redacted]
FIREARMS/TOOLMARK EXAMINER II

SUMMARY OF RESULTS

None of the shoes in Items 22-1 thru 22-6 made either of the shoe prints on Items 6-19 and 9-32.

DESCRIPTION OF EVIDENCE

THE FOLLOWING ITEM(S) WERE RECOVERED BY CRIME SCENE TECHNICIAN MICHAEL S. W[redacted] CRIME SCENE INVESTIGATION SECTION FROM 7009 MONROE ON 02/06/96 AND SUBMITTED AS LAB PAGE # 6 ON 02/07/96

ITEM #
6-19 A sealed box containing a piece of compressed bread exhibiting a partial shoe impression

THE FOLLOWING ITEM(S) WERE RECOVERED BY CRIME SCENE TECHNICIAN MICHAEL S. W[redacted] CRIME SCENE INVESTIGATION SECTION FROM 7009 MONROE ON 02/06/96 AND SUBMITTED AS LAB PAGE # 9 ON 02/07/96

ITEM #

9-32 A sealed paper bag containing one piece of linoleum exhibiting a partial shoe print on one side

THE FOLLOWING ITEM(S) WERE RECOVERED BY CRIME SC TECHNICIAN CHARLES F. [redacted] CRIME SCENE INVESTIGATION SECTION FROM 12 & INDIANA ON 02/14/96 AND SUBMITTED AS LAB PAGE # 22 ON 02/16/96

RECORDS COPY

PAGE 1 OF 2

A00231

Figure 2.5 A (redacted) Crime Lab Report #11 in the Bryant/Bridges homicide investigation *(Continued)*

96013994
REPORT# 11

DESCRIPTION OF EVIDENCE (CONTINUED)

ITEM #	
22-1	One pair of Reebok shoes
22-2	Six pairs of Nike shoes
22-3	One pair of Kani sandals
22-4	Two pairs of Fila shoes
22-5	One Fila tennis shoe
22-6	One K-Swiss tennis shoe

RECORDS COPY

PAGE 2 OF 2
A00232

Figure 2.5 (Continued)

KANSAS CITY, MISSOURI POLICE DEPARTMENT

PHYSICAL EVIDENCE/PROPERTY INVENTORY REPORT

Supp. CRN 96-013994

Approved By [redacted] Date 02/06/96 Page 23 Of 46

Type of Offense: ☒ Homicide ☐ Rape ☐ Robbery ☐ Assault ☐ Burglary ☐ Stealing ☐ Auto Theft ☐ Arson ☐ Forgery ☐ Other

To Be Used As Evidence? ☒ Yes ☐ No

May Property Room Release Or Dispose Of Property According To Approved Procedures? ☐ Yes ☒ No

U.S. Currency/Coin To Be Held In Original Form - Do Not Deposit - ☐

U.S. Currency/Coin To Be Deposited ☐ Authorized By

Victims Name Bryant (Last) George (First) A (MI)

Bridges Junior O.

Suspect (1) (3)

Suspect (2) (4)

Location of Recovery 7009 Monroe (Address)

Unit Handling Follow-up Investigation Homicide

☐ CPD ☒ MPD ☐ EPD ☐ NPD ☐ SPD ☐ Other

Vehicle Recovered From — Year, Make, Color

License Number/State — V.I.N. Number

Recovered From — Last, First, MI, Race, Sex, DOB

☐ Victim ☐ Suspect ☐ Finder ☒ Other Scene

Address 7009 Monroe Phone No.

Owner of Property — Last, First, MI, Address, Phone

Person Arrested — Last, First, MI — Booking Slip #/ GOS #/ UTT # (Circle One)

☒ Firearms and Toolmark ☐ Chemistry ☒ Trace Evidence ☐ Fingerprints ☐ Documents ☐ Other

Item No.	Bag No.	No. of Articles	Narcotics Field Test +/-	Description	Serial Number	Estimated Value
6	1	1		Copper jacket fragment		NV
7	1	2		Motorola Pager in black Holster		NV
8	1	1		Swab of apparent blood from		—
—	—	—		concrete garage floor		NV
9	1	1		Swab of apparent blood from		—
—	—	—		concrete garage floor NW of steps		NV
10	1	1		Copper jacket fragment		NV
11	1	1		Spent projectile from north		—
—	—	—		garage wall		NV

LABORATORY USE ONLY

Lab. Case #

Lab Page #

Exam. and Date

PROPERTY ROOM USE ONLY

Control

Location

Rec'd By

Date Rec'd

Disposition

TOTAL NV

Reporting Officer CST [redacted] Serial No. [redacted] 000048

Figure 2.6 A (redacted) physical evidence/inventory report in the Bryant/ Bridges homicide investigation

Chapter 3

Building My Murder Memo (Part 1): Organizing the Details

Before reviewing the raw data (i.e., Discovery) in Ricky Kidd's case, I already had 20+ years of exposure to homicide investigations. That's how long it took me to develop the ways I "investigate the investigation."

However, my thought process about reviewing complex criminal investigations had started evolving long before that. To begin at the beginning: My first interest in crime and mystery began as a young kid, reading *The Hardy Boys* books by Frank Dixon.

Fast forward to working in "The Cop Shop" at the Houston Police Dept. (HPD) as a reporter with the *Houston Chronicle* in 1983. At that time, Eric, Dan (a different Dan), and I covered three shifts at the Houston Police Department, seven days a week. Randy and Doug covered crime and violence for the two 24-hour-news/Talk AM radio stations. Jack, Susan, Mark, John, and many others covered The Cop Shop for the *Houston Post*. We reported on more than 500 violent deaths each year in Houston and the Harris County area. That year, the City of Houston exceeded 300 homicides.

I started out on the rookie shift – Thursday through Sunday 3 p.m.–1 a.m. On any given Friday, it was possible for Cop Shop reporters to make two homicide scenes before our dinner break. We might stop at KFC on our way back to the office to start filing our stories of mayhem, knowing it would get busier after 10 p.m. I worked at the cop shop full-time for two years and filled in for several years after. I could count the number of homicides I worked on, but I'd rather not. It was a large number, easily more than 1,000. Added to that were violent deaths caused by random, and not so random, accidents, bad behavior, poor choices, acts of God, all regrettable stuff.

Our physical office – "The Cop Shop" – was a large, rectangular room with five desks, a couple of bookshelves filled with outdated city directories, phone books, and Key Maps, and six wall-mounted speakers tuned to multiple police radio channels. Whenever we heard a request for a "body car," or the code for "homicide," we grabbed our notepads and listened

DOI: 10.4324/9781003543299-3

for an address. We took pride in showing up to report every homicide in the city or county. Despite our respective media outlets being in competition, we knew that getting to a crime scene minutes before our competition didn't matter much since both newspapers came out the next day. Sometimes we all rode in one car.

At the homicide scene we got the basic information from Raul or J.C, the department's Public Information Officers. Sharing daily visits to sometimes gruesome, always morbid, crime scenes made it easy for friendships to develop. J.C. and Raul knew we needed information. They usually tried to help us as best they could. They buffered us from the pairs of homicide detectives called out to each scene. We knew most of these detectives by name, but they seldom spoke to us while they worked in the field.

We knew one detective was designated as the lead detective. He concerned himself with the body and the immediate crime scene. The other detective worked the people, the obvious witnesses – anyone close to the victim, anyone who saw the crime. If he wanted a neighborhood canvass conducted for potential witnesses, he just asked the nearest patrol sergeant for help. Soon, patrol officers began knocking on doors.[1]

The *Houston Chronicle*, the city's *Paper of Record*, felt that each victim of violent death in Houston deserved public recognition and acknowledgment of their life and death. Our job was to describe to our 1 million readers the *who*, *what*, *when*, *where*, and *how* (but seldom *why*) – essentially, the *what happened*, on this individual's last day on earth. More often than not, we were asked to provide this information in two paragraphs. Two short paragraphs. On occasion, we were given much more room, on the front page, to explain what happened.

On Friday, June 10, 1983, I reported on the following five homicides in Houston:

- Jesus Banuelos, 25, address undetermined, was shot to death at 3:15 a.m. today during an argument with his girlfriend's brother at the woman's apartment at 3954 Arlington Square. Police said Banuelos was visiting his girlfriend and her brother was also in the apartment. The two men were drinking beer when an argument started. Banuelos was shot once in the chest and once in the arm with a small-caliber handgun and the girlfriend's brother fled. He was being sought today, police said.

1 During this time, there were zero female homicide detectives employed with the Houston Police Dept.

- A 36-year-old man was found shot to death in the middle of the street in the 4600 block of Alvin about 3:30 a.m. today. Police said the motive and gunman were unknown and no one they questioned admitted to knowing anything about it.
- Claude Wallace Celestin, 24, who lived at the Harbor Light Center, 2407 N Main was stabbed once in the neck at 6:15 p.m. Thursday and died in Hermann Hospital two hours later. Detective R. Holland said a man had entered the center's food line through an exit door, apparently bypassing the mandatory religious services. Celestin approached the man, told him about the center's rules, and said he couldn't eat without checking with the supervisor. Celestin and the suspect were walking down a hallway to talk to the supervisor when the man pulled a knife and stabbed Celestin, Holland said. He said the man fled, eluding others in the food line who pursued him outside.
- Carlton Dale Readeaux, 31, of 3906 Belgrade, was stabbed once in the chest during an argument in the 3200 block of Elgin in southeast Houston about 4 p.m. Thursday. He was dead at the scene. The suspect ran but was arrested later. Clarence Leroy Milsap, 37, of 3339 Elgin, was charged today with murder and was being held in lieu of $20,000 bond.
- The body of an unidentified Latin American male in his 20s was discovered under an abandoned sofa in a ditch in the 6000 block of Garrow Thursday afternoon. Detective S.A. Cain said the man apparently was killed nearly two days earlier. He had what appeared to be stab wounds in the neck and head.

only one seriously injured in the accident.

Police probe five unrelated homicides here

BY DANNY GROTHAUS
Chronicle Staff

Houston police were investigating five unrelated homicides, two of them fatal shootings which occurred today, and three fatal stabbings.

• Jesus Banuelos, 25, address undetermined, was shot to death at 3:15 a.m. today during an argument with his girlfriend's brother at the woman's apartment at 3954 Arlington Square.

Police said Banuelos was visting his girlfriend and her brother was also in the apartment. The two men were drinking beer when an argument started. Banuelos was shot once in the chest and once in the arm with a small-caliber handgun, and the girlfriend's brother fled. He was being sought today, police said.

• A 36-year-old man was found shot to death in the middle of the street in the 4600 block of Alvin about 3:30 a.m. today.

Police said the motive and gunman were unknown and no one they questioned admitted to knowing anything about it.

• Claude Wallace Celestin, 24, who lived at the Harbor Light Center, 2407 N. Main, was stabbed once in the neck at 6:15 p.m. Thursday and died in Hermann Hospital two hours later.

Detective R. Holland said a man had entered the center's food line through an exit door, apparently bypassing the mandatory religous services. Celestin approached the man, told him about the center's rules and said he couldn't eat without checking with the supervisor.

Celestin and the suspect were walking down a hallway to talk to the supervisor when the man pulled a knife and stabbed Celestin, Holland said.

He said the man fled, eluding others in the food line who pursued him outside.

• Carlton Dale Readeaux, 31, of 3906 Belgrade, was stabbed once in the chest during an argument in the 3200 block of Elgin in southeast Houston about 4 p.m. Thursday. He was dead at the scene.

The suspect ran, but was arrested later. Clarence Leroy Milsap, 37, of 3339 Elgin, was charged today with murder and was being held in lieu of $20,000 bond.

• The body of an unidentifed Latin American male in his 20s was discovered under an abandoned sofa in a ditch in the 6000 block of Garrow Thursday afternoon.

Detective S.A. Cain said the man apparently was killed nearly two days earlier. He had what appeared to be stab wounds in the neck and head.

Detectives ask that anyone with information on the man's identity or circumstances of his death contact police at 222-TIPS.

Figure 3.1 My news story in the *Houston Chronicle*, published June 10, 1983

These crime scenes could be horrific. I'm not surprised I can still picture some homicide victims and crime scenes from long ago:

- *Late one Thursday night, while talking to Raul and looking past him, under a distant streetlight, I could see a man lying on his driveway in his bathrobe, a puddle of blood beneath his head where he had been shot. He had heard a noise and walked outside to check on his car. He had lived in a nice one-story ranch house, in what appeared, in the dark, to be a nice suburban neighborhood.*
- *Early on a Friday evening, I saw three female office workers brought out on stretchers from their free-standing real estate office set back slightly from a busy street with its six lanes of steady traffic. Each victim had been shot and killed at their desk, about 5 p.m. No cash or valuables were missing. This case was never solved.*
- *One night, we saw a young man lying on a sidewalk next to some tables and chairs outside a trendy midtown restaurant. The recently added outdoor seating had become a new attraction. This customer, sitting outside with his date and two friends, had argued with an armed would-be robber before he was shot in the chest. The would-be robber, now a murderer, fled on foot.*
- *One cloudy, rainy afternoon, we saw a 7-year-old boy lying on a narrow street covered with a white sheet. He was running home from school on a typically narrow Houston Street with no curbs or sidewalks, just an open drainage ditch sloping down along either side of the narrow two-lane blacktop. He slipped and fell just as a garbage truck was backing up. The boy's head was crushed. This was a tragedy, not a homicide.*

Based on my experience reporting homicides back then, I recall that roughly 60 percent of all murders were committed by a relative or an acquaintance – someone the victim knew. And the other 40 percent of these homicides would initially appear to be more random, investigative *whodunnits*.

Before detectives left the scene of most of these homicides, they were likely building their case against the relative or acquaintance, seen by others committing the crime. Police were gathering forensic evidence and wrapping up eyewitness statements to deliver to the prosecutor's office before their shift ended.

These "acquaintance homicides" were strictly perfunctory investigations – a homicide investigation following an obvious set of facts, leading investigators quickly and easily to a valid suspect. The police were doing as they had been trained to do. Two or three witnesses saw a relative, or an acquaintance, argue with, then kill, another relative or friend and then flee in a known car, probably to a known location. Investigators simply followed the facts right to the suspect. They may have even found the murder weapon somewhere along the way.

An eyewitness who already knows and can "ID" the suspect represents strong evidence – as long as the environment allows the witness to get a good look at the assailant. Experts agree, it is dramatically easier to *recognize* a familiar face committing a crime than it is to *identify* a stranger hours or days after seeing that person commit a violent act.

These other homicides, the whodunnits, were often the result of a robbery, or some kind of criminal contact, possibly a random argument with a stranger which escalated.

Given the nature of this book, understand that many homicides which first appear "random" may represent the logical conclusion to a dysfunctional (yet, unknown) relationship. Not discovering the existence of that unknown relationship between victim and assailant during the initial investigation could lead to a wrongful conviction.

Deadly disagreements over drug turf, and turf in general, throughout the 1980s, represented a new homicidal trend. The record-setting mayhem I reported on was pre-gang-era violence. The handgun remained the weapon of choice in most murders, followed by the knife and blunt weapons – with one unique exception, at least from my news stories. One road rage murder I wrote about for Houston's *Paper of Record*, was committed with a 7-iron.

Among those homicides, which didn't solve themselves, I think homicide detectives, in a good year, cleared about half of the whodunnits.

Assuming my anecdotal figure (in Houston from the early 1980s) was roughly correct – that 60 percent of these homicides were solved immediately, or fairly easily – investigators then solved about half of the whodunnits for a formal clearance rate of roughly 70 to 80 percent. Investigators solved these whodunnits based on a hunch, maybe an eyewitness, maybe an anonymous "Crime-Stoppers" tip, or a snitch. More ideally, police solved the whodunnit with a latent print, or some conclusive physical evidence found at the scene. Any of these investigative events may lead to an admission, or a denial and a trial. This was also pre-DNA, c. 1980–1986.

Looking back, I found that my anecdotal instincts were pretty close to the nationwide statistics from that time period. The national homicide clearance rate in 1980 was 71 percent. By 2020, the clearance rate had steadily dropped since the 1970s to 54 percent and appears to have leveled off. Ref: FBI data, analyzed by the Marshall Project.

As for the association in homicides between victim and actor, the vast majority of homicides are committed by an associate, friend, or relative of the victim, according to the FBI's data from 1985, 1990, 2000, 2010, and 2020. The homicide numbers ranged between 20,392 (in 1990) and 13,420 (in 2020). Data consistently showed that strangers committed these homicides between 14 percent of the time (in 1985) and 10 percent of the time (in 2020).

The FBI's Uniform Crime Reporting (UCR) Program asks but does not require all Law Enforcement agencies to provide this type of supplemental homicide data (i.e., Victim's Relationship to Offender). The number of reporting agencies providing this detail of supplemental data has apparently declined.

In 1985, the relationship between victim and offender was listed as unknown in 30 percent of the homicides reported (with 14 percent of the cases identifying the offender as a stranger and 52 percent of the cases identifying the offender as someone related, acquainted, or associated with the victim.)

The number of "unknowns" among homicides reported grew steadily to 50 percent by 2020. That year, data indicated 10 percent of the homicides were committed by a stranger and 38 percent were committed by an acquaintance, associate, or relative.

When I worked in The Cop Shop, I wanted to think that all of those "cleared" cases at HPD represented cases they "probably" got right. However, I'm sure there are some "cleared" cases where they only, "maybe" got it right. Chances are their suspects were convicted at trial.

And we know about half of those whodunnits were never solved, meaning they were not able to get those right at all. One could argue that an *open case* is better than locking up the wrong person for the rest of their life. In this business, that question remains open to debate.

Unsolved homicide cases, in a back-handed way, told me the police were making an honest effort to get it right. Whodunnits are difficult. I saw, close up, the pressure, the tedious work, and the luck involved in solving a whodunnit. And I was especially aware of the added pressure, noteworthy homicides – crimes which we put on the front page – placed on investigators.

As reporters, we sometime played this competitive game by trying to create a "front page angle" and sell an editor with a novel lead. A few times we succeeded in bumping a "two-paragraph homicide" from the back pages onto page one with a creative phrase or news angle. Homicide detectives were not amused.

There were a few homicide detectives who, I believed, cut corners to get a suspect off the street or to clear a case. I later gained first-hand knowledge of that corner-cutting activity.

Yet, I still believed most Houston homicide detectives set out to get it right. And I think most homicide detectives went to sleep most nights believing they got it right.

It was enlightening to me, as a reporter, seeing how detectives built their cases. It was equally enlightening when witnesses approached a reporter, claiming detectives were getting it wrong. On occasion, I spoke to a relevant witness whom the police had never interviewed. Sometimes, detectives found out what this witness knew by reading the newspaper. Sometimes, this new witness contradicted a homicide theory, which detectives had already submitted to the prosecutor. Or sometimes, this new information helped investigators with a case they were – thankfully – still investigating.

As a reporter, I once contacted a person I thought might be relevant to a high-profile capital murder trial beginning that week in Houston. During our conversation about his former roommate – the defendant, now on trial – my interviewee became a key witness.

At his request, through a conduit, the former roommate's account was made available to both the prosecutor and the defense, simultaneously – mid-trial. This witness provided convincing and credible evidence that the defendant had voluntarily described to this witness, the defendant's role in the murder of the two people he was charged with killing. The murders, per this former roommate, were committed at the request of a third party known to the police but unsuspected – up to that point. Within 24 hours, the defense accepted a plea deal, and the state gained an indictment against the third party, with their original capital murder defendant now agreeing to turn state's evidence (in exchange for prison time instead of death).

The police had never contacted this person, despite his obvious relationship to many people involved in this crime.

Also, as a reporter, I learned that just because a witness comes forward, their story isn't necessarily true, or wholly true. And so, I began to realize there were many more sides to a complex crime, many more angles than what Raul or J.C. could offer at a crime scene. It seems there were always other witnesses out there whom the detectives had not contacted. Maybe the witness was initially reluctant to talk. Maybe that witness was at work when the police canvassed the neighborhood. Maybe the witness did not like, or trust, the police, or did not like the approach used by police. Whatever the reason, I saw that even a good homicide investigation might have gaps or lack the facts needed to know the complete story.

Eventually, I struck out on my own at homicide scenes. I gathered my own witness statements while waiting for Raul or J.C. to pass along the official version. I began finding discrepancies, then contradictions – sometimes small, sometimes significant – between the witnesses I interviewed and the information the police passed along. Not always. But sometimes.

With this understanding of the process, a few years later, in 1988, I began working for criminal defense attorneys. I was fortunate in Houston to work with some of the best criminal defense lawyers in the country. My first capital murder defense team was headed by Richard "Racehorse" Haynes. (A Houston lawyer, named one of the nation's top Criminal Defense Attorneys by *Time* magazine. Haynes was a Texas legend and a star of the legal world, after winning a series of high-profile Texas murder trials in the 1970s and 1980s.) I gained additional criminal defense experience under attorneys Kent Schaffer, Stan Schneider, George "Mac" Secrest, and other highly skilled Houston defense lawyers. Houston lawyers back then described local criminal defense work to me (jokingly?) as "professional mud wrestling."

During that time (the 1980s) in Houston/Harris County, the Death Row population of Harris County alone ranked third compared with the Death Row populations of all other states. Only the entire state of Texas and the state of Florida had more Death Row inmates than had come out of the Harris County Courts. Legendary Harris County Prosecutor, Johnny Holmes, was an avid proponent of the Death Penalty.

Prosecutor Holmes told me once, without evidence, that the existence and use of the Death Penalty prevented homicides. He simply knew that to be true.

After years of reporting on crime, covering homicide investigations and sitting through some lengthy capital murder trials, I became a participant in what I believed would be a minor role.

In 1988, as a fledgling criminal defense investigator, my professional evolution began. Early on, I learned, through observation, the importance of organization. Journalism requires short-term organization. I had that. Criminal defense work requires long-term organization; this degree of organization:

- Being able to locate a fact, discovered two years earlier and initially thought to be insignificant ...
- Being able to recognize context from 500+ pages of Discovery delivered in a random stack ...
- Being able to keep track of dozens of items – physical evidence – through collection, lab analysis, and forensic reports, to identify the one piece, which was misplaced, ignored, or never tested ...

- Being able to put one complex case aside, while working on two other cases for six months, then picking that case back up, exactly where you left off ...
- Being able to manage contact information on 50 to 100+ witnesses, not knowing until the last minute which 8 witnesses will be needed in court ...
- Being able to quickly find and share this information with attorneys who have their own mountain of legal information to maintain.

(Sadly, and to their clients' detriment, not all criminal defense teams hold organization in high regard.)

Years later (in 2006) in Ricky Kidd's case, I had a specific idea of how I wanted to organize his raw data/Discovery material and approach his claim of innocence.

First, I wanted to create an accurate (and brief) description of the crime and the relevant elements of the criminal investigation. This would be a reference tool, which I believed would remain useful for the life of the case. I wanted to create a user-friendly summary of the police investigation, so that everyone on the defense team could easily grasp the case and the issues as they developed (if they developed).

I knew what elements needed to be available (repeatedly) for quick reference.

I played with, and eventually created my boilerplate, making sure each of these elements of the crime had a place.

I found with Ricky Kidd's case, and with the 50+ cases to follow: the original police investigation developed certain "facts," which would never change. Then I found that my review of the investigation in chronological order would reveal additional, maybe different, "facts" and "elements."

I designed a format to be a fluid document. Throughout the life of any habeas case, I'm able to build and revise and expand this document until all raw data, all new facts, and newly discovered facts are added. Some homicide investigations last one or two weeks. Most investigations stretch out over several months. I have reviewed homicide investigations and their supplemental reports spanning multiple years. This document is not completed until I have reviewed the last police report and the last lab report, the last piece of raw data gained before trial.

I began calling this summary document, in Ricky's case, my *Murder Memo*. As my approach and review of these cases became consistent, my summary work product retained the same label, adding the victim's name out of respect. In Ricky's case, the *Bryant & Bridges Murder Memo*.

These *subject areas* offer brief descriptions based on my review of the raw data. Every relevant fact about the crime and the investigation has a place. I use the same subject areas for every case I review:

(Victim's) Murder Memo

CRIME:	[I create a *BRIEF* description of the crime itself. This brief summary is similar to my Murder Widgets at the *Houston Chronicle* – a very simple, what, when, where.]
CRIME SCENE:	[*BRIEFLY* describe geography and physical characteristics of the crime scene, weather, lighting, exact physical location, relevant surrounding area, etc. in specific and accurate terms.]
VICTIM(S):	[(Always the most important person here) – ID victim at time of crime. List relevant physical characteristics, clothing, relationships to any principals (witness or suspect) prior to the crime. If multiple victims, list all injured here including fatalities and survivors (describe wounds).]
ACTOR(S):	[List (*BRIEFLY*) all physical characteristics or physical description given by eyewitnesses of the actor, soon after the crime. List descriptors only. (If actor is known by name or face, he is a suspect and goes below.) This list will also include "Persons of Interest."]
SUSPECT(S):	[List all suspects, named or described from crime scene witnesses, or other sources. All subsequent suspects named later and ID'd through investigative tips, informants, or lab work. Add physical descriptions. (A suspect may be named but cleared before being arrested. A suspect may be named but never charged.)]
VEHICLE:	[*BRIEFLY* describe any relevant or suspect vehicles ID'd by witnesses, or any vehicles ID'd by investigation as being relevant to crime.]

PHYSICAL EVIDENCE:	[*BRIEFLY* list relevant physical evidence recovered at crime scene. This will be only a partial list of physical evidence, relevant to the crime or tying suspect to the crime scene (i.e., cellphones, prints, shell casings, security video, recorded statements, any item connecting a possible actor to the crime scene).]
MURDER WEAPON:	[*BRIEFLY* describe murder weapon based on known facts, i.e., knife, sharp object, blunt object, apparent strangulation, handgun, 9mm, .45 cal., shotgun etc. Firearm may be ID'd based on caliber of shell casings found, or projectile recovered from victim(s).]
EYEWITNESSES:	[*BRIEFLY* list all eyewitnesses identified in initial reports. Add to list if necessary. Helps to know, at a glance, who claims to have witnessed the crime.]
AUTOPSY:	[*BRIEFLY* describe cause of death, including weapon, fatal injury, bullet(s) recovered, wound trajectory, time of death, toxicology (if relevant). Also list any speculation, any unknowns.]

This boiler plate information is followed by:

CRIME SCENE NARRATIVE:

[Begin notes summarizing initial crime scene investigation with more specifics, describing accurately and exactly who, what, when, where, and how... as much as police discovered at the scene.]

WITNESS INTERVIEWS:

[Summarize witness interviews in sequential-chronological order of contact, not when reports were written or transcribed. Develop consistent format:

At (time/date) (Witness name) was contacted and interviewed by police at (location). (Witness name) told police ...]

Of course, each case is different. Each of my Murder Memos is slightly different. The constants I strive for are *accuracy*, *thoroughness* (of relevant material), and *brevity*, with all relevant material being searchable and traceable (i.e., traceable back to the source = Bates #).

What follows are some examples from past Murder Memos, showing how I described that crime under each topic area. These are good examples of how and why I attempt to place all relevant facts of the crime somewhere in this boilerplate. (Some facts were fictionalized to protect privacy.)

Random Murder Memo

CRIME: ***[I create a BRIEF description of the crime itself. This brief summary is similar to my Murder Widgets at the*** **Houston Chronicle** ***– a very simple, what, when, where.]***

Crime: At about 1:47 a.m. on Friday, 10/17/2020, a triple shooting/double homicide/Agg Assault occurred at 3201 Roosevelt Ave. St Louis. Shooter/Suspect fled on foot.
STL PD Complaint#. 21041xxx
Crime Lab Case# LAB-21-005xxx

Crime: About 5:00 p.m. on 1/19/94 (Sunday), a gray auto stopped at 25th & Calvin. A b/m and b/f got out of the car and approached two b/m's, demanding their Jackets. One b/m offered his jacket, then when he reached into the pocket to retrieve his comb, was shot in the chest by the b/f. Both got back in the car and the car sped off.
Initial Incident #s:
92–165xx
92–165xx
92–165xx
92–165xx

CRIME SCENE: ***[BRIEFLY describe geography and physical characteristics of the crime scene, weather, lighting,***

exact physical location, relevant surrounding area, etc., in specific and accurate terms.]

Crime Scene: Shooting occurred in a vacant 4-family Flat (apt building), 3201 Roosevelt Ave. No utilities appeared to be connected. Officers arrived at 1:53 a.m. to "shooting." Upstairs police found K.S. who directed police to the bedroom where they found (fully clothed) C.W. (#1) and B.W. (#2) w/GSWs to their head/neck (deceased). K.S. taken to St Louis U Hospital critical/stable. Upstairs bedroom described as having a mattress on the floor and one battery-powered light on the south wall above the mattress. V#1 found on floor east of mattress. V#2 found on floor on east side of room. Open purse left on bed – cash visible/debit card visible.

Crime Scene: J.D. (victim) and R.A. (witness) were walking eastbound on 25th. The suspect car (Per R.A.) was westbound. The car turned left (south) onto Calvin in front of J.D. and R.A., then stopped on 25th St. (south side of the intersection). Police say J.D. and R.A. were approached while standing at the northwest corner, or north side of the intersection of 25th (east/west) [25′5″ wide] and Calvin (north/south) [30′5″ wide]. J.D. was shot near the northwest (or northeast?) side and ran to the northeast (or southeast?) corner where he collapsed at the curb.

The suspect car, reportedly traveling west on 25th St., had turned on Calvin and stopped, facing south. After the shooting, the car drove south on Calvin.

Temp was 42 degrees. Weather was dry and cloudy.

SUNSET occurred at 5:15 p.m.

VICTIM(S):	***[(Always the most important person here) – ID victim at time of crime. List relevant physical characteristics, clothing, relationships to any principals (witness or suspect) prior to the crime. If multiple victims, list all injured here including fatalities and survivors (describe wounds).]***
Victims:	**(#1) C.W.** (b/f, age 41, 5′2″ 120 lbs.) (suspect = x-boyfriend) Murder 1 [One gsw to left neck below ear w/needle in right hand + one GSW behind rt ear at hairline ... or exit wound + **2nd GSW** to top of rt breast (post-mortem?).] **(#2) B.W.** (w/f, age 33, 4′1″, 115 lbs). (did not know (Suspect)) Murder 1 (one gsw to rt temple). **(#3) K.S.** (B/F born 7/x/1973, 5′3″. 167 lbs.) [1 (or more) GSW to leg/thighs. (Knows (suspect).]
Victims:	J.D. (age 16) shot 1x in chest at 5 p.m. while standing in street (25th & Calvin) next to friend, R.A. Taken to hospital. Pronounced dead at 6:18 p.m.

ACTOR(S):	***[List all physical characteristics or physical description given by eyewitnesses of the actor, soon after the crime. List descriptors only. (If actor is known by name or face, he is a suspect and goes below.) This will also include "Persons of Interest."]***
Actors:	"two men wearing masks ... were waiting for us." (per A.R. (witness)) Shooter #1 – 5′7″–5′9″, wore black hooded sweatshirt, baggie blue jean w/yellow design on back pocket. "He did all the shooting." Shooter #2 – b/m 5′7″–5′9″, wore grayish hooded sweatshirt and light tan pants. Both wore ski masks. Both gangbanger-like, holding guns sideways.

Actors:	**Initial Metro PD**: Suspect #1) B/M, age 19–20, 5′9″ slim w/black hair in dreads, wearing a purple t-shirt and black dickies. #2) B/M, age 19–20, 5′6″ Medium Bld, w/black hair in a fade, wearing purple t-shirt and black dickies. **Initial Campus PD**: Suspect #1) B/M, 5′11″, 160 lbs, w/black hair in "long dread locks" wearing a "white t-shirt." No Suspect #2.

SUSPECT(S):	***[List all suspects, named or described from crime scene witnesses, or other sources. All subsequent suspects named later and ID'd through investigative tips, informants, or lab work. Add physical descriptions. (A suspect may be named but cleared before being arrested. A suspect may be named but never charged.)]***
Suspects Named:	Fred Savin Max George Dennis. Ripley – (Witness saw him w/gun running from shooting) Dean Preacher – (person of interest in photo spread) Ron. F. – (Mike H. heard from (unknown) @12:30 a.m., that Ron F. did it) #4 (in Dean P. 6-pak) "looked like suspect" per Tia C. A. Ripley, ID'd as BluDaddy = the killer, per CI Darious M., aka: D-1 Dan Dan (Anonymous Caller) Cricket (Anonymous Caller)
Suspects:	**Jonathan Blakely** (Driver) and **Marvin Post** (stopped in suspect car at 6:10 p.m.). **Eleanor White** spotted and arrested at 21st & Davis, also, at 6:10 p.m. **Jonathan Blakely** and **Eleanor White** ID'd on 1/30 as (by N Franklin) + **Eleanor White** and **Marvin Post** ID'd by Roger R on 2/3.

VEHICLE:	***[BRIEF description of any relevant or suspect vehicles ID'd by witnesses, or any vehicles ID'd by investigation as being relevant to crime.]***
Vehicle ID:	Gray Chevy Corsica, 4-dr, w/Ohio LP (???) [NO WITNESS ID'd this as the shooter's car.] ... or ... Older model gray or lt blue Chevy Caprice or Olds (1978–82?) with broken rear pass window (covered w/cardboard?) (per Wit 1, Wit 2, and Wit 3)
Suspect Auto:	1986 Chevy Corsica w/Ohio LP# xxx ###, [VIN: 1G1LT54GOLY######] (stopped at **6:10 p.m.** at 21st & Davis, after leaving 2802 W 18th St. Police arrested **Jonathan Blakely**, **Marvin Post** and **Eleanor White** at this time.) Reportedly involved in agg asslt ~~about 3:30 pm~~ **at 4 p.m.** at 23rd & Locust(?) Owner: Bravo Rental Co. WRONG CAR? See (Witness #1, #2, and #3)
Actor Auto:	Clean, white Olds Cutlass 4-dr. (Later ID'd): 1995 White Olds Cutlass Cierra (owner = Alamo Rental)
Suspect Auto:	1981 White Olds Delta 88

PHYSICAL EVIDENCE:	***[BRIEF listing of relevant physical evidence recovered at crime scene. This will be only a partial list of physical evidence, relevant to the crime or tying suspect to the crime scene (i.e., cellphones, prints, shell casings, security video, any item connecting a possible actor to the crime scene).]***
Physical Evidence:	– Six .22 cal and one .25 cal shell casings found at scene. – Three bullets recovered (a .25 cal and two .22 cal) had both left and right twist

	marks indicating two different firearms were present at the crime scene. – Money found in victim's sock, pants, and jacket pockets = $475. – #39 Blood? Sample from driver side hood of Misty B's car (OK LP# TPE ###) – #33 (Exh #14) bloody tissue paper found on 101st East Ave, south of Trapeze Lounge w/unknown DNA profile. DID NOT match victims or (witness). (SEE 0371). – [DNA?] Police found a tan and Black hooded coat in dumpster located in northwestern Parking Lot of apt complex southeast of Trapeze Lounge. (Exh 8) – Money Bag (containing $300) found in V's left jacket sleeve (@ Autopsy) – .22 Colt semi-auto pistol + ski mask + jersey glove (found together 7 months after crime in area lake) [NOTE: Sophia S. was sure (Victim) used a money belt for his cash, and stuffed paper receipts in his moneybag. No Money Belt found.] #37 – Nokia Cricket Cell phone obtained at hospital from surviving victim. Called "Angel" 402-50xx at 2:58 a.m. (SEE 0150, 0164)
Physical Evidence:	– Recovered at Autopsy: a "flattened, large caliber, copper jacketed bullet," located in right posterior shoulder (Photo G). – Gun Shot Residue Kit administered to **Eleanor White** at 7:00 p.m. on 1/19/94. Item E-3. (Tag # 92-12xx) – Gunshot Residue Kit administered to **Jonathan Blakely** (Tag # 92-12xx) – Intra Tec-9 semi-auto rifle + clip + 14 shells (SN#1329xx [Tag# 92-13xx] – A .38 Cal revolver #6918xx was submitted for testing. Tag# 92-16xx – MISSING: Any report or explanation for source of this .38 revolver.

MURDER WEAPON:	***[BRIEFLY describe murder weapon based on known facts, i.e., knife, sharp object, blunt object, apparent strangulation, handgun, 9mm, .45 cal., shotgun, etc. Firearm may be ID'd based on caliber of shell casings found, or projectile recovered from victim(s).]***
Weapon:	Initially described by witnesses as a revolver. (No shell casings recovered.) ME recovered two .38 cal bullets.
Weapon:	Per Lab/ME: Probably a .38 cal, (possibly 9mm or .380. (Witnesses ID'd "snub nose" revolver.) Lab confirmed the Tech 9 confiscated from Jonathan Blakely was NOT the murder weapon.
Weapon:	.22 cal bullets removed from V's abdomen and Rt Thigh. .25 cal shell casings also found at scene.

EYEWITNESS:	***[BRIEFLY list all eyewitnesses identified in initial reports. Add to list if necessary. Helps to know, at a glance, who claims to have witnessed the crime.]***
Witnesses:	Karla. B., b/f (age 4.5) (mom = S. P., of 73xx Wilson). George. W., b/m (age 70), of 7007 Monroe (neighbor) Shannon. H. (?) (neighbor) Anonymous Caller #1 (= Phyllis D?) Richard H. (?) (neighbor) Earl R. (?)

Witnesses:	Henry P[redacted] (Campus Police) Joseph P[redacted] (Campus Police) 7 Campus officers inside Gentry Hall, per Henry P. 5 Campus officers outside Gentry Hall, per Henry P. Campus Video Camera Operator, per Thomas Pxxxxxx.

Charles C. (gsw victim) (Unnamed Witness #2?)
Alfred C. (uncle)
Tia C. (mom)

Kya W. (3rd party)
Marquetta C. (aunt) (Unnamed Witness #4)
Jasmin M. (3rd party)
Sherica G. (Shooting rt in front. Saw nothing – ran.
Met G.B. outside
Faye Y. (Saw shooting, w/Sherica G.)
Unnamed Witness #3 (= Allie B.???)

AUTOPSY: ***[Very BRIEF cause of death, including weapon, fatal injury, bullet(s) recovered, wound trajectory, time of death, toxicology (if relevant). Also list any speculation, any unknowns.]***

Autopsy: (#298) Two bullets removed from (victim's) body consistent w/a .22 cal gun. #55 was an "intact bullet" recovered from abdomen. #56 was a "markedly deformed projectile" recovered from the right thigh.

Cause of death: First shot struck the heart through the Victim's left side.

(Per FSI 2011 memo) – Med Records of surviving victim stated: Evidence recovered also included #24, a .25 metal jacketed bullet w/6 lands and grooves bearing a right twist w/dried blood and tissue (cleaned). Bullet recovered from (victim) at crime scene. Bullet had sufficient markings for inclusion in NIBIN.

Autopsy: Case# ME09-08xx – Autopsy by Dr. Bruce L.

Cause of Death = Two GSW into left torso and left back. One bullet penetrated left lung and right common carotid artery. Both bullets recovered. ("medium caliber") Two thru-and-thru GSWs of left arm may be from same bullet(s), or different bullet or bullets. Multiple scars. Multiple tattoos on face and both arms. Toxicology was negative for alcohol and/or drug use.

Oklahoma v. Karl Fontenot

My review of Discovery in Karl Fontenot's case was one of the oddest example of my innocence cases. Clearly, these cases seldom arrive packaged the same way. By necessity, my review of this case was done piecemeal. Only the end results mattered.

That's what I meant in Chapter 1 when I pointed out, I can only review what I have to review. In June 2012, Attorney Tiffany Murphy asked me to work on this case with her and her students at the Oklahoma Innocence Project. I literally started with John Grisham's non-fiction book, *The Innocent Man*, published in 2006. I began building my Murder Memo with what facts I derived from Grisham, believing his sources were official records of some kind.

I then learned that Grisham relied heavily on a previously written book: *The Dreams of Ada*, by Robert Mayer, originally published in 1987. I read that book – still lacking a complete set of police reports – and made notes which also contributed to my Murder Memo and my growing list of questions, aka: *Queries/Needs/To Dos*. (At one point, I called and spoke to the author, Robert Mayer, who very generously discussed his sources – all officials and public records.)

I made a preliminary trip to Oklahoma City, and met with Tiffany and students on Thursday, June 28, 2012. Students and I traveled to Ada, Okla, that weekend, to contact some *alibi witnesses*. This sequence may be the exception, but it is not uncommon to initially approach alibi witnesses, who *should* be friendly, to assess a client's alibi and "pick the brains" of friendly witnesses. It's a good way to "jump-start" an investigation, gain some traction, and get students or new investigators some experience with "friendly," albeit, very important, witnesses. We began learning the lay of the land and started gaining context for the Discovery we were about to digest.

Tiffany obtained the first 860 pages of Discovery (paper photocopies of microfilm) from the Oklahoma State Bureau of Investigation (OSBI) using a standard Open Records request. She Bates-stamped the pages, then forwarded that Discovery to me in early August. The reports were in random order. For instance, the initial crime scene report was found at Bates "OSBI #330."

My Day Timer notes indicate I began organizing in chronological order, then reviewing Ada Police reports on Tuesday, August 14. I spent 34 hours reviewing those police reports, making notes, and building my Murder Memo. I spent another couple of hours reviewing and editing my Murder Memo before delivering my summary review (i.e., Haraway Murder Memo) to Tiffany on Saturday, August 25.

Over the next few years, we obtained additional Discovery. So, my original Murder Memo grew with additional, investigative facts. (This *additional* Discovery wasn't necessarily *new* Discovery. By comparing newly

Haraway Murder Memo

[LAST UPDATE 8/28/12]

Crime:

Store clerk Donna Haraway was apparently abducted (and store robbed) sometime between 8:30 pm and 8:45 pm on Saturday, 4/28/84, from McAnally's Convenience Store at 2727 East Arlington, Ada, OK. She was reported missing at 8:50 pm by store customer Gene [redacted] w/m of Ada, OK.
Ada PD Case# 84 - 98

Crime Scene:

McNally's Convenience Store at 2727 East Arlington, Ada Ok. Customer walked into store around 8:45 pm and clerk/Haraway was gone. Mgr determined $167 missing from register. (5s, 10s, 20s.) Bag with larger bills -- $440 -- untouched beneath drawer. And $500 cash untouched in the safe. Haraway's purse undisturbed behind counter containing her ID and car keys. No sign of struggle inside or outside the store. Tape showed last item rung-up was a Tall-Boy beer. Rung up, but register count indicates the 80 cents was not placed in register. Last credit card purchase made by [redacted] at 7 pm.

Weather:

High was 82 degrees, low was 57 degrees. No precipitation.

Daylight:

Actual sunset was 7:09 pm, with Civil Twilight ending at 7:36 pm. By 8:45 pm, it was night-time with a dark sky. There was only a waning crescent moon on 4/28/84.

Victim:

Donna Denice Haraway, ([redacted]/59) w/f age 24, of 202 East 14th St., Ada OK.
Spouse: [redacted] Haraway
Physical ID: [Ref: Missin Person report completed 4/29/84 by stepfather, Robert [redacted]] 5'5" 110 lbs, brown eyes, w/long curly sandy brown hair. ("dyed blonde/brown w/red tint") Last seen wearing (size 7) plaid blouse – color unknown (possibly Lavender w/blue flowers, lace around neck line. (size 7) blue jeans (Levi's 501), (size 6.5) white canvas tennis shoes, white anklet socks, gray zip-up, long-sleeved warm-up w/hood. Wore diamond engagement ring +wedding band. Wore small post-type earrings, hypoallergenic. Wore Timex watch w/brown band.
POE: 2727 East Arlington, Ada, OK. Non-smoker.

Grothaus Investigations - 1 -

Figure 3.2 My Haraway Murder Memos, pages 1–3, based on 800+ pages of police reports *(Continued)*

NAMED Suspects:	Thomas Jessie Ward, w/m age 24, 5'8" 145 lbs, lt brown hair/blue eyes Karl Allen Fontenot, w/m age 19, 5'8" 132 lbs dark brown (black) hair/green eyes (Neither had access to a vehicle) Odell Titsworth, w/m age 25,
Actors: (Initial Suspects)	Suspect #1 (Seen at JP's) -- w/m approx 6', slender, collar length light brown hair, no facial hair, about 22 – 24 yoa, wearing blue t-shirt, faded blue jeans, white tennis shoes. Suspect #2 (Seen at JP's) – w/m 5'8" – 5'10" lt brown or blonde hair, ear lobe length, shorter than #1, about 22 – 24 yoa, wearing white t-shirt, faded blue jeans, tennis shoes.
Vehicles:	Suspect vehicle described many ways. Official description (0003) in 4/29/84 BULLETIN: early model Chevy pu truck w/light gray primer color, **narrow bed** w/oversized tires on rear. Rear end was jacked up.
Physical evidence:	Store Cash Register Tape. Video of T Ward and K Fontenot Interview/Confessions Polygraph Data (?) Remains of Donna Haraway reportedly located on 1/21/86 in Hughes Co. The location is 24.1 miles EAST of Ada on Hwy 1, 8.9 miles south of intersection of Hwy 43 and Hwy 1, back to the east on a county road .4 of a mile. The body was located 500 yards north in a wooded area along side of a hill. Cause of death listed as one GSW to back of head. Condition of skeletal remains unknown. Some clothing remnants recovered. Some jewelry recovered. Photos (2 rolls) of immediate area where remains discovered. Unknown if any hair found with the remains.
Autopsy:	xxx
Police/Investigators:	Original report, Mike [redacted] (219) OBI agent Harvey [redacted] (composite drawings

Grothaus Investigations - 2 -

Figure 3.2 (Continued)

OBI Gary [redacted] original eye-witness interviews
OBI Dennis [redacted]
OBI Agent Jackie [redacted] hypnotist

Initial Police Report

Original report quotes a ? witness who saw suspects in store approx 1.5 hrs before leaving store at 8:30 pm, presumably with Haraway.

Reporting parties = **Gene [redacted]** of Ada, OK and **Lennie [redacted]** (?) of [redacted] N [redacted] Moore, OK.

[redacted] pulled into parking lot and saw a w/m w/brown hair and a w/f w/blonde hair got into driver's side of a grey older model pu and drive EAST on Arlington (into Ada). He detected nothing suspicious, until he went inside the store and there was no clerk. He called PD.

Karen [redacted] of [redacted] W 13th, Ada, OK is a clerk at JP's convenience store at 2904 E Arlington (2 blks ~~west~~ of McAnally's). She saw 2 men in JPs that night playing pinball machines. (Actually located 2 blocks east of McAnally's on opposite side of street.)

They drove a primer gray pu **w/possibly a narrow bed**.

[redacted] described the men at JP's and these became the descriptions of the "Suspects 1 & 2" in the apparent abduction 2 blks away.

[Suspect #1 -- w/m approx 6', slender, collar length brown hair, no facial hair, about 22 – 24 yoa, wearing blue t-shirt, faded blue jeans, white tennis shoes.]

[Suspect #2 – w/m 5'8" – 5'10" lt brown hair, shorter than #1, about 22 – 24 yoa, wearing white t-shirt, faded blue jeans, tennis shoes.]

With ambiguous evidence, Police immediately advised five states that between 8:30 and 8:45 pm, 4/28/84, "TWO SUBJECTS: robbed the McNally's convenience store located at 2727 E Arlington in Ada, Ok. $167 missing. Clerk is missing and assumed abducted by the robbers.

"These two suspects were in a convenience store across the street from the store robbed, about 10 minutes prior to the robbery. "

Suspect vehicle is "early model pick up poss Chevy with gray primer color, oversize tires (????? Rims). Rear end was jacked up **w/narrow bed**."

This NCIC Bulletin refers to other previous abductions of female clerks from convenience stores.

Grothaus Investigations - 3 -

Figure 3.2 (Continued)

acquired police and lab reports with my Murder Memo, I knew immediately if this was a uniquely *new* or a *duplicate* report. Our ability to identify *New Discovery* was critical in future litigation.)

My completed Murder Memo represented 36 pages of summarized, chronological, searchable notes, traceable back to the original police investigation (by Bates #s). Much of this summary became relevant and persuasive in helping Tiffany convince a judge to grant Karl Fontenot his freedom. However, on August 25, of 2012, I had no idea which police report, or which part of this Murder Memo would get us there.

Let's Discuss ...

Few cases I have worked, probably *none*, had so many original contradictions between the standing conviction and the initial crime scene reports. I realized early on the absolute necessity for detailed and accurate fact-gathering from the original police reports. My Murder Memo needed to identify facts as facts, and speculation as speculation, using attribution when possible, and a liberal use of the modifiers, *reported* and *alleged* and *apparently.*

Starting off with CRIME, I really wasn't sure there had been an abduction, and if so, when it occurred. If the store clerk was abducted, was that abduction witnessed by the reporting witnesses? The man and woman seen leaving the store may or may not have included the store clerk, Denice Haraway. Circumstantial evidence is often ambiguous – like the purse and schoolbooks left behind, the cash left untouched, the cigarette left burning in the ash tray, the open, unfinished can of beer on the counter, the lack of duress shown in the exiting woman's demeanor, and the casual nature of the couple's exit into a pick-up truck.

What qualifies as "relevant facts" about the CRIME SCENE may change as an investigation continues. The "Haraway disappearance" represents an extreme case of random details which may or may not be relevant. I knew this review was my one and only chance to capture and document what may be important, as determined later ... much, much later.

This was the case when additional Discovery provided by the state to Karl's habeas team (... years after the original convictions) included critical crime scene details, never before shared with the defense. This new material included the store's cash register tape, which, initially, helped police identify and contact "customers of interest."

These previously undisclosed police reports were *not* Brady Material, because they did not prove innocence. However, they did open doors and provide leads for our investigation of "what happened," leading to some startling revelations.

A careful review of the newly acquired Discovery begged the question: *what* constitutes a *Suspect*? As in the Haraway case, police reports of such a crime will include physical descriptions of "suspects" and "presumed suspects." Someone seen near a crime scene, immediately before or after a crime, could be either, or neither. Thus, the artful term, *Person of Interest.*

Good police work may turn a *Person of Interest* into a *Good Witness*, or a *Good Suspect.* Or, sometimes, a *Person of Interest* becomes a *Wrongful Conviction.*

In all cases, I use my Murder Memo as a Quick Reference Guide to compare the "raw data" contained in initial witness interviews – often conducted just hours, or even minutes, after a crime occurred – with the suspect, later charged and convicted. These initial, spontaneous descriptions may also be found on a 9-1-1 call or much later during a Defense Team investigation – when a review discovers that the eyewitness provided a physical description, a useful description, which was not included in the police report.

In the Haraway case, the initial *Suspects* were the physical descriptions of two men seen at a different location, at a different time, who were described as, "acting suspicious." The fact that an artist sketch was done only added to the public perception that these two men abducted Denice Haraway. The physical identifiers of the two men seen at a different place appeared to influence the physical description offered by the three witnesses who saw a woman "casually" leave the store with a man (possibly the abduction of Denise Haraway).

And so, the physical characteristics of the arrested suspects, Karl Fontenot and Tommy Ward, become relevant.

In general, I have seen arrest reports and police reports offering physical descriptions of actors/suspects/arrested parties, which are inaccurate – but they happen to match the eyewitness' physical description. Weight can change. Height can change sometimes, depending on one's age. Hair can change. So, it's critical to find some official documentation for height, weight, and hair – *at the time of the crime.*

I'll look for a driver's license, a recent arrest, a prison record, anything official, to compare with the police reports – especially when I find, or I suspect, a discrepancy. Mug shots of *that* arrest can be helpful, but not so much if the arrest comes months after the crime, as in the case of Karl Fontenot and Tommy Ward. Ward and Fontenot were arrested October 18, and October 19, 1984 – almost six months after the crime. That was enough time for their hair length to change.

Remember that preliminary June trip to Ada with Professor Tiffany Murphy's law students? Turns out, one of the first witnesses we contacted easily recalled giving both Karl Fontenot and Tommy Ward haircuts in April of 1984, so they could begin their new jobs. Karl had just gotten a job at a Wendy's Hamburgers franchise which required "short hair." The job started the week after Easter Sunday (April 22, 1984). Ms. Haraway disappeared on Saturday, April 28.

This witness recalled taking several Polaroid photos of Karl and Tommy, including photos taken on that Easter Sunday. She also recalled giving all her Polaroids from that time period to police investigators. Police never returned the photos. Nor were those photos ever found in Discovery.

Chapter 4

Building My Murder Memo (Part 2): Reviewing the Police Investigation

My goal in reviewing the raw data is to begin investigating the investigation, while also investigating the crime. But *what* am I looking for – in general?

Do patterns of behavior exist in wrongful convictions? Are there certain factors consistently found in most wrongful convictions? Are there statistics? Of course there are.

Beyond the 30 cases I investigated, in which we were able to prove innocence,[1] two highly regarded, national databases exist. Both databases offer solid statistical evidence on how wrongful convictions occur.

First, the Innocence Project (IP) reviewed its own cases from the first 25 years of DNA exonerations. Between 1989 and 2014, the Innocence Project reviewed trial transcripts, police and lab reports, and court records from their first 325 exonerations – exonerations based entirely on irrefutable DNA evidence.

Since these exonerations represent criminal convictions formally overturned, based on undisputed scientific evidence, their data is understood to be the *gold standard* for evaluating wrongful convictions.

This data was evaluated and discussed in volume 79 of the *Albany Law Review*, published in December of 2016.

Second, that *Albany Law Review* article refers to the other national database for exonerations – the National Registry of Exonerations (NRE). This registry, also dating back to 1989, is a project of the University of Michigan School of Law, and the University of California Irvine Newkirk Center, which grew out of work conducted at the Northwestern University School of Law Center for Wrongful Convictions.

The NRE data includes the Innocence Project's DNA exonerations, as well as convictions overturned on innocence claims, based on evidence

1 Confirmed by 6 jury acquittals, 9 Prosecutor's Dismissals, and 15 exonerations/prison releases.

DOI: 10.4324/9781003543299-4

other than DNA. The NRE reviewed its 1,529 cases of proven innocence gained through 2014. Some of the NRE's data is included in the *Albany Law Review*'s analysis of wrongful convictions – mainly in discussing the *contributing factors*.

Although the IP's database of DNA exonerations holds the gold standard title, I feel the raw data gained from the NRE's database may more aptly represent the wrongful conviction landscape.

In viewing these statistics, I'm not as interested in the demographics of the wrongfully convicted, or the demographics of the victim. (Although, I agree that race is a factor – defendants of color are far more likely to be wrongfully convicted.) Gender and race are just not my interest here.[2]

My interest over the years has always been: *how* does someone get wrongfully convicted? Or maybe, *why* does someone – anyone – get wrongfully convicted? That's my sole interest.

I looked at the cases represented in both of these national databases. IP's 325 DNA exonerations represent 64 percent sexual assault charges, where the victim survived. Another 27 percent of their innocence cases were homicides which included a sexual assault. Only 9 percent of IP's DNA exonerations involved the lone crime of homicide.

Understand, these DNA exonerations required – by definition – that the actor's DNA be found at the crime scene. That is the case more often in sexual assaults, and less often in homicides.

The NRE's list of 1,529 exonerations (through 2014) includes IP's 325 DNA exonerations in their totals.

Of the NRE's exonerees, 45 percent were convicted of homicide and 23 percent were convicted of a sexual assault (victim survived). About one-fourth (26 percent) of the NRE's exonerees were convicted of crimes that never happened (e.g., a homicide later determined to be suicide or an accident, a false sexual assault allegation, etc.). In comparison, only two (less than 1 percent) of IP's DNA exonerations represented crimes which never occurred.

Looking back over my 30 cases representing wrongful convictions and false charges, my records allowed me to review 25 of those cases, and identify the *contributing factors* discussed here. (Of those 25 cases, 24 represented homicides and 1 represented a sexual assault; as it turned out, a crime which never occurred.)

The *Albany Law Review* touches on speculation that the number of exonerations discussed here may represent only a small portion of wrongful convictions nationally. So believes University of Michigan Law Professor Sam Gross and many others who have spent time in criminal defense and habeas work.

2 Looking at my 30 cases (in Mo., Ark., Tenn., Okla.., and Ks.), 17 were African Americans (16 men and 1 woman). Thirteen of my cases represented white men (10) and white women (3).

I worked with Sam Gross and others on an interesting wrongful conviction project back in the early 2000s. Gross researched and authored a study in 2008 explaining how difficult it is for the wrongfully convicted to gain meaningful attention to their innocence claim, let alone gain a habeas team to prove it. He adds that number (of potential exonerees) to those habeas defendants who plead guilty to a lesser crime – a crime they did not commit – for time served, rather than remain in prison waiting for a full exoneration.

And it is reasonable to assume another significant number of innocent defendants, found guilty at trial of lesser crimes and shorter prison terms, lack the resources and/or never bother trying to challenge their wrongful conviction. (Even that number ignores those innocent defendants who decide to plead guilty to a lesser crime, pre-trial – to avoid a much harsher sentence, if convicted at trial.)

Those convicted of major crimes, serving life sentences, have quite the uphill climb ahead of them. A wrongfully convicted inmate must find a legal team willing to help, able to help, with the time and resources to help. And *luck*, both good and bad, will come into play.

The habeas investigation must be lucky enough to find the right piece of evidence, or find the right witness (still alive) who, years later, is now willing to cooperate, or recant, or identify the true actor, or identify another critical witness, long overlooked.

Bad luck: Between 2004 and 2010, the Innocence Project said they had to close almost 25 percent of their case investigations because physical evidence could not be found, or they confirmed that the evidence they wished to test had been destroyed.

Good luck: Of the Innocence Project's 325 exonerations based on DNA analysis, 28 of those cases were almost closed, after IP was told the biological evidence they wished to test had been lost or destroyed. Only an investigator's persistence, and some sheer luck, led to the eventual location of the biological evidence, which led to a DNA analysis, which led to a court's ruling to exonerate.

It is literally and statistically impossible to project how many current or former inmates in the United States of America were wrongfully convicted. The *reasons* these wrongful convictions occur are what suggest, to me, the number of wrongful convictions may be widely underestimated.

So, how did these wrongful convictions occur? Knowing these were all cases in which the police, the prosecutors, the courts, the juries – everybody – got it wrong. And they got it wrong presumably using the same methods and standards and justice system protocols they depend on to get it right.

I looked first at these "gold standard" (DNA) conclusions. Then I looked at the broader NRE sample. Then, I compared those factors with my anecdotal experience (25 cases).

Contributing Factors

Looking at 25 years of exonerations and data, researchers found certain identifiable factors at play in all of their wrongful convictions. IP settled on what they saw as the four major *contributing factors*:

- Eyewitness Misidentification (72%)
- Misapplication of Science (47%)
- False Confessions (27%)
- Use of Informants (15%)

Slightly more than half of these wrongful convictions were based on two or more of these contributing factors. Researchers attribute the added second or third factor (i.e., multiple factors) to what they call "cognitive bias." They believe it is the human, hard-wired tendency for investigators to seek information and interpret information in a way that confirms their newly acquired beliefs.

Later in the book, I refer to this tendency as an "agenda-driven investigation." Same thing.

An example would be when a coerced confession leads to police influence placed on a witness trying to identify the actor. Or vice versa, bad science or a misidentification by a witness could lead to police coercing a confession.

As likely, a false and/or malicious tip from an informant could influence the police in a suggestive eyewitness misidentification, or encourage the lab to misinterpret or "overstate" an analysis.

Authors of the *Albany Law Review*'s analysis state that cognitive bias, in this instance, "is not the product of intentional dishonesty or malice but is simply a side-effect of the way in which human brains are wired."

I disagree.

I believe trained professionals who investigate and prosecute complex crimes resulting in life (or death) sentences, must strive to avoid this investigative cognitive bias, by making more of an effort to be objective and professional. Otherwise, we are accepting that "mistakes" are simply baked into the process.

Eyewitness Misidentification – 72%

The IP analysis suggests all or almost all mis-IDs are innocent mistakes, not deliberate mistakes. The NRE analysis counts only innocent mistakes in their mis-IDs and counts deliberate mistakes under a perjury/false allegation category, a category IP does not acknowledge.

Under *Eyewitness Misidentification*, the NRE saw that as a factor in 34 percent of their wrongful convictions, compared with the 72 percent of the IP's wrongful convictions. The NRE analysis determined that in these cases (34 percent), the mistaken identification was accidental (i.e., not deliberate or intentional). The NRE category for Perjury and False Accusations is discussed below.

In reviewing my 25 cases of innocence, I counted misidentification as a contributing factor in 56 percent of those cases. My mis-ID cases counted both malicious and mistaken misidentifications.

There are volumes written about the difficulties the human brain experiences in accurately identifying another person under criminal circumstances. Even more volumes have been written describing methods police investigators might use to avoid mistaken identification.

Perjury and False Accusations

I believe these two factors (misidentification and false accusations) may sometimes be related. The NRE analysis found that *Perjury and False Accusations* was a contributing factor in 55 percent of their proven wrongful convictions. The NRE includes *false informants* in this category.

Based on the NRE analysis, *Perjury and False Accusations* is the leading contributing factor in their wrongful convictions database.

The Innocence Project does not attempt to measure perjury and false accusations.

In my sample of cases, I found *Perjury and False Accusations* a factor in 68 percent of those wrongful convictions/innocence cases.

One entire commandment, from the Old Testament's 10 Commandments, was dedicated to those who would "bear false witness" against a neighbor (e.g., knowingly make a false ID in a criminal case). This problem has literally been around longer than Moses. I believe our criminal justice system could do a better job recognizing that possibility – that witnesses might be willing to testify falsely against their neighbor.

Note to Reader

Remember, that in each database – the IP, the NRE, and my much smaller anecdotal sample – more than one factor was found in most cases of wrongful conviction (or in my cases, wrongful convictions and false charges). That explains why the total percentages are greater than 100.

Misapplication of Science – 47%

The Innocence Project describes the types and examples of *Misapplication of Science* as (honest) scientific error, overstatement, gross negligence, and lab personnel misconduct. These "types" of mistakes can apply to all the forensic disciplines. I have seen examples, in various scale, of all four types.

As a non-scientist, I have never challenged the findings in a lab report. But I have learned to organize and review lab reports in a way that helps me identify scientific conclusions which logically call for a second opinion (if additional testing is an option). Even better, my method of review has identified missing lab reports, which clearly suggests a problem.

One example of bad science/overstatement would be the claim that a "hair comparison" can identify an individual (used in two of my cases) tying the defendant to a crime scene. Science may be able to show one hair is "similar to," or "consistent with" another hair. For an expert to describe two hair samples to be "identical" or "a match" is both "overstatement" and "bad science."

IP identified 47 percent of its cases where *misapplied science* contributed to a wrongful conviction. The Innocence Project, in my mind, represents the last word in science expertise.

The NRE's database found misapplied science a contributing factor in 23 percent of its cases.

I found *misapplied science* a contributing factor in 20 percent of my cases.

As a criminal defense investigator, it is important to recognize that mistakes can be made (with and without malice) by these third-party forensic experts.

False Confessions – 27%

A *False Confession* is certainly the most surprising and the most counterintuitive contributing factor. I know, because I've dealt with three false confessions. Two led to their wrongful convictions. One false confession led to a Capital Murder charge, which was overcome just two weeks before trial, when the prosecutor dismissed charges.

One other case of mine could fulfil IP's definition, in that a false admission was reportedly made, and used against the defendant at trial. The courts in that case determined the false admission was never made or, rather, that the police report describing this admission had been falsified and then shared with the jury.

The making of a false confession only makes sense after understanding the psychological pressure applied by professionally trained investigators against vulnerable, isolated individuals. These interrogation techniques are nearly 100 years old and replaced the physically violent techniques used by police as late as the 1930s.

These interrogation techniques may not be universal, but they have appeared in several wrongful convictions. (My false confession cases occurred in four different jurisdictions in two states.) The techniques include isolation, lying about incriminating evidence which does not exist, and encouraging confessions as a way to "set themselves free" (i.e., essentially avoid more oppressive interrogation). All claims of innocence by the suspects are initially rejected by investigators.

Experts describe the next investigation phase, following such a "confession," as "confirmation bias," and "tunnel vision." Once police obtain a confession, no matter how outlandish or detached from reality, the investigation focuses solely on conviction and guilt, ignoring better evidence to the contrary. (That may not describe all investigations, but it describes the steps leading to a wrongful conviction.)

What I don't see mentioned in discussions of the false confession is the prosecutor's willingness to accept a confession which is uncorroborated and bears no resemblance to the crime scene or other known facts. (That was the case in each of my false confession cases in four different jurisdictions.)

The IP found false confessions to be a factor in 27 percent of their wrongful convictions; showing how persuasive these interrogations can be, when years later they were compared with the DNA results.

The NRE found false confessions in 20 percent of their wrongful convictions, indicating to me that these confessions did not match the existing case facts.

My smaller sample size of 25 dealt with 3 false confessions (12 percent) and a fourth, in which the false admission was presented to the jury.

A great deal of research and scholarship exists on how false confessions are obtained, and what our system could do – if it chose – to eliminate *False Confession* as a contributing factor.

Informants – 15%

Only the IP data considered the *Informant* to be a contributing factor. The IP determined that the use of informants (and their false or misleading information) led to 15 percent of their wrongful conviction cases. An informant was described as either a "jailhouse snitch" or a civilian who hoped to gain a reward or some type of "deal" in exchange for their "tip."

I have found both categories of *Informant* are involved in many wrongful conviction cases. And their influence *is* difficult to measure, when looking at contributing factors in an investigation which ends in a wrongful conviction. Like *false confessions*, these "anonymous tips" may lack verifiable substance. I've seen, in some of my cases, where the tip did not really match the crime, but it did expose the person named by the tipster to more scrutiny and suspicion – simply because an anonymous tipster weighed in.

I have seen some "tips" which merely identified a person of interest, a person who may know something of value. That person then became a suspect, maybe out of convenience. And I have had cases in which the "tipster" was purely malicious, attempting to direct the police toward an enemy, or away from themselves – the actual assailants.

Jailhouse snitches can also create false evidence used to confirm an investigator's hunch or bias.

The prosecutor, in cases I have developed, did not appear inclined to question the veracity of a "tipster" or a jailhouse snitch, if that person helped them convict.

So, the gold standard database of wrongful convictions found those four factors: Misidentification, Misapplication of Science, False Confessions, and Informants to account for the wrongful convictions they have been able to disprove, beyond doubt.

That's a good baseline to keep in the back of the mind when beginning to review an innocence claim.

Two additional factors – major factors – found by NRE's database were also major contributors in my smaller sample size.

Perjury and False Accusations (discussed above) and *Official Misconduct* (by police, prosecutors, or other government officials).

Perjury/False Accusations – 55%

The NRE defines this contributing factor to include any victim, witness, or informant to make a knowingly false accusation. The NRE includes *informants* and *jailhouse snitches* in this category. It is important to note that a false accusation can contribute to a wrongful conviction without that person's testimony.

A witness might make a false statement against someone, motivating an investigation to determine that person's guilt, which I guess might make that person an *informant*.

An eyewitness can falsely identify a suspect as the actor in a crime. As likely, based on my cases, a person can falsely claim to have been an eyewitness, before falsely identifying a suspect in a crime they never witnessed.

As I mentioned earlier, there is nothing new about *neighbors* bearing false witness.

In my sampling of wrongful convictions and wrongful charges, perjury and false accusations were contributing factors in most – 68 percent – of those cases.

Official Misconduct – 46%

The Innocence Project believes this factor is too difficult to define, and thus does not include *Official Misconduct* as a contributing factor.

The NRE's definition bears quoting: "[includes] cases where police, prosecutors, or other government officials significantly abused their authority or the judicial process in a manner that contributed to the exoneree's conviction."

The NRE database, which includes IP cases, determined official misconduct was a factor in 30 percent of the IP cases and, overall, found official misconduct a factor in 46 percent of the NRE's total wrongful convictions.

In my sampling of 25 cases (none of which were DNA cases), I felt official misconduct was a factor in 44 percent of those cases.

The *Albany Law Review* noted (and I concur) that the higher rate of official misconduct identified in the NRE cases was due to the fact that the defense investigators in non-DNA cases had to "dig deeper into the case" in order to prove innocence. By "digging deeper," these investigators found official misconduct "more often."

Beginning My Review …

My "digging" always started with my review of the police reports in chronological order.

During my review of habeas cases and claims of innocence, I never consciously looked for *contributing factors*. Partially, because when I started reviewing most of my cases, beginning with Ricky Kidd's case, there was no Wrongful Conviction data. No contributing factors had been widely identified.

So, I never looked for contributing factors. While reviewing a case and using my method of review and organization – the contributing factors found me. The areas of concern in my innocence cases – if any existed – became evident.

When I start reviewing the police reports (in chronological order), I am actually beginning four specific tasks. I am …

- Investigating the investigation
- Investigating the crime
- Creating a searchable and traceable work product (my Murder Memo)
- Creating a list of people relevant to both of my investigations, whom I may need to fully ID, locate, and contact

I never thought of this as multi-tasking, but I guess it is.

Back to the crime and my review: Based solely on my observations and experience (and review of 100+ homicide cases), homicide investigators normally approach all crime scenes the same way. They start at the body, start with the victim, and work out. They begin gathering facts like any investigator conducting any research project. Who ... What ... When ... Where ... Why ..., and How ...?

At a typical homicide, one investigator (or team) will focus on the crime scene itself including the body and all physical aspects of the crime. A different investigator, or a different team, will focus on witnesses (people related to this crime). This second investigator, or the police under her direction, will canvass the area around the crime scene, interviewing individuals who might have seen the crime or known the victim. They look for who might have last seen or had contact with the victim. They are gaining initial impressions and recollections.

A typical homicide investigative report will include some type of *crime scene summary*, along with initial witness contacts and brief witness statements made at the scene. Or, the homicide investigative report may include a specific and detailed crime scene report, followed by specific reports based on initial witness interviews, and maybe an area canvass. The homicide investigative report will eventually provide more detailed witness interviews (written reports) and follow-up reports on investigative leads.

Within the next 2 to 24 to 48 hours after the initial crime scene investigation, these initial witnesses will likely be interviewed again, formally, and more extensively. If there is still no suspect – or no specific suspect-ID, these witnesses will be pressed for more detail. Without an initial suspect, the investigation may expand organically (identifying additional witnesses who may know something relevant), wait for some specific lab analysis, or stall out – while waiting for a tip from the community.

During my review, once I see that a suspect has been identified, or even suggested, I look at all subsequent witness interviews to see if the interview is about the crime, or about building a case against this "named suspect."

As my review progresses from the crime scene descriptions, to witness statements (in chronological order), I look for investigative patterns ... as well as any illogical steps. The patterns I like to see are investigative steps, leading logically from one fact to the next. An oddity or aberration would be a break in that pattern. When a witness appears out of nowhere, with no logical connection to the existing investigation – that is odd. I consider it an investigative aberration if reports indicate investigators ignored the next logical witness, or I see a "suspect" named without any apparent factual basis (i.e., without explanation, a named suspect appears in a written report – with no known context). When reports are reviewed in chronological order, there should not be any surprises like suspects appearing out of nowhere. That suggests to me that an anonymous tip, or someone's casual mention – not included in any reports – has become the agenda driving the investigation.

I am always looking for indicators of a fact-based investigation. That way, I will recognize the aberration – an investigation suddenly based on someone's speculation, not fact.

No matter what investigative aberrations I may find, I continue to objectively investigate the investigation. Moving forward, I may find more indications of investigators no longer investigating the crime, but instead, building a case against a *speculative* suspect. Building a case – gathering evidence of one's guilt – was their job. My job is to determine whether their investigation, or their case-building, was fact-based or agenda-driven. (By reviewing the entire police report chronologically, I may find later in the investigation a fact-based reason for a suspect ID – or I may confirm the suspect ID was based on pure speculation.)

I too must avoid creating my own agenda-driven investigation. If I see the police building their case before they have completed their investigation of the crime, I know better than to think my "agenda-driven" investigation will be any better. The police "hunch" may have been right. The state may have convicted the right person. To know that for sure, my investigation must remain fact-based.

When I am asked to look at a potential case of innocence, I am not only looking for signs of innocence. To do my job, I must determine *what happened* at the crime scene, and *what happened* in the investigation which led to this person being charged. Was the investigation fact-based? Was the conviction based on *all* of the facts? I will later compare the "facts" used in court with the facts developed during the original investigation. Were the same facts used? Not always.

As a journalist, I learned to objectively gather and sort through facts, and then report on "what happened." I developed a fact-based, investigative mindset. A related trait I developed was to always act as if I had no dog in the fight. No matter how emotional a crime or a crime scene might be (or how sympathetic the defendant's claim may be), I worked to remove myself from the emotional equation.

Exploring a theory is one thing; falling in love with that theory is quite another. Did this homicide investigator become invested in his own theory and lose sight of *what happened*? That's where the transition begins, from *investigating the case* to *building a case*. I saw agenda-driven news stories written for the *Houston Chronicle*. I eventually left that paper for the *Houston Post*, which did not practice agenda-driven journalism – as often.

When investigating a crime, it's always tempting to develop a theory, which leads to an agenda-driven investigation. It's like picking a horse. It may satisfy the ego to develop a theory, then build a case to support that theory (i.e., confirmation bias).

But once objectivity is tossed aside, so is the ability to recognize plausible, alternate theories. Facts, which don't support that theory, may be ignored, or discounted.

A technique I have found helpful in removing my ego from my investigation of the investigation: I focus on the victim.

I make my investigation become a show of respect for the victim. This does not require any religious conversion, just human decency. I then think about the defendant. I try to respect both with an honest investigation. Both the victim and the accused deserve that.

Even if I find the defendant is actually guilty (and that has happened), I feel like I have served a purpose by taking ambiguity out of the conviction. I believe my objective diligence keeps the playing field level for my current defendant, as well as the next defendant – who might be innocent.

One thing I've learned in reviewing scores of homicides and assessing dozens of suspected wrongful convictions is "stuff happens." Weird "stuff" happens. "Stuff" happens out there, which makes no sense to those of us grounded in our rational world. For example, partners will sometimes argue and, in a rage, one person kills another. But sometimes the random burglar, the unstable neighbor, the door-to-door salesman, the weird uncle, the undisclosed drug connection, or the drug dealer's cousin, visits the soon-to-be-deceased – unannounced. The odd and unforeseen sometimes happens. These awful acts may happen for *a reason*, but it's a reason not obvious to most of us. And it may be a reason that the homicide detective did not consider.

I've learned to count on at least one other predictable aspect of habeas work. In most homicides I've explored, once I determined the conviction (the state's theory) was not fact-based, my investigation will quickly mushroom. My *investigation of the crime* grows, because the list of plausible, fact-based, alternate theories grows. And the number of witnesses needing to be questioned – for different reasons – grows accordingly.

In some complex cases, I have found myself dealing with only one accepted fact: the victim's death and the cause of death. She was killed at a specific day and time (if that is known), and in a certain way. But that really may be all that is known with absolute certainty. I must ignore all witness speculation on who was, and who wasn't, capable of committing such a crime. I've seen more than one wrongful conviction seemingly based on opinions, rather than facts, or even someone's first-hand knowledge.

My job ... the fact-finder's job: identify the facts of the crime, then find a reasonable theory (or theories) which fit the facts – *all* of the facts. In the real world of habeas cases and wrongful convictions, I don't need to solve the crime. But in a true case of innocence, I must prove absolutely, convincingly, beyond any doubt, that my client did not commit that crime.

Beginning with the Crime Scene Report ...

Whenever possible, I begin my review of a homicide investigation with the crime scene report. (This is also where a chronological review should begin.) One of the lead detectives normally writes this report. This crime scene narrative generally follows standard protocol, even if the written report *format* may vary. This report will describe the weather, the physical location, ambient light, significant times, the location of the body, and – if obviously relevant – the location of related criminal activities leading up to the homicide or following the homicide.

This crime scene report will likely describe what the crime scene looked like when these trained investigators arrived. The report, full of specifics, should create a mental picture.

Normally, police patrol officers "preserve" the crime scene for these investigators. Any disruption to the crime scene (i.e., emergency medical technicians rendering aid or even removing the body to the hospital) will be noted. It becomes significant if a homicide goes undetected for hours or days, leaving that crime scene unpreserved for any period of time, (i.e., a residence, a vacant lot, an open field, etc.). That delay and the obvious disruptions will be noted in detail.

The initial crime scene report constitutes *raw data*. The homicide investigation begins with a blank canvas. These professional investigators are trained to record certain observations about the physical characteristics of a crime scene.

(Only rarely have I reviewed a homicide crime scene report so inadequate and unprofessional as to practically redefine negligence. Fortunately, in my experience, reports of that caliber are extremely rare and merely serve to insult the law enforcement profession. For that reason, I always assume the initial crime scene investigators are trained professionals, trying to get it right.)

The crime scene report will be loaded with salient facts, all related to who, what, when, where, why, or how. As I review, I organize these relevant facts onto my *Murder Memo* boilerplate. Every relevant fact has a place on that boilerplate.

I know of no shortcut here. Reviewing an innocence claim, I must review the crime scene line-by-line to gain a complete understanding of the crime, and the investigation of the crime. (Investigating a case pre-trial is no different.)

I can't be sure, but I often wonder if prosecutors read the entire crime scene report line-by-line, or the entire police report for that matter. Police may provide a written summary of their investigation, or offer a verbal summary, while delivering a copy of all police reports. Speculating again, I believe the prosecutor may only read the witness statements handed to her – which fit the police theory and support the criminal charge. If prosecutors are aware of any doubts revealed by the police investigation, it never shows in their prosecution of the case.

A cynical explanation would be that the less the prosecutor knows about the existence of exculpatory facts, the better she can prosecute this case. Then there are exonerations based on Brady Material, suggesting I'm not cynical enough. There have been exonerations, throughout the country, revealing prosecutorial misconduct, often involving exculpatory facts discovered during the initial police investigation. The courts discovered – 20 years later – these facts were simply pushed to the side, and not shared with the defense (i.e., Brady Material).

My experience tells me some defense lawyers may also exhibit short attention spans when it comes to reviewing police reports: "Not enough time. Just tell me what happened." All summaries of an investigation, whether verbal or written, may save time, but at the expense of *detail.* And detail, from what I have seen, is the primary ingredient to proving innocence (or guilt).

"Details" will be used by the state to prove their case – when they've got it right. Selective "detail" will be used by the state when they have it wrong or they are not sure. My methodical review identifies the missing details, the details which contradict the state theory, or the detail which supports a different theory. A methodical review looks for details the state chose not to share – maybe Brady Material, maybe not. A methodical review looks for the details investigators overlooked or ignored. A methodical review also finds details the original defense team never noticed or never recognized as significant.

A critical detail won't be labeled as such. Reviewing and then placing every relevant detail of the crime into the Murder Memo boilerplate will help recognize details ignored, or later found missing from the state's theory. (*As an aside, I'd like to mention that the very best criminal defense lawyers I have worked with shared at least two traits: they were organized, and they were all about detail.)*

A *fact* in the crime scene report might not appear relevant until I review a witness interview on page 273. It makes no sense to simply re-write an entire crime scene report into my Murder Memo. But using the same topics repeatedly (i.e., Crime, Crime Scene, Victim, Actor ID, Suspect, Vehicle, Weapon, Physical Evidence, Witnesses, etc.), I believe there is a place, somewhere among those topics, for all facts relevant to who, to when, to where, to what, and to how.

The investigation may speculate on various "facts" and initially provide multiple facts describing when, or where (or what, how, or why), but eventually the investigation (and science) settles on specific facts. I think it has value to organize these facts (and speculations), so that they are available for review when the investigation settles on one "fact" over another "fact." That also allows my investigation to determine if investigators used *facts* or *speculation* to reach their conclusion. For instance, the exact time a crime or assault occurred may begin as speculation, and changed later, based on science.

That's why I put "speculative facts" in my Murder Memo however succinctly, so they are there when needed later. I want to review these police reports so carefully, line-by-line, making notes accordingly, so that I only need to review them one time. After a careful review, I want to be able to refer to my Murder Memo – exclusively – for all relevant facts.

If a fact improves my mental picture of the crime scene, it belongs in my Murder Memo. Even though my general categories help me organize most homicides (and most crimes), a unique crime might require a tweak or two to my format. An example would be if the victim's remains are discovered months or years after a disappearance. Or a crime might have more than one crime scene. A habeas case might involve more than one homicide or involve a series of crimes which investigators believe were connected (i.e., the defendant committed Crime A, then Crime B, before committing Crime C). Each crime and each factual link to the subsequent crime, becomes part of my investigation. My Murder Memo will likely create a boilerplate for each crime, and I will review the police reports for each crime, chronologically and in sequence. That way, I can determine whether the links between these crimes are fact-based, or speculation.

By breaking each crime down into its own Murder Memo or Crime Memo, I may find alternate theories. If a suspect is convicted of several crimes, or a related sequence of crimes, my objectivity becomes more valuable. Each crime must be reviewed and assessed separately. Several times, I have found a seemingly related sequence of crimes dumped on a suspect based on speculation, maybe circumstantial evidence and, maybe, convenience. My objectivity forces me to look at each crime separately and determine if police were following facts or chasing theories.

Crime Scene Details …

The Who (victim) and What (homicide) are often obvious. Sometimes the real investigation must focus on the When and Where.

Facts dealing with *time* are often critical to who may have committed the crime. When did the witness hear a noise? Calls to 9-1-1 offer precise times. How many gunshots did he hear? When? What time, exactly? During what TV program? Was it daylight or dark? How long after the kids got out of school? What time does the witness normally get home from work? Did the relevant event occur before or after some routine activity? How do we know *those* gunshots the witness heard are related to *that* homicide?

In an isolated assault, or an abduction, when the victim's body is recovered after-the-fact or the body is moved after death and discovered later, time of death might help determine the What and the Where.

If the body had not been moved, but discovered some extended time later, the crime scene may still help identify the Who (assailant), the What, and the When.

For witnesses, what was the ambient lighting at the time of the crime? Who could have seen what?

All physical objects, both stationary and moveable, are relevant to the crime and the crime scene, and might help prove guilt, or innocence.

All documented crime scene observations become empirical facts. Any theory, any criminal charge, any confession, any conviction, should fit all of these facts – as if comparing a latent impression to a known print. If the theory doesn't fit these crime scene facts, either the initial observation was wrong, the report was in error, or the theory is off.

Details.

When I read the crime scene report, I want a visual of the crime scene in my mind. If necessary (and if no police diagram exists), I'll draw my own diagram of the crime scene based on this report. If I find a crime scene diagram, I will confirm that the diagram matches the crime scene report. A small detail, like the victim's head "lying to the north, feet facing south" can matter.

Reviewing a case in Little Rock, Arkansas, I saw a "North" indicator on a crime scene diagram, which was actually pointing "West." In that case the error did not impact the investigation, although it suggested every other detail about the investigation needed to be verified.

A tiny mistake can matter but might not be immediately recognized. Details are vital. Any correct verdict down the road is ultimately based on the initial investigator's attention to detail, the accuracy of that raw data in their reports, and the defense team's understanding of that detail.

Over time, crime scene photos have become easier to include in police reports and Discovery. In the past, crime scene photos were not always available.

Sitting at my desk, I am limited to the facts provided in these police reports. This crime scene description on paper, and in my head, must portray a complete incident, occurring at a specific time and place. There cannot be any gaps or contradictions between what did happen, and what could possibly have happened. As if I was writing a screenplay, the director won't tolerate any ambiguity in my shooting script. The lighting, the environment, the movements of all actors must be plausible, physically possible, and in perfect sync.

Note to Reader

Much of my casework was conducted before Google Maps and other useful Internet tools became available "at my desk." I now use Google Maps and street views often in becoming oriented to a crime scene – before my personal visit.

Sometimes a crime scene report, followed by witness interviews, may reveal contradictions. There may be mistakes in the crime scene report, or gaps in the witness observations, or problems with the written report. Any gaps in any observer's understanding of this crime shouldn't be overlooked. Any gap or contradiction involving the crime scene represents a "red flag," which will need to be resolved somewhere later in the police reports – or not.

Hopefully, any initial contradictions will be clarified by subsequent witness interviews or lab reports.

Otherwise, these gaps and contradictions become red flags in my investigation of-the-investigation. I have learned to document my red flags and will discuss later.

Details.

Best Evidence ...

Best Evidence was the title of a 1981 Kennedy assassination conspiracy book, a bestseller, written by David S. Lifton, and my first exposure to this term. Without debating Lifton's conclusions, I got his point that the *best evidence* in any complex crime was comprised of those "facts" with the least amount of speculation and ambiguity. *Best Evidence* was seldom circumstantial. *Best Evidence* was almost always *physical evidence*. And even *Best Evidence* may contain some ambiguity and lend itself to some speculation. In the case of John F. Kennedy's assassination, as in the case of many homicides, the *best evidence* exists with the victim's body itself.

Note to Reader

This may be a good time to point out – in my humble opinion – this is not a competition. There is no "us-versus-them." Whether you are a cop, a defense attorney, a prosecutor or a criminal investigator, a family member of the victim or of the accused, we should all be on the same page. We all should be concerned with "what happened." We all should be focused on finding the person who harmed the victim, and the victim's family and loved ones. We should all want to isolate that person from society for a period of time decided by the courts.

I am not ignoring the defense attorney's ethical obligations to their guilty client. One of those ethical obligations is to "presume innocence." But, ultimately, when a fact-driven investigation indicates guilt, a guilty client might be best served through mitigating evidence used to gain a fair sentence. And that client's attorney might be best able to serve her client, by knowing all of the facts.

Once the autopsy and toxicology and the criminal investigation are completed, charges are filed, warrants served, the Defense can start critiquing the state's work. In habeas work, that critique might start 20 years later.

The victim's body is sometimes the best evidence, especially in *whodunnits*. Sometimes the body is the only evidence. Often, the body starts out being the only evidence, and from facts found with the body, a fact-driven investigation begins.

The first aspect of this *best evidence* investigation involves the body found at the crime scene. The physical placement of the body relative to permanent fixtures can be relevant. A good crime scene report will place the body relative to a street curb, a sidewalk, a light fixture, the northeast corner of the house, the bedroom doorway, something permanent. A reference to a piece of furniture only offers clarity if photos are available. Furniture can be moved. Doorways remain in place.

Always verify that any crime scene photos correspond with any scene diagrams, and written descriptions in the report. For example, I always check to make sure the body's placement and other items described in the crime scene report match the photos, or the report's diagram.

When the body is found with the head facing north and the feet facing south, this could suggest the direction from which the attacker came. Maybe. It depends on whether the body was found face up or face down. That suggests two different directions. Was the body found by a friend or passerby? Was the body turned over before police or paramedics arrived? Who first touched the body? How did that person find the body? Then again, if the victim was surprised by an attacker and had no chance to react, then his direction of travel at the time of the attack might only suggest his assailant came unannounced – which could be a significant fact.

The body's position might suggest an execution (certainly when hands are tied) or a surprise, leading to an impulsive, or a targeted, attack. Body placement could suggest that the victim was trying to protect another, or was in a self-defensive stance, or was a third-party (unintended) victim.

I have reviewed cases in which witness interviews made all these questions about the body placement extremely relevant in determining "what happened."

Details.

Two recent cases come to mind which demonstrates the value of "body placement."

Late one Saturday morning in 2004, the owner of an auto repair shop in a small Georgia town was shot and killed in his repair shop office. The shooter had walked into the shop, virtually unnoticed, as mechanics were closing up in the auto bay area.

The owner was sitting at his computer with his back to the front door of his office. Although not described sufficiently in the crime scene report, the crime scene photos showed the owner had turned his entire wheeled chair around to face the shooter before he was shot 13 times. Although it is pure speculation, it appeared to me that the owner knew, or was familiar with this shooter, and apparently not fearful of him. The shooter presumably surprised the owner by pulling out a gun and firing 13 shots. The shooter then walked out of the shop and fled the area on foot, crossing the street outside and into a crowded shopping area.

This remains an unsolved homicide, even though a physical description was offered by one shop employee, and this shooter's presumed "familiarity" with the victim provided police several possibilities.

In another case outside of Kansas City, in 2007, a man had pulled into his own driveway in a suburban residential neighborhood at about 12:30 a.m. He had been out earlier, socially with friends. Crime scene reports indicate the man was found minutes later with one fatal gunshot wound, still sitting behind the wheel of his car, with the engine running. The car (in reverse) had slowly rolled backwards into his neighbor's yard and stopped when the car rolled up against the porch foundation.

Additional notes indicate the driver's window had been lowered by the driver before the shooting occurred. (The temperature was a chilly 20 degrees.)

Although it is pure speculation, those facts suggest the possibility that the driver, in his car, sitting in his driveway, having just arrived home at 12:30 a.m., very likely rolled his window down to greet a familiar person. This crime was investigated as a robbery/homicide.

The Autopsy...

Throughout this book I suggest the value of chronological order. The one exception is the autopsy report.

In this case, I take advantage of hindsight. The autopsy is the only part of the investigation which I may study out of sequence. In my Murder Memo, I put a summary of the autopsy (mainly the cause of death, and basic wound descriptions) at the end of my Crime Facts format (i.e., boilerplate) and just ahead of the Investigative Narrative/Witness Interviews. If there was a question about the cause of death, at the initial crime scene, or there was a surprise found during the autopsy, I consider that the initial investigation was conducted without that knowledge.

Sometimes, autopsy findings will contradict initial observations, or witness interviews at the crime scene. I've seen an entire investigation based on initial interviews and witness statements, which did not match the autopsy (or the crime scene). That investigation and the state's theory took on a life of its own, resulting in a wrongful conviction. Facts from the crime scene and autopsy were overlooked as if they were *irrelevant*. Not surprisingly, in such a complicated convoluted case, details were lost in the confusion, ignored by the state, overlooked by the defense.

Generally, the autopsy report contains few surprises. In most cases, autopsy results confirm initial crime scene observations. The toxicology report, normally completed 7–10 days later, provides a drug screen and potential level of intoxication (if that is even relevant). Any suspected poisoning is certainly an exception. (None of my 100+ cases have involved a homicide-by-poison.)

Only when the person's body is discovered some time after the crime, does the autopsy become more critical in determining cause of death and time of death.

The Medical Examiner's analysis of the wounds could be an informative element of the autopsy. These notes and diagrams describing wounds, wound patterns and directions can really drive a fact-driven investigation. This is one area of the autopsy which might contain the surprise, or the contradiction, to initial crime scene observations. I have seen homicide investigations in which investigators gave more credence to witness statements and less attention to cold, hard facts offered by the Medical Examiner's report.

The Medical Examiner's wound analysis can help define the number of attackers. With an expert, that analysis might even suggest the type of participant (strong or weak, left-handed or right-handed). Factual observations may include gunshot wounds (GSW), a bullet's trajectory, projectiles recovered, all details which may describe the number and type of gun(s) used, the weapon's proximity to the victim, maybe the shooter's angle (or position of the victim).

I often rely on my common sense, basic physics, and simple geometry. These facts must be considered in the context of the crime scene described by police. Experience matters in this area. I have learned when to call an expert.

I always compare any wound analysis from the Medical Examiner with the crime scene report. I make sure all facts from the crime scene report match facts described in the autopsy. The sooner a contradiction is identified, the sooner I may see how a wrong assumption or misapplied science may have impacted the investigation moving forward.

When the only witnesses to a homicide were the victim and the assailant, investigators must diligently and creatively (and accurately) explore the victim's body and the crime scene for all available facts.

At times, a second or third look at an autopsy report or a crime scene photo might produce an "ah ha" moment.

With experience, I have gotten better at identifying any contradictions. Once I have assembled and organized all the facts, I, or an expert, will see how they fit. With all the facts organized, I should be able to write an accurate "screenplay," describing this crime, knowing the What, When, Where, and How, possibly leading to the Who (assailant). Or I identify a "red flag contradiction" amid these "facts." I make a note of that in my Murder Memo.

Details.

Objects ...

Next in importance to the *Best Evidence* offered by the victim's body is the environment surrounding the crime.

I consider the placement, the existence, or the absence of all objects in the immediate area of the crime to be relevant, until additional information tells me otherwise. There will be obvious items: the cigarette butts in the ashtray, the beer cans nearby, the bed cover, the missing pillow, the empty gun box in the victim's bedroom (which matches the murder weapon).

Every inanimate object in the immediate area surrounding the victim's final resting place – is either *in place*, or *out of place*. (The "immediate area" is relative to the crime. That area could be limited to the victim's bedroom, or include items found in the garage, the driveway, or back yard, depending on the crime and the circumstances which may have led up to the crime.)

Exterior crime scenes can be more challenging to investigators. They will likely try to determine boundaries for the victim's immediate environment, or some reasonable boundaries for the crime scene, to be studied.

Again, the state's theory must fit and explain the placement or movement or absence of all "relevant," inanimate objects. Relevance may be subjective. I keep an open mind regarding these objects. If I am uncertain, then the relevance of an object might increase or decrease in value based on a witness interview I have not yet reviewed. Relevance might be determined 20 years later during a habeas investigation. Understand that a fact deemed "irrelevant" to the state's theory and prosecution may become "relevant" to proving innocence.

Investigators seldom have a perfectly "finite" crime scene. Unknown persons, animals, and weather conditions could affect items within a crime scene. The state may develop theories to explain *unknown factors* from a crime scene. The Defense (or an Innocence Claim) may depend on these unknown factors to create reasonable doubt or prove innocence.

A habeas investigation may be limited in expanding that searchable (crime scene) area, maybe not. In either a pre-trial or habeas case, the criminal defense investigator may want to go outside the crime scene boundary and explore. That "investigation of the crime" may require locating a fact which contradicts the state's theory and supports an innocence claim.

There are a variety of ways to look beyond the crime scene tape, whether the crime occurred the previous year, or ten years earlier.

When I isolate the raw data from the legal file, I have also identified any photos or videos of the crime scene. In reviewing crime scene reports, I identify any reference to crime scene photos. Tracking and locating photos, along with physical evidence, can become an investigation within the investigation.

Locating evidence in Discovery, such as police crime scene photos, can also turn into litigation, to be directed by habeas team lawyers. My job as investigator is to confirm the existence of these items (i.e., photos, video, etc.) and provide context for their value and their importance in determining "what happened."

After I have gained my client's confidence and trust (see Chapter 6), I find out what she can offer about the crime scene. In many wrongful convictions, the defendant knew the victim or was familiar with the crime's location. I always consider my client to be a potential witness (or source) in both of my investigations.

Both the victim and the convicted client have friends and family. It may be reasonable to approach family or friends of the victim in the spirit of "getting it right." Family and associates of the victim and the defendant may be able to help me expand the crime scene boundaries. Family or friends or acquaintances might be able to explain discrepancies I have noted at the crime scene. I don't expect and have seldom seen Homicide Investigators talk to friends and family about crime scene inconsistencies, once they start building their case against their suspect.

There will always be good, valid reasons why I *do not* approach the victim's family (pre-trial or several years after a conviction). That will always be both a legal and humanitarian decision made by the lead attorney. I have always felt the victim's family deserves the utmost respect, no matter what may have led to a wrongful conviction.

More often than not, the victim's family has become invested in the notion that the state convicted the person who killed their loved one. It is a painful proposition to ask the victim's family to reconsider. Nor will that family want to consider that another victim of this crime is the defendant – now wrongly incarcerated. Civil servants told them the killer of their son or brother, or daughter, or mother has been identified, convicted, and punished. Despite solid evidence to the contrary, or merely based on a habeas team's whim, I do not expect the family members to willingly engage or easily change their minds. (If I hear that the family has "doubts" about my client's conviction, I add that to the lead attorney's thought process.)

The next level of potential information about the crime scene, or an effort to expand the crime scene, could come from friends of the victim, then neighbors, associates, and even casual acquaintances. These third-party witnesses can be good sources for background information and crime scene clarification. These peripheral witnesses will likely be on my witness list anyway. (see Chapter 8).

By noting all crime scene questions and inconsistencies in my Murder Memo (either under CRIME SCENE, or under my Crime Scene Narrative), I will remember and try to resolve these questions when I begin conducting my third-party witness interviews, weeks or months later.

In Texas v. Odell Barnes *of Wichita Falls, I reviewed that homicide investigation 25 years after-the-fact, identifying many discrepancies between case facts and Barnes' conviction. Most significant were the crime scene photos of the victim's bedroom where her body had been found. Photos showed a white cardboard gun box, which had likely contained the .38 caliber revolver the victim's son told police he had bought for his mom.*

In the crime scene photos, three bloody smudges could be seen on the box, which laid askew on the bedroom floor. The victim had been beaten, and then shot with a .38 cal handgun. The victim's gun was missing from her home. One could surmise that the victim was shot with her own gun taken from that gun box found in her bedroom. The investigation never located a murder weapon. Nor did police ever find the victim's stolen gun (the likely murder weapon).

Other police photos showed that one of the bloody smudges on the top of the white cardboard box was a partial latent impression suitable for comparison. This box was the size of a cigar box. This bloody smudge sat near the middle of the top lid, about where one's thumb would have touched while holding the box. The state theorized that Odell Barnes had acted alone in beating, then shooting this woman, whom he knew casually as a friend.

Pre-trial lab reports indicated these bloody smudges did not provide enough identifying "points" to be used as evidence against the defendant. However, an expert we contacted believed there may be enough "points" to eliminate a person – Odell. We suspected that enough of the latent print could be gained from photos and digital enhancement to confirm the bloody latent impression could exclude both the victim and Odell as the owner of that bloody fingerprint.

If true, such an exclusion could be definitive, without meeting the standard eight points of comparison needed to identify. We were merely trying to exclude specific individuals.

Unfortunately, the State of Texas had already executed Odell Barnes.

In 2004, I reviewed the physical evidence and the Court's Trial Exhibits, including this gun box, still in police storage. I wanted to access and photograph the bloody latent. The bloody smudge on top of the gun box had disappeared, as if wiped clean with a bleach. What I found was a very white spot where the bloody smudge had appeared in the crime scene photos.

In a wrongful conviction, I may find the state theory (i.e., the conviction) inconsistent with crime scene facts. These contradictions may be subtle, or they may be blatant. A crime scene fact, inconsistent with the state theory, might have been overlooked, or convincingly explained away. Once I have identified a meaningful contradiction, I may wonder how everyone missed it.

Mistakes happen, I guess.

Details.

Environment, Atmosphere, Lighting ...

I evaluate crime scene information using multiple Points-of-View (POVs).

Relevant POVs include the victim, the assailant, any co-defendants, eyewitnesses to the crime, witnesses who observed or interacted with the crime's eyewitnesses, and bystanders who saw nothing (or think they saw nothing).

At the time of the crime, all three – environment, atmosphere, and lighting – can play huge roles in what a witness was able to see, hear, comprehend, process, and retain. All of these are relevant factors in assessing credibility and reliability. All of these factors are relevant in determining "what happened."

Knowing the ambient light helps determine what an eyewitness was capable of seeing. Ambient noise and activity will also affect what an eyewitness could see, hear, and process. A bustling boulevard is a far different crime scene from a quiet residential neighborhood. And both crime scenes are starkly different at 3 a.m. and 3 p.m.

The police are looking for a good witness to a crime.

Witness statements won't necessarily reveal these other factors. If a witness claims they saw the shooter, that may be all that's reported in the witness interview. I can't recall ever reviewing a case in which any police or prosecutor questioned the credibility or reliability of an eyewitness, unless that eyewitness saw someone other than the named suspect or saw activity contrary to the state's theory.

Actual lighting, if relevant, may or may not be discussed or described in police reports. A diagram might show placement of streetlights, or parking lot lighting – maybe not. It's my job, while investigating the crime and the investigation, to determine the actual lighting at the time of the crime. If relevant, I determine the exact time of sunset and the end of civil twilight – darkness (30 minutes later).

I need to evaluate any level of distraction occurring at the time of the crime. I have never witnessed a homicide, but I still must understand the difference in witnessing a shooting in a crowded bar versus a shooting at the back of a church versus a shooting in a busy parking lot – at dusk.

From police reports, I must gather the necessary facts to evaluate whether the witness could see what she claims to have seen. Maybe the witness was there, maybe not. I need to verify that as well. I've worked on cases of both. My knowledge of the total environment surrounding the crime scene might help prove this witness is not being truthful about the crime he claims to have witnessed. Or facts might determine she may be exaggerating or embellishing what she actually saw. Maybe she is simply mistaken, and the environment prevented her from being more reliable. Maybe she was hampered by poor lighting, or distractions, which she never discussed with police (in her desire to be helpful).

I have proven innocence by contacting witnesses to the state's eyewitnesses, people who interacted with these eyewitnesses near the time of the crime. Sometimes, a secondary witness knows the eyewitness could not have seen what they claim to have seen.

Details.

One Last Word About the Crime Scene ...

Crime scene analysis is an art as well as a science. A good *crime scene analyst* can tell from a thumbnail description of the crime and crime scene, if his or her services might be helpful. The expert I relied on (Gene Gietzen of Springfield, Mo – now retired) would start asking questions I hadn't thought of and questions that I couldn't answer. That was my clue that his expertise could help.

I considered Mr. Gietzen a "forensic generalist." He knew what he knew and knew what he didn't know. He'd tell me what he could analyze, and, if necessary, he would direct me to experts outside of his expertise. His goal, like mine, was to determine "what happened" based on the placement of all animate and inanimate objects (... from ash trays to blood splatter). He told me where DNA might be found. He clarified my false impressions and assumptions.

It takes time to develop useful instincts in these investigations. I am forever grateful that I developed a working relationship with such a competent crime scene analyst.

Summary

Note to Reader

Your understanding of the crime scene may be the foundation for your understanding of the state's case – why a prosecutor believes your client is guilty. If the state made a mistake, you need to know every detail of the crime scene in order to find that inconsistency. A wrongful conviction may have been based on an error, or a misunderstanding of the crime scene. The prosecutor might knowingly or inadvertently ignore a piece of crime scene evidence because it doesn't match up with eyewitness statements. Police might have developed a theory based on an oversight, then built a case around that false premise.

That is why I suggest that both of your investigations (... of the crime and of the investigation), start with the "raw data," the physical facts describing the victim and the crime scene.

The victim and all things related to this crime help describe the *where*, the *what*, the *how*, and, if necessary, the *when*. These facts can help ID the *who* (assailant). Some facts may not help the state determine who, but those facts might help the defense, or a habeas team, determine who it *wasn't*. Facts can eliminate a suspect – maybe your client – without proving who committed the crime.

The crime scene is your only glimpse of the assault and the assailant(s). You will be comparing crime scene data to all future witness interviews. When raw data contradicts the state's theories based on witness statements, you might have a wrongful conviction. These contradictions between crime scene and witness statements become your "red flags." Any inconsistencies between the state theory and crime scene facts – leads you to additional investigation, until the inconsistency is resolved.

It is important to use what little empirical evidence you have – crime scene analysis and raw data – when you evaluate eyewitnesses. Use this raw data in understanding the environment, and the crime scene, and what a witness could have seen or heard. That is the only way I have found to assess an eyewitness' credibility as well as their reliability.

Raw data implies detail – sometimes, lots of detail. Organizing this detail on your Murder Memo is critical to your ability to compare that raw data to the dozens of witness statements you are about to review – and the witness interviews you will later conduct.

Chapter 5

Building My Murder Memo (Part 3): Reviewing Witness Interviews and Lab Reports While Creating My People List and To Dos

Reviewing Police Witness Interviews (in Sequence) ...

Repeating myself, I prefer starting my review with a crime scene report, if found, or simply the first police report of the crime, if that is how that department organizes its investigation. I start assembling my raw data about the crime and crime scene first and start building my Murder Memo with those basic facts.

Reviewing the police investigation in chronological order, even reports from the initial crime scene reviewed in sequence, provides important context to every "next step" in the investigation. I like to follow that sequence and build my notes likewise.

Some crime scene reports include initial police contacts with witnesses. I may begin my "Witness Narrative" portion of the Murder Memo with notes from these initial witness contacts, depending on the reports and the nature of the investigation.

Sometimes, police conduct a massive area canvass, contacting all neighbors, store owners, residents, within a reasonable geographic area – people who may have seen or heard something relevant to this crime. This phase may involve dozens of witness contacts but only one or two witness interviews which appear relevant. This is a valuable window into the neighborhood on that particular day. My notes will reflect who was contacted (by name if available) and/or address or physical location (especially if no one was found at that location). The police report documenting this area canvass will likely include a brief narrative. I try to make my notes even more succinct. For example:

Witness/Neighborhood Canvass

Mae Cleaver, at 56xx Mercer, told cops she was in her bathroom at midnight, heard 4 gs from front of her house. She looked out, saw nothing.

DOI: 10.4324/9781003543299-5

Bonika Kay, at 56xx Mercer, told cops she was in her basement at midnight when she heard 4 gs in front. She did not look out.

Robert Cordes, of 56yy Mercer, told police he was lying in bed at midnight when he heard *several footsteps* running along his east gangway. 3–4 min later he heard 3–4 gs. Looking out his front door he saw no one. Went back to bed. *Few minutes* later his dtr told him kids next door were back on their front porch. Cordes looked out and saw VICTIM lying on ground.

Gloria Cordes, of 56yy Mercer, told police she heard *several footsteps* running along the east gangway of their residence. *Minutes later, heard 3–4 gs.* Several minutes later she looked out front, saw youths next door standing on their front porch.

Ralph Baker of 56xx Agnes, told police, he was visiting a neighbor at Greer and Clara. He heard gs from 56xx Mercer about 11:30 p.m. When he returned home he advised by cops of bullet hole in right side of his car parked in rear of 56xx Mercer.

Rod Slater at 56zz Mercer, told cops he heard 3 gs from front. He did not look out.

Police may return a day or two after a crime to conduct a neighborhood canvass. They are trying to contact everyone who may have seen or heard something. Given that scenario, their area canvass notes will appear later in my Murder Memo (in chronological order).

Normally, while some police are knocking on doors conducting an area canvass, homicide investigators are conducting initial witness interviews at the scene. The chronological order for each witness contact may become critical in determining when police hear for the first time a suspect's ID, or a physical description.

From Ricky Kidd's Murder Memo:

Initial Witness Statements –

Kayla [redacted] (age 4) initially told police at the scene that she heard the doorbell. George opened the garage door and let two men inside. The men argued with George. They pulled out guns and shot George, then left in a white car.

George [redacted] (Neighbor) told police at the scene that at 11:45 a.m., he was inside his house at 70[redacted] Monroe (next door to the north of Bryant's house). Washington looked outside his front window and saw suspects #1 and #2 running from Bryant's house to a white car parked on the street. He heard one more g.s and saw Suspect #3 running toward the white car. #3 suspect, who shot last, also drove the car away. The car backed up Monroe (northbound) and backed to the west on 70th St. up the hill.

Connie [redacted] [A 0247] told police at the scene that George took her daughter Kendra to school, then took Connie to her job at [redacted] downtown. George then returned to his home to help Oscar do work on their home. George only let friends in the house, and they likely paged him before they came over.

Kayla [redacted] with her mom present told police that two b/m came into the house. She twice stated that daddy's brother shot daddy, but she was unable to identify daddy's brother.

[NOTE: Page two of this two-page report containing the balance of Kayla [redacted] statement was located at [A 309]].

Kayla continued that two b/m in black hats and coats came over to the house in a white car. One man was fat and the other skinny. George raised the garage door and let them in through the garage. Both men had guns, and they wanted George's money. Oscar saw the men and ran downstairs. Next time she saw Oscar he was covered in blood.

Both men used lots of cuss words and one of the men told her she would be alright. She said they shot her daddy, and she didn't see them take anything when they left. After the men left she called the police.

Kayla said these two men came over to the house the day before when Sonny was at the house. Connie explained that Sonny was [redacted] – George's uncle.

Connie said the only skinny and fat people she knew that George would let into the house was Kareem(?) and Junior.

Initial Area Canvass –

(Police interviews conducted on 2/6/96)

Phyllis [redacted] of 70[redacted] Monroe was contacted by police about 12 noon. She said she heard shots (1 … 2 – 3 – 4), then she saw a white car back up northbound on Monroe. [A0297]

She SAW Shannon [redacted] in front of his house (70[redacted] Monroe).

She knew that Damon [redacted] and Eric [redacted] were in her driveway under a car when the shots were fired.

[NOTE: She was not asked, but apparently did NOT see Richard [redacted] anywhere on the street between her house and George Bryant's house.]

Jeffrey [redacted] (Michael?) of 70[redacted] Monroe was contacted by police about 12:08 p.m. He said he was inside sleeping around noon when he heard 2 shots, then 4–5 more shots. He looked out and saw neighbors outside across the street looking north on Monroe. [A 0298]

[NOTE: No mention of Richard [redacted].]

Sandi [redacted] of 70[redacted] Cleveland, said she heard shots in her apt., while watching TV. The shots came from the direction of her mom's house at 70th and Monroe (70[redacted] Monroe) and her son Shannon [redacted] who was standing across from the homicide scene.

Shannon [redacted] of 70[redacted] Monroe, told police he was an extremely reluctant witness. He told police he heard shots and heard tires screech but didn't see anything.

George W[redacted], of 70[redacted] Monroe, told police he was inside his house when he heard shots. He looked out and saw two b/m's wearing black coats and black stocking caps run from the yard to a clean, white, newer-model car facing south. Seconds later he heard another shot and saw a 3rd b/m run from the house and enter the white car on the driver's side. The car backed up northbound to 70th St. then backed up westbound on 70th St.

[NOTE: No sighting of Richard [redacted].]

Some homicides, where the area canvass was extensive, but fruitless, I might make a long list of residence addresses, followed by an occupant's name (if noted) and brief remarks, such as: "Saw nothing … Heard 3 GS, saw nothing … Sleeping, knows nothing … Heard/Saw nothing …Was Not Home … Saw nothing …, etc."

What I hope to accomplish with those notes is to create an inventory of potential witnesses/neighbors whom I find out later may have actually seen something, but did not want to cooperate at that time – for whatever reason. In those cases, I will want a searchable inventory (my Murder Memo), so a quick review may determine if a person ever talked to police and, if so, what they said.

As my review continues chronologically into the more formal witness interviews (from police reports), I may find additional, and maybe conflicting, *raw data*. I add that to the Murder Memo boilerplate as well as in the body of my witness summaries.

Specifically, eyewitness descriptions of actors may change, or police reports may add more specific observations about physical appearance, clothing, getaway car, etc. I note any contradictions and any significant additions. I also add additional specifics to my Murder Memos at SUSPECTS/ACTORS. Be aware these reports written by police at or near the time of the crime may reflect the chaos of the crime scene. An initial written report may contain mistakes, or inaccuracies. Additional information may be gained by police in subsequent interviews or simply added in subsequent reports.

I have the luxury of a calm, quiet environment while reviewing these witness statements. Police might have been standing at a bustling crime scene, initially interviewing witnesses in the midst of chaos. I also realize witnesses themselves are being asked to recall details of a traumatic, chaotic event they have not yet processed. Confusion can reign at a crime scene.

When I first began reviewing homicide reports, I filled notepads with summarizing notes, then converted my notes, via keyboard, to a Murder Memo. This way, I seared the case into my memory. Plus, I created an accurate, searchable word.doc. I have since learned to skip the handwriting step and go straight to the keyboard. I don't believe I have lost anything in the comprehension department. However, cognitive experts claim writing notes by hand increases one's recall and comprehension.

Building my Murder Memo, I attempt to use the same format for each witness interview (and each investigative event). My witness interview summary starts with the time and date, followed by the name of the witness interviewed and the location of the interview.

Documenting the time and date encourages my adherence to a chorological review. It may be significant to know the interview occurred at the witness' residence, or a neutral location, or the front seat of a Police Cruiser, or a state prison or county jail, or a police interview room.

My standard format includes the Bates stamp number for the first page of that interview (or investigative event).

I then attempt to summarize the police report of this witness interview at roughly a 10:1 ratio. That clearly depends on the quality of the police interview, the quality of the written report, and more importantly, the quality and relevance of the witness' information.

I'm looking for factual observations and relevant verifiable information. I include brief biographical information (i.e., cousin of victim). (I'll discuss witness identifiers later.) And I write my summaries with the intent of creating searchable material.

I attempt to summarize *what* they saw (or heard), *where* they say they were situated, *when* they saw (or heard) certain events, and *what* they were doing at the time. I generally (but not always) avoid summarizing any speculation offered by the witness, or what may be offered as community rumors.

I note any *verifiable* information related to specific activities. Verifiable information includes *who* they were talking to on the phone; *what* TV show they were watching; the weather at that hour; the status of daylight or dark or dusk; the identity of the neighbor they saw drive by right before, or right after. *Who* was standing next to them? What activity they attended immediately prior to witnessing the crime? What activity were they heading to *when* witnessing the crime?

If a witness' credibility falls into question, any specifics they offer, and noted in the police report, become part of my investigation (i.e., the person whom they claimed to be talking to by phone when the event occurred). This verifiable information can also be used to better define the time an event occurred.

From experience, I now know that the witness summary in my Murder Memo must be sufficient for me to glance at, months later, as I'm preparing to walk up to his front door, knock-knock, introduce myself, and ask him about the crime he witnessed 18 years earlier.

Any activity a witness describes, which involves another human being, or human event (i.e., a job, a tv show, a sporting event, a manicurist appointment) is a *verifiable* event. Many environmental descriptions are also well documented, and so they are also *verifiable* (i.e., weather, daylight, wind, precipitation, community mood).

If the witness said she was brushing her teeth when she looked out her window and saw something significant, relevant to the crime – that is not verifiable. Unless she brushed her teeth at the same time every morning, as her routine, 30 minutes before leaving for work. Her arrival at work that morning – on time – is verifiable.

If the witness said he was watching his favorite NFL team play the Green Bay Packers, and it was in the fourth quarter when he looked out the window and saw something relevant to the crime – that is *verifiable.* (In a follow-up interview, I would casually ask him if he had money on the game. If yes, his answer would suggest to me how closely he was watching the game and keeping track of the score. Years later, he might know almost precisely where the game clock stood when he was interrupted by this crime outside his window. That information would be *verifiable.*)

Seldom do police interviews I have seen include follow-up questions, verifying specifics: (... witness was watching a football game on TV ... witness was driving west on Baylor Ave ... witness had just gotten out of bed when she heard ... witness was on the phone ...).

I will want to ask those follow-up questions during my interview: (Which NFL game and the games status? ... Driving on Baylor Ave., going where, coming from where? ... What time did you get up and to do what? ... go to work, go to school? ... on the phone with who?).

When I later interview a witness, my Murder Memo summary of their police interview is normally enough to remind me what she recalled during that police interview – at least what information made it into the police report.

In some cases, the accuracy of these police reports/witness interviews become an issue. In those cases, I bring the actual police report with me.

That's another reason why it helps to list the Bates stamp page number next to each of my written witness summaries (and other investigative incidents) on my Murder Memo. Inserting "[#0032]" in the line above the witness name on my Murder Memo is easy enough. Being able to quickly pull page #0032 from Discovery saves time when, years later, the witness offers a largely different narrative from my opening questions. Or I may find that associates of this witness offer a different understanding of what they believe their friend (the witness) actually saw or heard.

With a Bates stamp page number noted on each witness interview, summarized in my Murder Memo, it becomes a simple task to find and review the actual police report and confirm the *exact wording* relevant to her honest, candid recall.

Note to Reader

I understand the police report itself may be in error. I must first gain the witness' cooperation, confirm what she recalls telling the police, and then show her what the police report claims she said.

Back to My Review …

Initial witness interviews contained in the crime scene report, or the original incident report, can be brief and (likely) incomplete. Understand the initial report of this crime may be written by patrol officers who were first on the scene. Homicide investigators will arrive later and begin creating their own reports, probably beginning with their initial crime scene report. This patrol officer's incident report will likely be included in the Discovery, along with the complete homicide investigation. It may be loaded with important initial observations – raw data.

Whatever the source for these initial reports, I begin my *Witness Narrative* summaries in my Murder Memo with these initial police contacts – in strict chronological order. I note any salient facts the witness may make in this initial, albeit brief, interview and assume a more complete interview will follow.

It suggests (to me) a competent investigation, when I see an eyewitness interviewed briefly at the scene, followed by an in-depth interview a few hours, or a few days later, once investigators have developed broader understanding. It may suggest a less than competent investigation if only some of the eyewitnesses from the crime scene are formally interviewed later.

Whenever there are multiple interviews of the same witness, I summarize each interview report in chronological order while comparing the witness' observations for consistency. Two interview reports, with the same witness, within hours or days, may show that specific facts have changed.

Reports may show her description of the assailant went from "tall and skinny" to "average height and medium build" (or something equally inconsistent). Both of these interview reports provide raw data – and may become an issue to pursue.

Maybe one of the reports was in error. Maybe she misspoke. Maybe her second interview was more "suggestive" compared with the initial police contact at the scene. Either way, I carefully make sure those contradictions from this eyewitness are reflected on my Murder Memo and move on. After reviewing the entire investigation, I will better understand the relevance of these initial contradictions.

As I review these investigative reports, I understand that every homicide investigator has his or her own writing style. Some are better than others. When reviewing their reports, I try to determine if the interview is *suggestive* or *fact-gathering*. Because I have noticed that once police gain some understanding of the crime, they may (inadvertently) start suggesting answers by the way they ask their questions. Investigators may start seeking affirmation (versus information) from the third or fourth eyewitness they interview, relevant to what the first or second eyewitness told police.

And I have found another significant issue, most likely to be revealed in these initial reports. I may find a brief reference to a person, possibly a witness, who may not be fully identified. This person may have been an eyewitness or simply have some knowledge about some aspect of this crime. But the police never pursue this person. I use the term "ghost witness" to describe these individuals who appear to have fallen through the cracks. This person may be totally irrelevant. This person may know exactly what happened. Who knows?

I flag the person's name and add whatever ID is available to my People List (described below), and continue on with my chronological review and Murder Memo building. I expect homicide investigators to also flag these names and eventually interview all potential witnesses. That's not always the case. In wrongful convictions, that omission can become an issue.

By reviewing these reports in chronological order, I discover, eventually, whether police ever contacted this person. If I don't find a witness interview, she will go on my list of things to do, because, who knows?

Any person possibly related to a crime, or a crime scene, could be critical to my understanding of *what happened*. Especially if the person was never interviewed by police. Maybe that person left town, or moved out of the neighborhood, or gave a bad address to the investigator, or the police wrote down the wrong address, or misspelled the witness' name and couldn't locate her later. Callbacks aren't always called back. Follow-ups may not be followed up. Stuff happens. I've encountered all of these scenarios.

And there are other, more sinister, explanations. Maybe police had already identified their suspect and were "building their case" before getting back to this witness. Maybe what this witness saw, or said, contradicted the theory they were pursuing. Maybe police never wrote a report from their interview with this witness. Maybe the police challenged what this witness claimed to have seen. I am aware of investigators pressuring a witness to the extent that the witness just decided, "I can't remember ...."

If the witness was interviewed, and the police report was written, but the prosecutor did not include that report in Discovery, I may be working on a wrongful conviction, based on prosecutorial misconduct and a Brady Violation. If that witness was never interviewed by the original defense team – but could have been – that might become an Ineffective Assistance of Counsel (IAC) claim.

During my review of innocence claims, I have found several of these, what I call, "ghost witnesses." In at least two of my wrongful conviction cases, I found a "ghost witness" who credibly and convincingly refuted the state's entire case.

In the homicide leading to Mo. v. Chris Dunn, *a 15-year-old Recco Rogers was sitting on a friend's porch with friends, late one night, in May 1990, on a residential street in North St. Louis. Several gun shots from nearby shattered their evening. As the boys jumped off the porch to run away from the gun shots, Recco was struck in the back of the head and fell to the ground. He died about an hour later at a nearby hospital.*

Police interviewed two of the boys that night who had been with Recco. Both Mike and Demorris told police that the shooter was a neighbor they both knew – Chris Dunn. They described his clothing.

When talking to police, Mike only mentioned himself, Demorris, and Recco being present before the shooting.

Demorris partially identified four other teenage boys besides himself and Mike and the victim, as being around when shots were fired. Reviewing the police reports, I was able to account for and find interviews for three of those four boys – everyone but "Gino."

When police came out to search for Chris Dunn the following day, they encountered a group of four teenage boys, including "Eugene W," who were also searching for Chris Dunn. According to the police report, these boys had heard Dunn may have been involved in their friend Recco's shooting. This report indicated police spoke to "Eugene W" (partially identified) and the boys discussed Dunn's whereabouts with the police. There was apparently no discussion or any questions about the shooting the night before.

Police found and arrested Chris Dunn that day. Dunn was charged with First Degree Murder, convicted the following year, and sentenced to Life Without Parole. The name of "Eugene W." was found on the state's witness list but he did not testify at trial.

I had been asked to review this case and assess Dunn's innocence claim. I eventually determined that "Gino" was Eugene [redacted]*., who at that point, appeared to be a potential "ghost witness," but not a priority. After tracking down several loose ends, confirming Dunn's alibi, and gaining recantations from the two eyewitnesses, I located and approached Eugene* [redacted]*. in April of 2016.*

Soon after Eugene answered my knock on his door, I confirmed that he still had excellent recall about the night Recco was shot. The second fact he confirmed was that no one had ever contacted him about that night. No police, no prosecutor, no defense attorney – no one had ever asked Eugene what happened the night Recco was shot and killed.

Eugene clearly recalled sitting on the porch that night and easily identified the others present. "Suddenly, someone started shooting at us, 'boom ... boom ... boom.'" The gun shots, he said, came out of the darkness, from in front of the house next door. "None of us could see the shooter."

Eugene had heard the others speculate that night that the shooter may have been Chris Dunn. Eugene had grown up with Chris Dunn in the neighborhood and said he never thought the shooter was Chris Dunn.

Eugene did not talk to the police that night because he knew he could not identify whoever shot Recco. Instead, Eugene stood in the crowd of onlookers with Recco's grieving mother. The day after Recco was shot, Eugene said he and friends were looking for Chris Dunn because they had heard the rumors. Eugene knew the rumor was not true. (And that was the only reason Eugene W.'s name appeared in the police report.)

Eugene signed an affidavit on my follow-up visit and later testified at two different habeas hearings, which led to Chris Dunn's release in 2024.

I found a similar witness in Ricky Kidd's case. I'll discuss that interview later in this book.

There is probably no one way to summarize police reports for a Murder Memo. It is a skill which will improve with practice and experience. With that in mind, I thought I would offer, on the following pages, two examples of the actual police reports and how I summarized these police reports for my Murder Memo in Ricky Kidd's case.

The first interview (with Clyde) shows my summary of a seemingly irrelevant witness. I include only what he knew, not what he had heard (Figures 5.1 and 5.2).

KANSAS CITY, MISSOURI POLICE DEPARTMENT

INVESTIGATIVE REPORT [CASE DOCUMENT]

Case #96-013994

TITLE OF INVESTIGATION	SUBJECT OF REPORT
Homicide #1 George A. Bryant B/M 4/27/63 #2 Oscar Bridges Jr. B/M 12/11/57	Interview of Clyde [redacted] B/M 11/[redacted]/66, [redacted] E. 71st. K.C.Mo. Telephone Number 333-[redacted]

REPORT BY:	ASSIGNMENT:	DATE:	PAGE 1 OF 2 PAGES
Det. [redacted]	Homicide	2/27/96	

On 2/27/96 at 2115hrs. Det. Thompson and I responded to [redacted] E. 71st. to contact the abo described subject. Several telephone calls were made to the victims residence on the caller I.I from this address.

Upon arrival we contacted the above described subject. He has known of victim #1 (Geor Bryant) for about ten years. He related that his seven year old daughter [redacted] made seve calls to victim #1's residence to talk to the victims daughter [redacted]. His daughter and t victims daughter would read to each other on the telephone and Kindra was his daughters be friend. Since the victim was killed the victims daughter has moved from the school that she we to and his daughter is not allowed to make any more calls to the victims residence.

He stated two weeks before George was killed he would frequent the house at [redacted] College a daily bases. He thought George was supplying the residence at [redacted] College and knew th George was dealing drugs. He described [redacted] College as being a brown house just South of 72 street. The person at the residence drives a 1978 Blue colored four door [redacted] a 19 Champagne [redacted], and a 1972 Chevrolet [redacted].

He related that a Sam [redacted] who lives on [redacted] and College knows would know the people i name at [redacted] College and would probably know George.

He related that a black male with the street name of "[redacted]" owed George money. He is curren refusing to pay since George is dead and the word of the street is, that there will be anoth Homicide. The people in the brown house are trying to collect the money from "[redacted]".

When asked what he thought about this offense he related that the word on the street is, th offense was a "drug deal". He heard that George witnessed a white guy get killed, which was o story. The second story he heard that several guys just rode up while George was outside and sh him.

Supervisor: Sgt [redacted]

File Page #

A00030

Form 107 P.D.(10-80)

Figure 5.1 A (redacted) KCMO PD report of an interview with a subject named Clyde in their Bryant/Bridges homicide investigation quite sure he would have noticed a report of a witness to the crime who specifically did not see Richard [redacted] in front of George's house.]

2/27/96

[0030]

On 2/27/96, at 9:15pm, police interviewed **Clyde** [redacted] (born 11/[redacted]/66) at his residence, [redacted] E 71st St., KCMO (333-[redacted]). C[redacted] had been a friend of victim George since 1986. C[redacted] knew George was a drug dealer. C[redacted]'s daughter was good friends with [redacted]. [redacted] had no knowledge of the crime.

On 2/27/96, a **Crime Lab Report** indicated the following:

A partial shoe print in apparent blood was found on a piece of linoleum, which was photographed several ways. [SEE 3/13/97 apparent comparison with all of R Kidd's shoes.]

2/29/96

Gary [redacted].

On 2/29/96, **Gary** [redacted] called KCPD Det Kent Morton from DeKalb, GA

25

Figure 5.2 The brief passage in my Ricky Kidd Murder Memo summarizing Clyde's police interview

The second witness interview report with Maurice, which follows on the next page, was far more significant, in what he knew, what he saw, and what he heard relevant to the crime (Figures 5.3 and 5.4).

Depositions Review (When?)

Only in state criminal cases, and only in certain states (including Missouri), does the defense have the opportunity, or at least the option, to depose a state witness prior to trial. In federal court, depositions of witnesses are not generally conducted prior to trial.

If I am reviewing Discovery in a habeas case in a state which allows defense team depositions of state witnesses prior to trial, I definitely want to gather those depositions for review. But they will be my dessert. I will review depos only after I have completed review of all police reports in chronological order.

I will review these depositions after gaining a full understanding of the police investigation. These depositions are often conducted mere days or weeks before the actual trial. These depositions may take place a year or more after the actual crime and the completed police investigation.

KANSAS CITY, MISSOURI POLICE DEPARTMENT

INVESTIGATIVE REPORT [CASE DOCUMENT]

Case #96-013994

TITLE OF INVESTIGATION	SUBJECT OF REPORT
Homicide #1 George A. Bryant B/M 4/27/63 #2 Oscar Bridges B/M 12/11/57	Interview of Maurice [redacted] B/M [redacted]/70, [redacted] E. 114 Terr. K.C.Mo. Phone number 763-[redacted]

REPORT BY:	ASSIGNMENT:	DATE:	PAGE 1 OF 2 PAGES
D[redacted]	Homicide	2/24/96	

On 2/24/96 at 0900hrs. I was contacted by Det. Stockard who was interviewing the above described subject in the interrogation room. Det. Stockard advised me that the above subject wa present and heard the shots when this offense was committed. He was contacted and related that he thought George was killed because he witnessed a murder. A Terrell was charged and George was going to testify against him. That was information he heard through hear say. He stated if he could get out that he could find out some information pertaining to this offense because he knew the victim George and hung out in the same neighborhood that this offense occurred.

When asked the specifics of this offense on the day that it occurred he related that he was out in front of [redacted] hou[redacted] working on his vehicle. He admitted seeing a black male drive up to Georges house in a white Oldsmobile cutlass. The vehicle parked on the East side of Monroe, facing Southbound. He observed the garage door of Georges house open and related that everyone uses the garage to enter Georges house, no one enters through the front door. When the garage door opened he observed George motion for the black male to enter the residence. He observed the black male and the only way he could describe him was he was a black male wearing a lot of gold. When asked the specifics of what he was wearing he denied that he knew. After the black male entered the residence he heard three shots fired which sounded like it was from inside the victims residence. He then heard screaming or hollering then at first he stated, he observed George being chased outside of the residence by the black male, then later when asking for a description of the black male chasing George he denied seeing George run out and related that he only observed silhouettes running around the victims vehicles. He did admit that after the two shots outside he observed George fall to the ground. He then heard several shots outside, then heard several shots again inside of the residence. When the shots were being fired he was lying on the ground since he did not want to get hit. While on the ground he observed one black male enter the white Oldsmobile and drive South up the hill. At the time that the vehicle was coming up the hill another vehicle was coming from the South, which kept the white Oldsmobile from going South. The white Oldsmobile then backed down Monroe to 70th, then went West bound from 70th street.

Supervisor: [redacted]

File Page #

Form 107 P.D.(10-80)

A0[redacted]325

Figure 5.3 A (redacted) KCMO PD report of an interview with a subject named Maurice in their Bryant/Bridges homicide investigation *(Continued)*

CONTINUATION

CASE #96-013994

DATE 2/24/96

PAGE 2 OF 2 PAGES

He was asked if he knew Richard and he stated that Richard lives in the coroner house at 70th and Monroe. He stated that Richard and Dan [redacted] were together but denied that they were outside at the time that this offense was committed.

He was shown a photograph of Rod[redacted] B/M 3/[redacted]/52 and denied knowing him, Rod[redacted] is known as "Fat [redacted] to frequent victim #1 residence frequently. He was shown Andre [redacted] B/M 2/[redacted]/75 and did not know him by name but related that he has seen him in the neighborhood before. He was then shown the "Mug" show up folder consisting of six black males numbered one through six. He identified the fill in photograph in position #6 as seeing before but he could not remember where he had seen him. He stated that the black male in photograph #3 he thought was dead because he thought his picture was in the Call newspaper.

It should be noted that the "Mug" show up folder had Marcus [redacted] B/M 8/[redacted]/69 in the #3 position, Gary [redacted] B/M 11/[redacted]/73 in the number 2 position, and Ricky L. Kidd B/M 9/10/74 in the [redacted] position.

It should be noted that this subject was interviewed earlier in this investigation and basically denied seeing any activity at the victim #1's residence.

Form 106-B P.D.(10-80)

File Page #

A0[redacted]326

Figure 5.3 (Continued)

So, my summary of a witness deposition will go chronologically at the end of my Murder Memo, after all the facts have been gathered by police.

These depositions can be revealing in many ways.

What I hope to see is a competent defense lawyer who takes this opportunity to explore the state witness' background, discover context, find out

[NOTE: These interviews should have given police reason to at least consider Richard [redacted] as a possible suspect, rather than a confirmed witness.]

2/24/96

Exculpatory Evidence Alert/ Brady???

On 2/24/96, **Maurice** [redacted] was interviewed by police, at HQ apparently while in custody. [A 325]

[redacted] said that on 2/6/96 he was outside helping Earl [redacted] work on his car. [redacted] saw a White Olds pull up and stop in front of George's house. The car was parked southbound on the east side of the street (George's side).

[redacted] saw the garage door go up and saw George invite the men inside. Once these men were inside, Givens said he heard 3 gun shots. He heard yelling and then saw George outside being chased and shot twice outside.

The b/m's got into the white Olds and backed up northbound on Monroe Street and backed up westbound on 70th St.

[redacted] knows Richard [redacted] who lives at 7000 Monroe. Asked specifically if he saw Richard [redacted] and [redacted] said Richard [redacted] was not outside during the shooting.

[NOTE: Nor did Shannon [redacted] see Richard [redacted] in his narrative.]

[NOTE: [redacted] was standing across the street from Michael [redacted]'s house and south of George Bryant's house. If Richard [redacted] was in front of George Bryant's house during the shooting, [redacted] would have been directly in [redacted]'s line of sight. And [redacted] would have run back (south) toward [redacted], as he ran up the hill to Michael [redacted]'s house and 'bammed on the door.']

[redacted] was asked, but was unable to ID 'Fat [redacted]' who police had Id'd as Ro [redacted], a known associate (and bodyguard) of George Bryant.

[redacted] was shown the 'Mug' show up folder, apparently the same one shown Connie [redacted]. [redacted] offered no ID.

[NOTE: On 11/2/06, Ricky Kidd was positive he had never seen any report or interview on Maurice [redacted] (in his original discovery). He had never heard of Maurice [redacted]. Kidd is quite sure he would have noticed a report of a witness to the crime who specifically did not see Richard [redacted] in front of George's house.]

Figure 5.4 My Murder Memo summary of the police interview of Maurice

what the witness saw and heard, and knows (first-hand), in depth. I hope to see the defense attorney show an interest in what happened.

I want to see if the witness' answers about the crime match her police interview at the crime scene – 18 months earlier.

I understand the defense lawyer will have a strategy in mind when questioning this state witness two weeks before trial. That strategy may be different from mine, as a factfinder.

Looking at this deposition 20 years later, during a habeas case review, may reveal a lot about the competence of the defense team in what may have been a wrongful conviction. Of course, in some of these cases where depos were allowed, but *no* pre-trial depositions were conducted, it's easier to draw a conclusion about the defense team.

Reviewing the Lab Reports …

Having arranged the police and lab reports in chronological order, my review is not just focused on police witness interviews. It's important to look at *all* facts police gather during their investigation and look at them in chronological order. That includes facts from the lab, various business or phone records, facts from any source which add to the investigator's understanding of *what happened*. My Murder Memo becomes a searchable inventory of these gathered facts and allows me to further research those facts later.

My Murder Memo becomes a chronological summary of all *investigative events* – not just witness interviews.

Lab reports, in particular, can be especially useful in both my investigation of the crime and my investigation of the investigation.

Any homicide investigation will likely include physical items which are collected, inventoried, and sent to a lab for processing and analysis. Each step will be reflected by some type of report (i.e., a crime scene report, a police inventory, a crime lab report).

I summarize each of these events in chronological order in my Murder Memo. That allows me to monitor what happened to each of these (evidentiary) items. In a potential wrongful conviction, I may find that items were seized, tested, and the findings were "inconclusive." I will flag any ambiguous test results (from 20 years earlier), which could possibly *exclude* an individual (the convicted defendant) with current science and additional testing.

"Inconclusive" from 10 or 20 years ago could mean something far different today. More sophisticated testing procedures are developed every year – for all forensics and latent prints – not just DNA testing. In the Discovery material, I look for *bench notes* from a forensic lab, which may clarify the "inconclusive" finding. A lab's bench notes will always be helpful, if available. (Bench notes are the handwritten notes kept by lab personnel as they do their analysis or forensic research. These notes literally "show their work," which led to whatever conclusion they offered in their formal Lab Report.)

Note to Reader

I know from my pre-trial investigative work, forensic bench notes generally require a special Discovery Request, but they should always be requested. Sadly, I have never found bench notes in any habeas case I have been asked to review. But I keep hoping, someday, I will find a manila folder labeled "Bench Notes."

If the bench notes exist, or the Defense team can request them, those notes may indicate that a scientific conclusion had actually been reached (pre-trial). However, the lab decided to go with "inconclusive." There may even be a trace of prosecutorial misconduct behind that "inconclusive" finding. But first, the bench notes will need to be reviewed by an independent forensic expert.

"Inconclusive" may have been accurate for that time period. Current testing by either the state lab or an independent lab might develop better results. That would be the only way to determine that "inconclusive," 18 years earlier, may have been code for "not incriminating."

Any lab finding of "inconclusive" should also trigger a search through the trial transcript for the lab technician's testimony. It is improper for the lab tech to offer any opinion based on an "inconclusive" test result. Sometimes, the prosecutor may be able to get a lab tech to offer into testimony some quasi-opinion. In doing that, the jury may see that quasi-opinion as a "possibility" when, in fact, the lab result suggests *no opinion* which – I've been told by experts – should mean "no opinion."

Depending on the case and the physical evidence involved, I may also do a line-by-line inventory of relevant items seized and processed, just to identify what evidence *was*, and what evidence *was not* presented at trial. Prosecutors, like defense attorneys, are human. They can make mistakes. They can misinterpret or misread lab reports and, unfortunately, they are also capable of cheating.

We may never know which occurred when the prosecutor in Ricky Kidd's case implied to the jury that Kidd's latent print had been found in the shooter's getaway car – a white 1996 Oldsmobile. When, in fact, that latent had been found by a Crime Scene Tech in Ricky's own white 1981 Olds Delta 88. (See "Ricky Kidd's Latent Print," below.)

There is at least one other reason why I sometimes inventory and track each relevant item of physical evidence from collection through testing. Not all relevant items from a crime scene are always tested – for anything – no matter how obvious or significant such testing might appear to a layman, such as me.

I've never gotten a straight answer as to why a relevant item related to a crime is not sent to the lab. My guess is the reasons are both practical and financial. Most crime labs are over-worked, under-staffed, and underfunded. Every lab test takes time and costs the state money. Once a confession is gained (coerced?), or an eyewitness comes forward – the investigation often stops.

Lab tests on existing evidence costs money. If the state can make their case without additional testing, they don't bother. If testing could corroborate a shaky eyewitness, it may or may not be done. (The state may worry that a lab test might discredit the state's theory, based on one shaky eyewitness. A lab test might make the state's case go "poof," and the lab analysis becomes exculpatory evidence. Why would the state take that chance?)

Once the state stops investigating and starts building their case, they don't want a lab test challenging their theory. At that point, the state is only interested in conviction. That could also explain a lab result being termed "inconclusive."

Also, when I inventory evidence, I also inventory each item sent for processing to make sure a lab result came back. I have reviewed habeas cases where I determined a lab report was missing from Discovery. I saw that an analysis had been requested, so a lab report should have been delivered to the prosecutor or the investigative agency – whoever requested the test. All items sent out for processing should have a corresponding lab report of the analysis. That scenario (a missing lab report) could represent a clerical error, or Brady Material, or some other element of misconduct.

That's why I track every piece of evidence removed from the crime scene and follow that evidence through testing, analysis, and final report.

I would never assume that sloppy paperwork or a lab's clerical mistake represents a conscious effort to convict an innocent person. That said, I have seen disorganized and confusing paperwork make it unlikely the average defense attorney can keep up with every piece of critical evidence. At that point, it really doesn't matter if the state is consciously playing a shell game with evidence, or if they are merely careless and unprofessional, the result could be the same.

Details.

Ricky Kidd's Latent Print

After reviewing all police and lab reports in Ricky Kidd's case, and creating my chronological Murder Memo, I met several times with Ricky – through confidential "legal" calls. We discussed his case and the police investigation. Ricky identified certain significant police reports that he was sure his original defense team never received, reports that he had never seen before (i.e., possible Brady Material).

Ricky also shared helpful background and observations he made at his own trial. I recall one claim was that the prosecutor had implied to the jury that his fingerprint was found in what the police identified as the shooter's getaway car. When, in fact, that fingerprint was found inside his own personal car.

That fact alone would not prove Ricky's innocence. But it bothered Ricky.

When I read that portion of the trial transcript, compared with my understanding of the issue, I saw he was right. And it would later become a real issue.

During Ricky's trial, the prosecutor put the state's fingerprint expert, Kathy Hentges, on the stand. She began testifying about the 30 fingerprints, or "lift cards," processed from the crime scene at 7009 Monroe, which Hentges received on February 12. Of those 30 cards, 13 prints of value were identified, and all but one matched the victims, George Bryant and Oscar Bridges.

The prosecutor then asked Hentges about three fingerprints, or lift cards, Hentges received on February 20 from Crime Scene Tech (CST), Charlie Johnson. These cards were created at "12th and Indiana ... a warehouse facility ... where vehicles are towed to ... and processed...."

Of those three fingerprint cards, Hentges found one print of value. Asked if she was able to determine who left that print, Hentges answered, "I was able to identify Ricky Kidd, the right index finger impression on the interior of the right front window."

The prosecutor's questions immediately move on to two more fingerprint cards sent to her on February 22 by another CST. Hentges testified that one of those two latents, found "on Item 24-6, a Carmex Package," was suitable for comparison. The latent matched suspect Gary Goodspeed Sr. (a person suspected but never charged).

Hentges was not asked, nor did she offer, where that Carmex Package was found.

During a very brief cross-examination, Ricky's defense attorney asked Hentges to confirm that she received three latent cards from CST Johnson on February 20, and that those cards had been processed inside a police garage at 12th and Indiana.

Neither the prosecutor nor the defense counsel ever established that the latent print matching Ricky Kidd was recovered from Ricky Kidd's 1988 Olds Delta 88 (which was never connected to the crime). Ricky's Oldsmobile was processed at the 12th and Indiana Police garage with Ricky Kidd's written permission on February 14, after he was stopped for questioning.

What follows is a page from the official trial transcript, showing the brief cross-examination of Ms. Hentges, conducted by Ricky Kidd's defense lawyer (see Figure 5.5).

State v. Kidd & Merrill **Multi-Page™**

Page 1014

Q. And in that particular fingerprint card, was it of any comparison value?
A. Yes. There were two prints of value on that item.
Q. And were you able to compare it with the known prints that you had?
A. Yes, I did.
Q. And were you able to determine, in your expert opinion, the person that left those prints?
A. No, I was not.
Q. Those particular prints did not match either the two victims or the five persons that you were asked to compare those to?
A. That is correct.
Q. Did you receive any other fingerprints or fingerprint cards that we have not yet spoke about in this case?
A. No, sir.
Q. And that was the extent of -- your extent of involvement in this particular case?
A. That is correct, sir.
Q. You, yourself, did not lift any of these prints; is that correct?
A. That is correct.
Q. And your role in this case is simply to compare the known print cards that you already have to those fingerprints that have been lifted either at the scene

Page 1015

or by the Regional Crime Lab?
A. That is correct.
MR. NASTEFF: If I might just have one moment, your Honor? No further questions.
THE COURT: All right. You may cross-examine.
CROSS-EXAMINATION BY MS. ANDERSON:
Q. Just to make it very clear, you did a total of four comparisons on cards that were given to you, a number of cards, but four separate occasions, right?
A. There were cards received on five separate occasions.
Q. Okay, five separate occasions. The first -- there were 30 received initially on this case?
A. That's correct.
Q. And then you received another one on the 20th; is that correct?
A. On the 20th there were three cards received from crime scene technicians.
Q. Okay. Now, you've written a report dated February 20, 1996, with regard to a location 12th and Indiana. Do you recall that?
A. Yes, ma'am.
Q. Okay. And so that was taken -- these prints were taken from 12th and Indiana, which you understand to be like a police garage?

Page 1016

A. That's correct.
Q. And it was taken from, your understanding, a car that was contained within the police garage?
A. I couldn't answer that question as to exactly the location of where the car was.
Q. Okay.
A. Just other than the address of 12th and Indiana.
Q. And this is the interior of the right front window?
A. That's correct.
Q. And later from another card you wrote a report dated February 22, 1996. You got it?
A. Yes.
Q. And that was taken from the location 969 Tel Aviv?
A. That is correct.
Q. Okay. And that's a Carmex package?
A. That is correct.
Q. And there was another one after that of another window that was taken from a car; is that correct? I think that's the very last one you testified about.
A. On the same date, on February 22, there was one card received from Crime Scene Technician Lane, and there was two lift cards received from Steve Warlen from the crime lab.
Q. Okay. No matches. Is that -- prints of value, but no matches to any of the people you were asked to compare

Page 1017

to?
A. On the card received from Crime Scene Technician Lane there were two prints of value on that and not identified.
Q. Okay. Thank you.
MS. ANDERSON: I don't have any further questions.
MS. LADESH: No questions.
THE COURT: All right. Anything further?
MR. NASTEFF: No, your Honor, nothing further from the State.
THE COURT: All right. You may stand down.
THE WITNESS: Thank you, sir.
MS. MCGOWAN: At this time I call Detective Jay Pruetting to the stand.
JAY PRUETTING,
having been sworn by the Court, testified as follows:
DIRECT EXAMINATION BY MS. MCGOWAN:
Q. Detective, good morning.
A. Morning.
Q. Could you state your name for the jury, please?
A. Jay Pruetting.
Q. Where are you employed?
A. Kansas City, Missouri, Police Department.
Q. Where are you currently assigned?

Becky Hook, RPR, CCR, CSR Page 1014 - Page 1017

Figure 5.5 Transcript from Ricky Kidd's trial showing the cross-examination of fingerprint expert, Kathleen Hentges

I then reviewed my Murder Memo and found the source of the confusion. (Using my Murder Memo, a search of "Indiana" or "Johnson" or "Latent" all led me to the relevant lab and crime scene reports.)

From my Murder Memo:

<u>On 2/14/96 at 7:15 p.m., police processed both of Ricky Kidd's cars</u> at Police Garage, 12th & Indiana. [A00201 + A00191]

Both cars transported from Armour and Holmes (Kidd's apt) to Police Garage. Police obtained a Consent to Search, signed by Ricky Kidd. [A0087]

A luminol search of the Olds Delta 88 found no blood.
The Olds Delta 88 was dusted for latent prints.
From Ricky's Olds Delta 88, police recovered the following:

9 pair of athletic shoes
2 non-matching athletic shoes
1 pair of sandals

<u>On 2/14/96, police Evidence Inventory</u> created with items removed from Ricky Kidd's 1981 white Olds (LP# K6W-064). [A00203]

Includes Hinge Lifts (Items 7–10).
Tech = CST Charles Johnson

(In Ricky's defense, I must point out that he was literally moving into a new apartment when he was stopped by police and arrested on February 14, 1996. That explains why his car was full of his shoes.)

My Murder Memo indicated that on February 19, 1996, police had located the suspected shooter's car, a 1996 Olds Cutlass, at an Alamo Rental Car dealership. This car had been rented to Gary Goodspeed Sr.

2/19/96

<u>On 2/19/96</u>, KCMO PD **<u>Crime Lab</u>** (CST Heather L Lane (13036) processed the white 1996 4dr Olds Cutlass Cierra Alamo rental car (LP# MZC-796) Police recovered:

Physical Evidence Inventory [A00211]

Water bottle under driver's seat
Feathers found in the trunk
"Carmex" w/GoodToGo sticker (Under L side front pass seat)
Rear Trunk Mat
Hinge lifts
Latent prints
Swab from passenger side handle

2/20/96

On 2/20/96, a **Crime Lab Report** (#5) indicated the following [A0184]:

Items 24-5 and 24-6 were recovered by Heather Lane at 969 Tel Aviv on 2/19/96 and submitted to PO Stephen Warlen.
24-5 = water bottle, recovered 2/19/96 in the Goodspeed rental Olds Cutlass, the lab found 3 latent prints of "possible value."
24-6 = Carmex container found 2/19/96 in the Goodspeed rental Olds Cutlass, the lab found 2 latent prints of "possible value."

This next Murder Memo entry for February 20, 1996, based on Kidd's comments, became more suggestive of possible misconduct:

On 2/20/96 a **Crime Lab Report [Latent Print ID]** [A 0208] states the following:

> "Examination and comparison of latent lifts received from CST Johnson on 2/20/96 reveals one print marked to indicate it was lifted from *'interior of right front window,'* is the same as the right index finger impression on a fingerprint card taken on 8/5/95 by Hertenstein and signed Ricky Kidd."

Report is signed by Kathleen M. Hentges #10410, Certified Latent Print Examiner.

[NOTE: The only ID for source of this latent is "12th & Indiana."]

Completing my review, I noted this last report pertaining to Hentges' trial testimony and the police lab's latent print findings:

2/22/96

On 2/22/96, a **Crime Lab Report** [Latent Print ID] indicated the following [A0190]:

> A latent print on the Carmex container (Item 24-6) matches the left thumb of "Suspect" Gary Goodspeed Sr, born [redacted]/56, KCPD Jacket# 135[redacted].

[NOTE: The only ID for source of this latent is "969 Tel Aviv."]

Whether this was malicious or not, these reports – compared with the trial transcript – showed me that the prosecutor was not tightly tethered to the facts. Nor was the defense attorney a devotee to detail. A copy of that misleading crime lab report I found at Bates# 0142 may be found on the next page (see Figure 5.6).

Building the People List ...

As I review police reports and summarize witness statements (in chronological order), adding summaries to my Murder Memo, I am simultaneously building my People List.

Criminal cases are based on evidence. Evidence presents in the form of *objects* and *people*. A thorough inventory of all relevant *people* is as important as a thorough inventory of all crime-related objects.

When I review police reports, I'm not only focused on facts, and witness observations, I'm also hyper-focused on any mention of individuals and their "identifiers." I seize on any miniscule piece of identifying information offered about any person remotely related to this crime, related to the victim, related to an eyewitness, or related to a suspect. I consider any person mentioned in a report to be worthy of my People List. For that reason, I do not call this my Witness List.

What are *identifiers*? Identifiers can be any unique descriptor besides a first and last name, which helps me distinguish that one person from the other 340 million persons in the United States. I look for identifiers such as a middle name or initial, date of birth (DOB), a Social Security number (SS#), a state driver's license number (DL#), a State ID number, a local criminal ID number, a state prison ID number (Mo DOC#), a federal

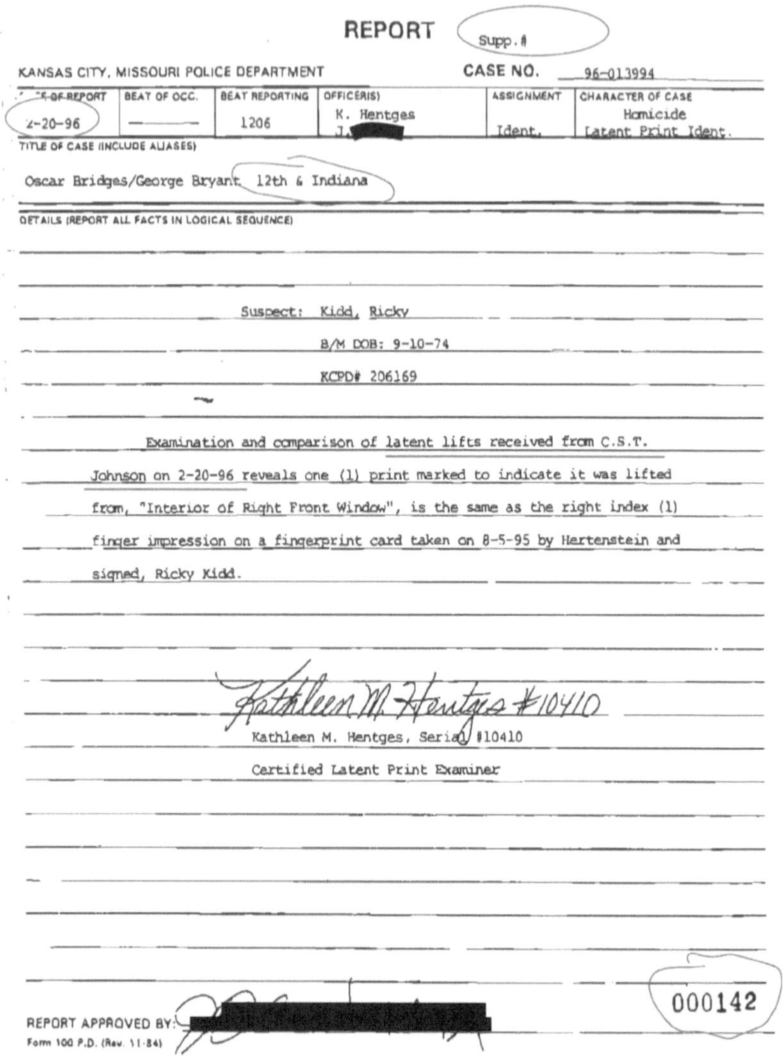
REPORT Supp.#

KANSAS CITY, MISSOURI POLICE DEPARTMENT CASE NO. 96-013994

DATE OF REPORT	BEAT OF OCC.	BEAT REPORTING	OFFICER(S)	ASSIGNMENT	CHARACTER OF CASE
2-20-96	———	1206	K. Hentges J. [redacted]	Ident.	Homicide Latent Print Ident.

TITLE OF CASE (INCLUDE ALIASES)

Oscar Bridges/George Bryant 12th & Indiana

DETAILS (REPORT ALL FACTS IN LOGICAL SEQUENCE)

Suspect: Kidd, Ricky

B/M DOB: 9-10-74

KCPD# 206169

Examination and comparison of latent lifts received from C.S.T. Johnson on 2-20-96 reveals one (1) print marked to indicate it was lifted from, "Interior of Right Front Window", is the same as the right index (1) finger impression on a fingerprint card taken on 8-5-95 by Hertenstein and signed, Ricky Kidd.

Kathleen M. Hentges #10410

Kathleen M. Hentges, Serial #10410

Certified Latent Print Examiner

000142

REPORT APPROVED BY: [redacted]

Form 100 P.D. (Rev. 11-84)

Figure 5.6 A KCMO PD lab report confirming a latent lift received on February 20, 1996 matches Ricky Kidd

prison ID number (BOP#), one's gender, race, one's known residence or last known address (LKA). I call these *primary identifiers.*

In these reports, police generally identify all main characters (i.e., witnesses). But a witness may mention a person who is not fully identified, not beyond their name, maybe only their first name. Maybe the report only mentions the person's relation to a known individual: "Raymond's cousin."

On my People List, that person would be initially listed as "Jaylynn LNU (i.e., Last Name Unknown) – Raymond's cousin." Only later will I find out if the police sought out Jaylynn, contacted, interviewed, and fully identified her.

For the purpose of creative searches (discussed later, in Chapter 7), I add any of these other "identifiers" offered in a police report, or mentioned anecdotally: place of employment (POE), a work phone, any personal cell or home phones, the names of any immediate family (i.e., mom, dad, sister, brother, son, daughter), a school attended, a graduation year, a place of birth (POB), height and weight, color of hair, or color of eyes. Any one of these identifiers may later help me distinguish one Joan Smith from all the other Joan Smiths out there. I call these *secondary identifiers*.

Placing a name on my People List takes up very little space. I build my list as a simple word.doc, using the alphabet (by last name). If I later learn this person is absolutely irrelevant to this case and a waste of my time, I use my delete key. Poof. It's easy to build an alpha list of every name mentioned in these police reports, and just as easy to delete them, if they prove to be irrelevant.

A seemingly irrelevant person (a shop owner near the crime scene) mentioned on page 27, or an acquaintance mentioned during a witness interview on page 132, may become relevant on the next to last page of the homicide investigation. If I don't put that name on my People List when they are first mentioned, I may lose important context when they are later deemed important.

It's also possible that an "irrelevant witness" is mentioned much later in one of my own witness interviews. I can then find her first mention in police reports, since I placed her name on my People List.

Details matter.

I learned the hard way to write down any relevant details I find while reviewing police and lab reports in a complex criminal case. Thinking I can commit everything to memory is a fool's approach. I will remember a lot, but not everything.

Some defense teams and some attorneys like to create their own *witness lists*, using an Excel spreadsheet. I suppose there are times when additional categories make that a useful tool. But I have found that a spreadsheet quickly becomes just that: a large, cumbersome, unwieldly spreadsheet.

Other defense teams fault on the side of careless and disorganized trial prep. How many wrongful convictions have resulted from defense teams unable to keep up with all the people related to a complex case – all the detail ... *who are they? ... where are they?... what do they know?*

I have created a standard format for my People List. I use the person's full name, including a middle name or middle initial, if available.

Immediately next to that name, I briefly describe this person's *relevance* to this case. Every person on this People List has a relevant relationship with the victim, or the crime, or the suspect/defendant, or an alternate suspect, or they had a relevant relationship with a witness to the crime or some other witness in the case. That allows me to create a brief, yet important, reminder of who this person is – relevant to some aspect of the case.

My People List serves three purposes. It is an inventory of everyone who may be relevant to my two investigations. It allows me to eventually locate those people for personal contact (by building and adding current versus prior residences). And this list will always remind me, at a glance, who this person is, relative to the crime (or the victim, the defendant, a witness, etc.). I will literally use my People List to refresh my memory as I'm walking up to their front door to pay a visit.

O **First, Middle, Last Name** – [RELEVANCE. Knows WHAT about the crime, the witness, the victim, the Defendant.]

Dob: age, or YOB, or xx/xx/xx (if relevant … race/gender (ht, wt, eyes, hair)
SS#: xxx-xx-xxxx
State DL: xxxxxxxxxx
LKA: xxxx Bourbon St., New Orleans, LA
Current Res: xxxx Main St. Baton Rouge, LA
Relative: (Mom: name, DOB, residence)
Cellphone#: xxx xxx xxxx

Understand, a person on my People List may be described with pure *speculation* as to their relevance. Based on a source in the police investigation, this person *may* know the victim, this person *may* know the suspect, this person *may* have witnessed all or part of the crime. She is on my People List based on what she *may* know – because the police never contacted her.

Additional identifiers found in the police reports go exclusively on this People List, so I don't need to duplicate all witness identifiers on my witness summary notes in the Murder Memo.

I assemble all relevant identifiers, past, present, and future on that list. A People List I developed in 2012 will still be useful in 2027, when witnesses need to be located for an evidentiary hearing.

Any one of those "identifiers" listed above might be helpful in locating a witness during the initial investigation, or 20 years later. If I learn that a witness moves, or changes their cellphone number, or changes jobs, that new info goes on the People List.

When attempting to locate a witness using today's robust database searches (see Chapter 7), certain identifiers are more helpful than others. But several of these secondary identifiers allow me to be more creative, if necessary, when searching for a witness.

Note to Reader

In this chapter, I'm asking you to collect any and all possible identifiers and keep them in one place on your People List. In Chapter 7, I will explain how and why these secondary identifiers might help locate a witness in the future.

While going through police reports, having noticed a brief mention of a third-party witness of interest, I have found the best *identifier of last resort* to be that person's relationship (by blood or social) to some other *known* person. I may review several witness interviews, before I can – anecdotally – ID a person's relationship to someone else; another witness who is more fully identified in police reports. These could be ex-girlfriends, or neighbors, or casual acquaintances whom I understand from the police reports can positively identify this third-party witness. However, I still must contact that known witness directly, gain their cooperation, and ask them to identify this unidentified third-party witness.

I have been able to ID and locate critical witnesses who were mentioned only anecdotally in innocence cases and ignored by the police investigation. Sometimes, these unidentified witnesses proved critical to my investigation once I gained their identity.

Maybe an eyewitness ran into this unidentified person immediately after the crime. Maybe this eyewitness recalled seeing her at the crime scene. Maybe the known witness described being on the phone with this unidentified person, when the crime was discussed. If I deem this person the least bit relevant, I put that name, or some description, on my People List. "Frank ... the old man who lived in the house on the corner."

Once I've gone through all police reports and confirmed the police never identified or contacted this person, it becomes my job to do that.

If necessary, I start with the generic, FNU LNU (first name unknown last name unknown). Given the example above, if I can figure out the cross streets for that "old man," I can ID Frank's residence as "LKA: House on northeast corner of Mercer and Clara." I have learned to ID and find witnesses with scant information. It starts with noting every scrap of identifying information and constantly adding minutiae to my People List. For example:

> * **Frank LNU** – [WITNESS? Could have seen shooting from inside his house. Knew victim. Knew eyewitnesses? NOT contacted by police.]
>
> Dob: (age 50+ at time of crime)
> LKA: xxxx Mercer (ne corner @ Clara), STL

I understand that this "unknown person/witness" is only *unknown* to me.

If a person exists, then that person can be identified by some other person, or by some record, or by some other method. A witness can be "identified" several different ways, by using a partial name, physical description, residence, occupation, place of employment (POE), status in the neighborhood, status in the community, or by association with another person. Once I have established some type of definitive witness identity, it will be possible to locate and contact that person.

Here is an example of an actual witness I hoped to identify in Karl Fontenot's case:

> * **FNU LNU** – [WITNESS. May have been in store immediately after abduction. Possible Aunt to Jackie S[redacted] (Joe H[redacted]'s x-girlfriend). Sister of Miriam L[redacted]. Possible maiden name might be C[redacted]. School Teacher in Enis(?). Info, per Ralph B.]
>
> Dob: (age unknown)
> LKA: Enis, Ok?

And it is not always complicated. In Ricky Kidd's case, I was told, or maybe I read in a police report, that the person living at 70xx Monroe saw the shooting of George Bryant. I had no identifiers. I was simply looking for the person living at 70xx Monroe who saw someone shoot George Bryant. (I had already confirmed that no police reports indicate police contacted any witness from that residence.)

Ten years after that shooting, I knocked on the door at 70xx Monroe. I asked to speak to the person who saw the shooting of George Bryant, who lived just down the street. That person came to the door. She was willing to cooperate and identify herself. She went on to tell me a lot more about what she saw that day. Problem solved.

In a St. Louis Death Penalty habeas case, the client's alibi relied on three sisters he had spent time with but could not fully identify. While sitting in Terra Haute USP, the client was able to describe the house on a specific street between two cross-streets, which had only three houses on one side, due to the street's odd configuration in the Central West End.

A few weeks later, I drove down that street, saw the three brick townhouses just as he described. I found the one in the middle burned out and boarded up. I searched the address for that middle house through a database. In looking over a list of prior occupants, I found three females with the same last name, with similar ages – possibly "the three sisters." I located two of these three women, who were "the sisters," and interviewed them the following week.

In another case of Innocence – still unresolved – out of Kansas City, the complainant told police about – and later testified to – a phone call with an acquaintance, in which she acknowledged discussing the alleged molestation of her daughter, and several critical events leading up to her discovery of incriminating evidence.

Neither the police nor the prosecutors ever attempted to ID or contact this "corroborating witness." In both the police reports and the trial transcripts, the first and last name of this telephone witness were spelled phonetically, and – I eventually discovered – inaccurately.

The only ID I had to start with was that (inaccurate) phonetic spelling of her name. Since she was a co-worker of the complainant, I also knew her POE (a municipal government). Through public records, I was able to obtain an accurate spelling of the first and last name of this telephone witness and confirm her work history in the department where they both worked.

Through court records and public records database searches, I was able to locate this witness in Colorado. I later contacted and interviewed this telephone witness, whom no one had ever bothered to contact for corroboration. (The defendant's conviction and Life Sentence occurred 13 years earlier.) What this telephone witness told me contradicted almost all of the complainant's narrative, which had been offered unchallenged and uncorroborated to both the police and the jury.

If my understanding of what a person knows is speculative, I use "(?)" when I write that the witness is the victim's girlfriend(?), or the witness is a co-defendant's aunt(?), or the witness contacted the eyewitness immediately after the crime(?). If necessary (and available), I will source my speculation with a simple "per Josh" or "per police." These notes remain "speculation" until I interview this witness and discover – firsthand – their relationship and what they know, saw, or understood.

Often, the information I initially ascribe to a person is incomplete. But I start somewhere with something. As I read through the reports (in chronological order), any mention of "Robert Crawford" in a police report or in a witness interview, prompts me to search my People List for "Robert Crawford." I can quickly determine if this is *new* information, or does the info in this police report *confirm* what I had speculated about Robert Crawford? I'm able to quickly search a name on my growing People List, making it easy to keep up with scores of people, what they know, might know, or don't know.

As the police investigation progresses (and I continue my review, while building my Murder Memo), I may add or delete what this witness knows, or what this *witness may have seen(?)*, or what this *eyewitness saw, "per police."* His relevance might also change from "eyewitness" to "standing next to eyewitness." Or, from "seen at crime scene" to "eyewitness." I diligently keep these descriptions and comments *very brief*.

Example I

- **Gary Tyrone B[redacted] Jr** – [AT GRADUATION? RW's friend. RW sez Gary B can ID Anita and Gerald.]

After reviewing police reports describing her two interviews, followed by her viewing a photo-lineup at Police HQ, my People List description for Faye Y. evolved to this version, before I knocked on her door:

Example II

- **Faye Y[redacted]** – [EYEWITNESS. Sherica's aunt, Holding her son's hand. Shooter brushed past her immediately before he shot Taylor directly in front of her. Shown photospreads 6/30/09 of RW and A L[redacted] [redacted]. No ID of either. She standing w/Montez G[redacted] and Danny B at time of shooting. CONFIRM exit path taken by shooter. (SEE P 8344).]

  Dob: [redacted]/74 b/f (37)
  Lka: [address]. N'Ville, Tn
  Res: ('07–'11) [address], N'ville, Tn
  Dtr: Gladys Y[redacted] born 1991

This brief description was the sum total of all I knew or needed to know about this witness (Faye Y.) before I knocked on her door 20 months after the shooting and 3 months before trial began.

The formatting and information I have settled on and used the past 20 years in my People List began with my organizing and review in the Ricky Kidd Case. Here are the first two pages of that People List from my initial review of the police reports:

Mo v. R Kidd – PEOPLE

[RE: The 11:45 a.m., 2/6/96 robbery/murder of George Bryant and his friend Oscar Bridges, at Bryant's house, 7009 Monroe, by "three black men" who left the scene in a newer white Olds.]

* **Paul L A[redacted]** – [Friend of Ricky K, arrested 2/14/96 while helping Ricky and Monica move to a different apt.]

Dob: [redacted]53
Res: [redacted] Manchester #9, KCMO

* **Shalonda A [redacted]** – [Longtime R. [redacted] friend, who Richard went to see after G Bryant shooting on 2/6/96. She wit his call to police?]

Dob: [redacted]70
SS# 492-[redacted]
Res: (Mom) [redacted] Lydia Ave #A, KCMO 64131
Cell: 816.822-[redacted] (9/07)

* **Teresa B[redacted]** – [Saw Damon H[redacted] at 7000 Monroe immediately after the shooting.]

Dob; [redacted]59
Res: [redacted] Indiana, KCMO
POE: [redacted] School Cafeteria, [redacted] Askew, KCMO

* **D[redacted] B[redacted]** – [x-wife of Junior Bridges, adds nothing to the investigation.]

Res: [redacted] Cambridge, KCMO (767-[redacted])

* **Oscar "Junior" Bridges Jr**. – [Victim, killed 2/6/96 at 11:45 at Bryant's house]

Dob: [redacted]/57
SS# 515-[redacted]

* **Andre [redacted]** – [Apparent suspect, victim's nephew? Video line up done 2/9/96.]

Dob: [redacted]/75
KCPD# 201[redacted]
Res: ('96) [redacted] E 61st St., KCMO

* **Connie [redacted]** – [Victim's wife, mother (or stepmom?) of [redacted]
dob: [redacted]/[redacted]/65

'96 LKA: [redacted] Monroe, KCMO (822[redacted]) w/George B
'96 POE = [redacted] (911 Main St.)
Res: ('07) [redacted] E 85th Ter #106, Kcmo 64138 (816/356-[redacted]) w/Ke[redacted] C[redacted] and K[redacted].

* **K[redacted] [redacted]** – [Eyewitness, Victim's daughter, 4.9 yoa on 2/6/96.]

Dob: [redacted]91
Mom(?): [redacted] [redacted], [redacted] Jackson, KCMO

* **George A Bryant** – [Victim, killed 2/6/96 at 11:45 a.m.)

Dob: [redacted]/62 (63)
SS# 488-[redacted]
Res: [redacted] Monroe, KCMO (822-[redacted])

* **[redacted] Bryant** – [Bro of George, at Jean [redacted]'s 2/6? Killers from Ks?]

O **Henrietta [redacted]** – [Goodspeed's x-wife, mother & their Alibi Witness?]

Dob: [redacted]/56
SS# 491-[redacted]
Res: ('96) [redacted] Tracy, KCMO (523-[redacted])
Res: ('09–'14) [redacted] E 49th St., KCMO 64130 (921-[redacted] or 861-[redacted]r 361-[redacted] c/o Lacerine Bynum) **w/Gary Goodspeed JR???**

Alt Res: ('09[redacted] Jackson, KCMO (361-5753)
POE: ('96) [redacted] & Assocs., [redacted] Paseo, KCMO (892-[redacted])
Nicole's b.f. = Reggie W[redacted] Both at [redacted] Tracy on 2/6/96???

* **Marvin B**[redacted] – [Apparent suspect? Probably Victim's bro-in-law.]

Dob: [redacted]/77
KCPD# 206[redacted]

O **Lashanda R**[redacted] **B**[redacted] **Aka:** [redacted] **or R**[redacted] **R**[redacted] **m**) – [Henrietta's niece, [redacted] G's cousin.]

Dob: [redacted]/76
SS# 489-[redacted]
Res: (2/96) [redacted] Tracy (w/Henrietta and her small children)
Res: (2/96) at [redacted] Wabash, KCMO (523-[redacted]
Res: ('02) [redacted] Jackson, KCMO (w/Lacerine and Cecil [redacted] (ages 77 + 76)
Current Res: ('07–12/14) [redacted] Fremont Ave., KCMO (Hm: 816-966-[redacted])
Cell: (?) 816-606-[redacted]

Note to Reader

When creating a People List, you may be inclined to list everything a witness knows, next to their name on the People List. Don't. Everything they know about the crime belongs in the Murder Memo from their police interviews. Their name is searchable and easily referenced on that word.doc. The People List is not intended to provide a full bio of that person. The People List should tell you what the person's relationship is to one or more of the big six: the crime, the victim, the defendant, a co-defendant, a witness, or an alternate suspect.

Insignificant or Irrelevant Witnesses …

Every good (or bad) homicide investigation will probably contain interviews with witnesses who appear irrelevant, or witnesses I describe simply as *know-nothing* witnesses. (They *know nothing* relevant to this crime or this investigation.)

As I review police reports while building my Murder Memo, I generally keep track of these witnesses on my People List as "relevant(?)." On my Murder Memo, I'll note when and where police interviewed *Judy Simpson*. In my narrative, I'll say something like, "*Simpson* appears to know nothing about the crime, or the victim, or the witnesses."

I'll also place Judy Simpson on my People List with all known identifiers and the descriptive: "– [KNOWS NOTHING(?) about crime.]"

This is why I bother:

After finishing my review, I may still consider these *know-nothing* witnesses to be irrelevant. Or, through a late witness report I may see how a *know-nothing* witness might – *might* – know something relevant. After I begin my own investigation, one of my witness interviews might suggest that a *know-nothing* witness actually witnessed part of the crime. Maybe that witness just didn't want to cooperate with the police – and he literally pretended to *know nothing*. Or a *know-nothing* witness shows up later in the investigation claiming some peripheral knowledge of my client's guilt. This *know-nothing* witness might evolve into a very relevant witness.

Based on experience, if we could always take police reports at face value, defense investigations would be much easier, and we would see far fewer wrongful convictions. Normally, I believe I *can* take a police report at face value. I also understand it is impossible to know when I can't.

So, I generally end up with a subset of *know-nothing* witnesses whom I ID and leave on my People List. That way, these witnesses are ready for me to locate and contact, in case I need to confirm what they don't know, find out what they may know, or delve into what they later claim to know.

Putting my Murder Memo to Work ...

Note to Reader

If it is just not possible to create a paper file of your Discovery and arrange the police and lab reports in chronological order, you must arrange your Murder Memo summary notes of these police reports (i.e., witness interviews, lab reports, investigative events) in their proper sequence by date and time. Create your word.doc. and build your Murder Memo so that it tracks the actual investigation – all investigative events, everything the police and lab did. Cut and paste. Insert. Re-arrange. Whatever.

After completing my review of all police and lab reports and adding my last witness summary to my Murder Memo, I take a break. I put my Murder Memo aside for a day or two. Then, when I know I can start fresh, I carefully begin reading my Murder Memo, from the start, reviewing each report describing this investigation of this crime – as a new project. I will also edit and revise my Murder Memo, which forces me to go line-by-line, absorbing the entire investigation, just as it unfolded, in strict chronological order. (If I find summary notes from an interview or an investigative event out of order, I stop and cut-and-paste, so that I am reviewing all events in sequence.)

Reading this completed Murder Memo – fresh – allows me to step back and look at the homicide investigation as it progressed in real time. I believe that is the best way, maybe the only way, I recognize any problems which may have occurred in the initial investigation – problems which might otherwise go unnoticed.

My ability to succinctly summarize these police witness interviews and lab reports has improved over the years. I have learned to more readily recognize what facts are important and relevant and how to make my summary searchable. My focus continues to settle, objectively, on *what happened.*

My review of this Murder Memo tries to comprehend every relevant fact revealed by each witness, each lab report, and each investigative activity. I want to see if those facts logically led police to this defendant (my client). If necessary, after my Murder Memo review, I will check the trial transcript. Were those same facts used to convince the court of the defendant's guilt?

I am conducting a stress test on the state's theory.

If a witness offered a narrative or a set of factual claims that don't fit the state theory, or those claims don't match the crime scene, I *flag* that witness and his claims. A witness interview may appear incomplete to me or suggest a "gap" exists in what she claims to have seen and what she may have actually seen. I flag that witness and her claims for later contact. I flag all potential witnesses who were never contacted by police. I do my best to inventory and confirm that all known lab reports were included in Discovery – as summarized in my Murder Memo.

My understanding of what is important and relevant must remain objective.

At some point during the police investigation, the defendant was arrested and a "Probable Cause Affidavit" was used to apply for that arrest warrant. Does that probable cause match up with the facts developed in this investigation? Were any facts left out? Did police do any investigation following this arrest, to "build their case"? Was any objective fact-finding investigation conducted after the defendant's arrest? Looking objectively, were any obvious investigative steps skipped by police?

As I reach the end of my Murder Memo review, I should have a clearer understanding of what facts are *important* and *relevant*. As I gain a clearer picture of *what happened*, I may become more aware of contradicting witness interviews, or "facts" seemingly based on speculation. I may identify *investigative conclusions* which – objectively – don't make sense to me.

As I come across any person who needs to be flagged, or any conclusion which I don't see as "fact-driven," anything that stands out to me – objectively – I make a written note. I may create a list. I may start a memo-to-self. I leave nothing solely to memory. I leave nothing to chance. These are complex cases with dozens of moving parts. Maybe I'm not that smart. Maybe I'm a genius. It doesn't matter. Anything that stands out to me, anything I think to flag mentally, I create a written record – or a list.

I am investigating both the crime itself *and* the police investigation. The Homicide Investigators who wrote these initial reports were in their first few hours and days of their investigation. They were still working with a blank canvas. They should have been open-minded and objectively gathering all information to help them determine *what happened*. They may have made a mistake. Or they may have prematurely settled on a bias.

If the police did not investigate this case in that open-minded, objective manner – it is still my role to investigate this crime objectively – through the facts offered in those police reports, summarized chronologically in my Murder Memo.

By keeping an open mind, I am more likely to recognize if, when, and where this initial investigation stopped being objective, and became agenda driven. Did the police narrow their focus and begin building their case – maybe, too soon?

My Lists: Queries, Needs, and To Dos ...

As I read my completed Murder Memo for the first time, questions always occur to me about the Homicide Investigation, questions about a witness, questions about reported facts or alleged evidence – questions about this case which I'm hoping the police reports may later clear up. But if 400 pages later – by the end of my Murder Memo – the police reports have not clarified my concern, will I remember the question?

Or maybe, days earlier, while reading and summarizing police witness interviews for my Murder Memo, a specific question occurs to me, and I don't want to forget it.

I create another word.doc and add these questions to a growing list – in real time. The more complex the case, the more beneficial I've found these lists of searchable *Queries* ... or *Needs* ...or *To Dos*. While reviewing the police reports, or while reviewing my completed Murder Memo, a random *observation*, or a random question I had not previously considered, may pop into my consciousness. With all of these moving parts, I literally need to write out that observation or that query as it occurs. Because, by the time I reach the bottom of that page of my Murder Memo, I may have two more questions I now need to remember. If these issues are later answered by the police investigation, great. It always helps to eliminate an issue before my investigation begins.

But if that question or observation remains unanswered by the police reports, that random thought, or query, or observation, might become an issue in my own investigation (i.e., did witness Rachel know the defendant before the crime? Did police ask Rachel if she personally knew the person they now suspect as the assailant?).

My *observation* or my *query* may be a question for the attorney or anyone familiar with the case (i.e., does our client know Rachel, the witness? Did our client and Rachel grow up together, or go to the same high school?).

When I carefully review my Murder Memo for the first time (if my Murder Memo is well constructed and in chronological order), the *Questions* and *Needs* and *To Dos* which occur to me – once tabulated – will create a comprehensive investigative strategy. Without trying, my fresh review of my Murder Memo develops questions which – to me – are both obvious and intuitive and need to be answered – by somebody.

What follows is part of my initial *To Do List* in Ricky Kidd's case after my review of the police and lab reports. I knew that no one else had looked at Ricky's case following his conviction ten years earlier. I had no lawyer or defense team to query. These were the *Questions*, *Queries*, and *To Dos* that appeared obvious to me, in my investigation of the crime and my investigation of the investigation. These represented my attempts to determine *what happened*:

Kidd To Dos

[updated 6/22/07]

- Locate and contact Betty Jean C[redacted] re: what she saw and heard 2/6/96. Did she call 9-1-1? Does she know who did? What does she know about Richard [redacted] POV?
- At 70[redacted] Monroe, contact Vera [redacted] re: 2/6/96 and what George W[redacted] saw. Determine status of George W[redacted]. Any other witnesses to shooting?

- Locate and contact Letha [redacted], x-wife of Richard [redacted] re: her knowledge of the 2/6/96 incident and Richard's POV. (They were married 11/97–7/99.)
- Obtain missing document (records check) conducted 2/6/96 at 1:30 p.m. by Sheriff's Deputy relative to Kidd's gun permit application.
- Obtain missing reports from homicide and/or TIPS pertaining to all missing anonymous calls and tips, specifically including the anonymous calls made on 2/8/96 and 2/10/96, described in police reports.
- Locate and contact Eugene [redacted], friend of Marcus [redacted], with whom Marcus stayed the first week of Feb 1996, before getting a room at the Adam's Mark. Eugene reportedly gave Marcus a ride to the airport 2/11/96.
- Obtain suspect-photospreads used by police throughout this homicide investigation.
- Locate and contact Phyllis [redacted] re: 2/6/96, Richard [redacted] POV, what Earl [redacted] saw, anonymous calls to PD?
- Locate and re-contact Maurice [redacted], (c/o his mom) friend of Earl [redacted], visiting Earl 2/6/96, saw shooting, but did not see Richard [redacted].
- Locate and contact Earl [redacted] re: his POV on 2/6/96, and his knowledge of Richard [redacted] and what Richard saw that day
- Locate and contact Shannon [redacted] re: the 2/6/96 shooting he witnessed, and Richard's POV.
- Locate and contact Sandi [redacted], re: what her son Shannon told her about the shooting.
- Locate and contact Damon [redacted], who was working in driveway with Earl [redacted] on 2/6/96. What did he see?
- Contact Vivian and Eugene [redacted] at 70[redacted] Monroe re: their knowledge of 2/6/96. Only Cory [redacted] contacted by PD. Cory said she was at work. Determine their knowledge of Richard [redacted] POV and Shannon [redacted] POV.
- Contact Luther [redacted] re: his knowledge of 2/6/96 shooting, Shannon [redacted] POV, Richard [redacted] POV. Who was the b/f who called 9-1-1 from that residence?

More About My Lists....

If the attorney has had this case a long time, and I'm coming in late, I might create a list of questions for the attorney, based on my completed Murder Memo. It's a necessary conversation to make sure the attorney has seen *this* or thought about *that*. This query list helps me catch up on the thought process and any existing investigative strategy. If the lawyer had already explored an investigative area I flagged, or a previous defense investigator had already contacted that witness, then we can move on. If I see something no one else had noticed, that's a good time to raise the issue. Any good defense lawyer should welcome the observations from a fresh set of experienced eyes.

This scenario should also occur with any wrongful conviction class, or any Innocence Project volunteer, asked to review a case previously reviewed by others.

Routinely, I am always looking for witness observations which don't make sense, or don't match the crime scene. I instinctively look for witnesses whom I suspect may know more than the police report indicates – along with the witnesses I find who may not have been interviewed at all.

However, when I'm asked to review a case which has already been reviewed by others, I develop different sets of observations and questions. I expect (or hope) anyone who has plowed this ground before me will know what exists, what's been done, what's been queried. Sometimes I'm right.

A witness interview may suggest the need for phone records to verify a story. Were his phone records collected? Are the phone records somewhere in Discovery? Did the police contact the cousin, *Jolene LNU* to verify a statement made by another witness? I make a note about whatever and whoever attracts my attention. Sometimes *Jolene LNU* will simply go on my People List. Sometimes I'll add the query to be shared with the existing defense team:

- Did police ever interview Jolene LNU (victim's cousin)?

I may develop questions about physical evidence – whether an item was tested or even collected. This scenario may occur in an older habeas case, before evidence collection and testing became more common. (In some jurisdictions, that might still be a problem.)

Another reason to make such a list of observations in older habeas cases is the possibility of missing lab reports which were later obtained or discovered in the legal file by the current team. The same goes for apparent missing evidence inventories or missing investigative reports in general.

Not surprisingly, in wrongful conviction cases, *file organization* may have been a problem for the original trial team. Missing, lost, and misplaced reports become part of the challenge of identifying and resolving a wrongful conviction. The same issues may be relevant in recognizing constitutional issues involving IAC claims and Brady Material.

The first challenge is locating these records. Identifying whether these records were in original Discovery and were simply misplaced or mishandled by the original team. Or were these records obtained by a later habeas team? These issues create a subset of the "investigation of the investigation."

In my Ricky Kidd investigation, I knew I was starting from scratch when I reviewed the police and lab reports and created my Murder Memo. At that point, I created, mostly, a To Do List, with some queries for Ricky.

In other cases, which had passed through many hands before I was asked to participate, I was interested in what had already been *observed*, what had already been done, or attempted. I wanted to know if I and the current defense team were looking at the same set of issues pertaining to this case of possible innocence.

All of that explains why my written lists and notes, which grow out of my Murder Memo review, may consist of *Observations* or *Queries* or *Needs* or *To Dos*.

What *Observations*, *Queries*, or *Needs* remain unresolved (after my complete review of existing Discovery)? At that point, I share my observations and queries with the current defense team. What they are not able to resolve (assuming they are interested) may go on my To Do List. Those unresolved observations or queries must now be answered by witnesses, which may include my client, the convicted defendant.

Recently, a law firm asked me to help review and investigate a case of possible innocence, resulting from a gruesome 1996 homicide in a major Midwest city. Supervised college students had conducted an extensive investigation several years earlier.

The file of Discovery material I was asked to review consisted of roughly 3,000 scanned pages, divided into dozens of PDF files. These PDFs were mostly random duplications of roughly 400–500 pages of actual police and lab reports.

I created my Murder Memo, which attempted to recreate the investigation in chronological order. Out of that Murder Memo, I developed several Observations and Queries, which mainly focused on what I hoped the current lawyers knew and what the previous student investigators had also observed or done or attempted to do.

This is my typical approach to any case which has passed through several sets of eyes and hands. These are my actual queries. They prompted important discussions which contributed to the direction of our investigation. For several reasons, I fictionalized the names and identities:

Tatum OBSERVATIONS/NEEDS/QUERIES –

1. After reviewing John Tatum's notes – does Russell confirm he was shown a lineup including Craig Roberts?
2. Do we have the lineup photos in which a suspect had a beard, described by C. Sinovic and Ralph B. on 11/20?

3 We NEED a copy of the composite and whatever description was fed to the media on 10/24/96? (Composite apparently based solely on witness Raul C.)
4 Do we have the lineups and lineup photos used for Craig Roberts, Russell T., Denny T.?
5 Did Denny T. or Russell T. wear glasses?
6 Was Craig Robert's photo provided to the media upon his arrest?
7 NEED to assemble all reports related to Russell T.'s "confessions" on 11/14/96 and try to arrange them in chronological sequence. What can be corroborated?
8 Were exact clothes described by Russell on 11/14 ever found in their home?
9 DO any audio recordings of any police interviews exist?
10 Need South Bend IN PD Rpt 96-1-649 RE; stolen LP 8573988 (reported on 10/23?)
11 Were any, or all aspects of Russell's' description of man on Manchester, offered in media reports?
12 I never found a lab analysis of Tatum shoes/clothes indicating no blood, no sand grains, etc. Was analysis done?
13 Doubtful, but was Russell's description of blue jacket and skull cap worn, and actual blue jacket found at home – ever shown to witness Cathy Sinovic who clearly saw actor wearing brown jacket?
14 I found no lab reports after the **2/13/97 lab report** indicating that human blood was detected with multiple nail clippings and also found on Roberts' blue sweater.
15 I don't recall seeing the FBI Inventory Log, from their 11/16/96 search warrant at the Tatum House.
16 Any effort made to run unknown latent prints obtained in victim's car through AFIS?
17 I did not see any police report indicating the three eyewitnesses ever viewed a LIVE Lineup including Russell.

My FINAL Word on Lists ...

When I review a case, it doesn't matter if I have an idea, see a problem, or have identified something I *need* to know. I begin a list. There is no reason to get caught up in semantics. My lists are as varied as my cases. Each case calls for its own set of lists.

I create these lists as I *feel* they are needed. I may create a list of *Observations and Queries*, which include some *To Dos*. I may create a To Do List, which includes a note to ask the lawyer about a defense witness who refused to cooperate – technically a "Query," or maybe an "Observation." My To Do List might include a *NEED* to find out if any analysis was conducted on a piece of physical evidence.

One case might call for two lists. On another case, I might start a list of "Observations" plus a long list of "Questions" about what I think needs to be done, before I determine what may have already been done.

My lists are simply tools to help me organize the clutter.

By organizing the clutter, I feel I'm better able to identify the Homicide Investigation's holes – theories not objectively explored, or conclusions apparently based on speculation or assumption.

Not long ago, I reviewed my one hundredth complex murder case. I can now say with confidence, each homicide case is unique. And my review and investigation of each case seems to take on a life of its own.

I normally build my To Do List as I review my completed Murder Memo. But I am free to create and construct whatever work product I deem necessary to organize this complex case and its moving parts.

In my mind, this is my secret sauce. As I review my completed Murder Memo (with its summarized witness interviews, lab reports, and all investigative findings in chronological order), I'm generally able to determine whether this was a fact-driven or an agenda-driven investigation. This is when I recognize any big or small inconsistencies (if any exist).

When I review all the "investigative facts" in sequence in my Murder Memo, I am almost always able to determine whether innocence is a possibility. At this point, I begin to see the framework of a potential wrongful conviction. I begin to see what still needs to be known, and what needs verification. All this before speaking to one witness.

Chapter 6

Time to Get Out: My First Client Visit

I view my first meeting with the client to be my first witness interview.

Ideally, I have reviewed the police reports and completed my Murder Memo before that meeting. (If it turns out, I meet with the client before I've seen any police reports, everything here still applies, just without the context of the entire criminal investigation.)

There may be a benefit to viewing the crime scene *before* meeting with any witnesses – including the client – but I don't see that as a hard rule.

Interviewing the client as the first witness is ideal, but not always practical. Logistics and circumstance rule the sequence.

If I live in the same city as the *crime scene*, and my client is incarcerated out of town, then I will visit the crime scene first. If convenient, I might visit the crime scene as soon as possible – even while reviewing police reports. Visiting the crime scene, no matter when, and no matter how many years after the crime, is useful.

Visiting the crime scene first might help me ask better questions of the defendant. Visiting the client first might create a more productive crime scene visit. Either way, I can always revisit the client, or the crime scene, or both, to follow up on new insight.

I will discuss the client visit now, and the *crime scene* visit in the next chapter.

Note to Reader

My experience includes working on both pre-trial and habeas Murder I cases. This book is primarily concerned with evaluating wrongful convictions as a habeas case. However, in this chapter, I offer observations about the factfinder's relationship with the client/defendant in both pre-trial and habeas circumstances. There could be slight and subtle differences in approach.

DOI: 10.4324/9781003543299-6

The First Client Visit: My Mindset …

Some may want to first create a checklist of things to remember, things to do, and things to ask a habeas client, especially during that first visit. I think it's better to first develop the right mindset.

I want to think of this new client as a brother, or a sister, maybe like a daughter, or a son. (Although most of my clients have been men or teenage boys, I have helped defend five women in Murder I cases. I helped one woman gain an acquittal at trial and helped three other women gain exonerations or release from their Life Sentences. The fifth woman was found guilty in Federal Court and is currently serving a Life Sentence.)

Pre-trial: if this defendant was my brother, I'd want to know what happened. I would give him time to explain what happened, and time for him to explain his role, if any, in the crime. If he was involved, I would try to understand. Compassion may come later. I'd want him to get the best legal counsel his lawyer could provide – given the facts of the case. That's what I would do for my brother or my sister, my daughter, or my son.

The tricky balance here – as it is with family – is showing compassion without acting naïve or gullible. It's been my experience that the best legal assistance results from knowing what actually happened, not just blindly believing the defendant's narrative. I have never taken my client's version on faith and then set out to "prove his case."

As a factfinder, in both habeas cases and pre-trial, I don't consider it my job to *prove* my client's innocence. I do consider it my job to obtain my client's version of events and then attempt to verify the accuracy of her story. It's my job to gain her entire narrative, her description of all relevant events.

Initially, at that first meeting, I tell my client that I will give him the benefit of the doubt, especially where his narrative conflicts with his criminal charges. I assume he is giving me a truthful version of events, until overwhelming facts suggest otherwise.

In all cases, I must first gain the client's trust. Circumstances might require multiple visits before I can gain this trust. But I have found, with the right mindset – being sincere and showing genuine respect – I can gain a working level of trust with most clients during that first visit.

It helps that I can look a client in the eye and tell him that I know, first-hand, police and prosecutors are not always truthful. I have reviewed and verified that police reports (of witness interviews), in multiple cases, were fabricated. I am aware of police techniques which include lying to witnesses and suspects about non-existent evidence. As a journalist, I had seen homicide detectives testify falsely about events of which I had first-hand knowledge.

I also have personal experience with witnesses who have lied – some who lied maliciously, some for self-interest, some maybe after subtle coercion. I'm aware that witnesses can simply be mistaken. I let the client know that I know it can happen.

I can tell the client, with conviction, that I will not assume the accuracy of the state's criminal allegations, or the accuracy of the incriminating witness statements, until I have verified them to my satisfaction.

I want to convince the client: he is starting out fresh with me. I literally presume his innocence, until verified facts (or his own admission) indicate his guilt. He does not have a steep hill to climb – to convince me that the state might have it wrong.

Once he sees that I have no bias or preconceived notion of his guilt, he may start to relax.

Note to Reader

A new factfinder will start out with no track record or experiences to share with a convicted felon claiming innocence. And yet, you still have a lot to offer. You have your life experiences. You have your education. You have your sincere willingness to listen carefully and investigate his case and his claims thoroughly and objectively. You may have an organization, or a school, or a supervisor/lawyer backing your efforts. Even if you just have you, that's a lot to someone locked up, wrongfully convicted, asking for help.

Pre-trial: that same attitude of presumed innocence should be a given. But I have seen that it is not.

A habeas defendant, claiming innocence, will *want* to trust whoever offers to help. Gaining trust with pre-trial defendants may depend on their experience with broken promises from people in the criminal justice system – police, prosecutors, even defense lawyers.

A pre-trial defendant's ability to trust may depend on how much of his criminal history resulted from guilty pleas to false charges for a lighter sentence, or probation. This scenario happens when a young defendant pleads guilty to a misdemeanor, reduced from a felony, for a crime he did not commit. That defendant may have even been told, "This is a good deal."

Sadly, if my client, (pre-trial or habeas) has that history, he may already believe that "lying" and "presumption of guilt" are just part of the relationship between defendant and defense counsel – period.

Understand, I'm just describing the hurdles which may exist, but not be clearly visible, between a defense team and a new client.

I'm also aware that the trust must flow both ways. I cannot lie to a client. I don't feel I have that option. With my mindset, I refuse to lie to my client. I may dodge a question and defer to the attorney. I may offer diplomatic answers. I may say, "I don't know." I will say, "Maybe." But I can never lie to a defendant and then expect him to trust me.

Even for *strategic* reasons, I have never lied to a client.

Besides, I'm not a good liar. Maybe that character trait makes me more believable and trustworthy. I consider my trust and my integrity to be important tools in my toolbox.

Losing that trust, in this kind of a short-term relationship, it's nearly impossible to ever regain.

Consider the day-to-day existence of a convicted felon (wrongful or not): I have visited most of my clients in jail or prison, multiple times. I am intimately aware that my client has lost access to everything I might take for granted. My client has lost all control over his daily activities. He can be shackled against his will. Strangers have the power, at any time, to strip him of his privacy, his dignity, his humanity, and his ability to freely communicate.

There have been times when my client's mere survival in jail or prison was a daily concern – of his. He may be scared. He may show me strength and stoicism. He may smile and feign casual laughter. He may even enjoy the brief sense of security my legal visit brings. For him, just being with me in that cramped and stuffy meeting room may provide him with a welcome break from the daily tension.

Sadly, on a few rare occasions, I have worked with clients who had previously been deceived and played by members of their own defense team. Cruel beyond words – I think.

The absolute worst example of this abuse of trust comes to mind:

I'm aware of a fact investigator who once met with our client on the fifth floor of Davidson County Jail in downtown Nashville. The client was facing the Death Penalty in a federal capital murder case. This jail is a horrid place for legal visits. The small, glass enclosed rooms reserved for legal visits have a small, anchored steel table attached to one wall and three permanent, hard metal "stools" on each open side of this table. Sometimes, if needed, a fourth plastic chair will be brought in, fitting just inside the thick, steel mesh door. It is a glass-enclosed closet, maybe 7′ × 7′. Everyone in the room is at arm's length.

This fact investigator was making a second visit to the client and, for whatever reason that day, decided to verbally challenge and ridicule the client. There was no fact gathering. There was simply a string of insults, a disgruntled rant. This fact investigator accused this client of committing far more crimes than were listed in the indictment. The entire rant had no obvious design unless it was to intimidate the client into submitting to a plea. The investigator told the client he did not deserve the free room and board and the free defense counsel being provided by the government.

It was mere coincidence that I visited with the client the very next day to discuss his mitigation issues. It was my fourth visit. The client had gone from friendly and trusting to stone cold, untrusting of his entire defense team, me included. The client's demeanor had changed from relaxed and engaged during three previous meetings, to beaten, sullen, quiet, and unwilling to even make eye contact.

I got this client to describe in some detail what had occurred the day before. I could not repair the damage that day. That trust had been destroyed. Outside the jail, I called the lead attorney to describe the damage. The fact investigator was a friend of that attorney. A full 30 days later, the attorney was able to gain confirmation from the fact investigator, that yes, he had "leaned on the client" that day. Apparently, the fact investigator confirmed most of the things the client had described to me in detail. To me, it was a jaw-dropping abuse of trust and power.

The fact investigator and the defense lawyer continued to work together in criminal defense. That was the worst case of defense team abuse of a client I have witnessed, albeit an exception to the norm.

Assuming a client is guilty, or *assuming* that a client is untrustworthy prior to any investigation, seems to me to be unprofessional, at best. I've never gone there or done that.

Likewise, I consider it unprofessional to ignore bad facts. This is a difficult job.

First Client Visit: Gaining Trust ...

I find gaining a client's trust to be a fairly simple exercise. True, some clients may require more time and effort than others.

I initially offer my background to the client. The legal system, or fate, has put his future in my hands (along with the rest of the defense team).

Pre-trial or habeas: A new client wants to know who I am. He may be too polite (or intimidated) to ask direct questions. He may not know exactly what he should be asking his investigator or asking the defense team now working on saving his life or gaining his freedom.

That's why I think it is my job to offer my client the background he *should* be requesting but may not know to ask.

Note to Reader

As mentioned earlier, if you lack experience in this field, even if you are just starting out, you still have a lot to share and a lot to offer. Your life experiences, your desire to help, whatever education you have or hope to have, these are all valuable to a wrongfully convicted inmate. You will quickly find your sincerity and willingness to investigate his or her claims of innocence is what matters most.

In a pre-trial visit, or a habeas case where lawyers are already involved, the client will need to be advised on how the attorney/investigator/client process works. Normally – and preferably – the lead attorney has already explained the attorney/client protections and the "team" concept to a new client. Sometimes, my first visit with the client is made *with* the lead attorney. Otherwise, my visit will almost always follow the attorney's visit or visits.

Note to Reader

If you are looking into a wrongful conviction case, without attorney involvement, such a prison visit on Visitor's Day can still be productive. I would consider "privacy" to be the primary concern – assuming you are able to visit in a non-monitored, "public" environment.

Some clients I have worked with thought they needed to be likeable, and easy going, so that I would do my job. Many of my clients were inexperienced in dealing with a competent defense team. The little experience some clients had with defense attorneys may have been a hurried plea deal – maybe to a crime they did not commit.

At times, I've tried to imagine how I would feel, standing in leg-irons, with arms handcuffed and chained to my waist, aware that strangers think I should spend the rest of my life in prison for something – maybe I did – maybe I didn't do. If that were me, would I know what questions to ask my defense team?

In a habeas case, this new client has already served five, ten, maybe 20 years in prison. In my 30+ years working with convicted felons, many guilty, some wrongfully convicted, I still cannot imagine their thought process.

Wrongfully convicted inmates have told me from prison that *hope* is their oxygen.

After offering my background, I explain – in an effort to keep it simple – that my main job is to find out *what happened*. That job includes finding whatever facts exist which may prove the client's innocence (i.e., good facts). Once I make that claim, I feel obligated to follow through on that promise. At that point, it becomes personal. I engage.

In the next breath, I tell the client that if evidence of his guilt exists (i.e., bad facts), I will likely find that too. Again (I repeat), I intend to find out *what happened*. It is the lawyer's job to figure out what to do with those facts, be they *good facts* or *bad facts*.

Pre-trial: I may explain that if he is innocent, it will still take an aggressive defense to prove innocence or at least prove the state's case against him is false. (This is not constitutional law. This is my opinion of the reality I have seen.)

In a habeas case, depending on the stage of appeal, I might attempt to describe what I, or the lawyer, must find to get the client back into court (maybe for a new trial, maybe a re-sentencing – either can lead to legal relief). As often, I won't know exactly what we must find. If I don't know, I'll say so. Often, in cases I have worked, the client is on her final appeal, or beyond her final appeal. At that point it has always appeared to me that constitutional issues and proof of actual innocence rested hand-in-hand. In most of my innocence cases, I understood my goal, in laymen's terms, was to find evidence of "absolute innocence" – whatever that meant.

In habeas cases, finding out *what happened* might not be the only path to habeas relief. I always defer to the attorney for clarity on specific fact-gathering goals. When I can, I describe our goals to the client, and I spell out exactly what I am trying to accomplish. Although I continue to believe finding out *what happened* will always help the lawyer know what options exist.

Throughout the investigative process, I try to maintain my client's trust. It may help if he believes I'm *capable* of finding out *what happened*. Likewise, he needs to believe in my *willingness* to listen and believe him.

I also advise him that any false claims he may make will eventually be recognized by me as false. When I have that conversation, I make it abundantly clear that it is to his advantage to be truthful with me in even the slightest detail.

Why a Defendant May Not Be Quick to Trust ...

Almost all of my habeas clients want to trust me, simply because I have offered to help. Most of my pre-trial clients want to trust me, because their options are also limited.

Unfortunately, I must always consider my client may have a history unknown to me. My client may have been truthful with his defense team in the past and was ignored, or just not believed. If I sense any hint of that, I ask directly about his past experiences.

Sometimes, defense attorneys allow a "presumption of guilt" into their mindset. I've never done their job, so I cannot know how or why that happens. Nor will I try to quantify how widespread that mindset is in the system. I have seen it, and I've seen it get in the way of a defendant gaining optimum representation. And I have seen a defense attorney's "presumption of guilt" contribute to more than one wrongful conviction.

On the flip side (pre-trial), I have worked on several defense teams where our objective fact-finding produced additional evidence, "beyond any doubt" of our client's guilt. That also resulted from gaining the client's trust. The result in each case was a fair trial, with the defense gaining the best possible outcome for our client (and the community).

When the defense attorney, or her investigator, carries a "presumption of guilt" into the case, there cannot be a positive outcome – not for the client. So, when habeas time rolls around, and my new client still recalls how his trial lawyer's presumption of guilt derailed his defense, how trusting will that client be? I will need to address that.

First Client Visit: Obtaining the Narrative ...

The client interview will likely be my easiest witness interview of the entire case (whether pre-trial or habeas).

> **Note to Reader**
>
> For the sake of this example, let's assume this interview is with a habeas client, claiming innocence. You have thoroughly reviewed the investigation which led to his conviction and reviewed your Murder Memo. You know the police investigation, beginning to end. You have introduced yourself and believe you have gained his trust – up to this point.

My client, as a witness, should be highly motivated. This is one witness who can be re-visited as often as necessary. Even when asking the tough questions, this witness (if innocent) will want to clarify any confusion and identify all sources. There should be very little "can't remember."

However, attitude and personality and emotion can sometimes impact this first client interview. Sometimes, getting to the truth can be slow going. That can happen in any witness interview. With my client, I know I have a built-in opportunity – over time – to develop trust.

I expect my first client contact to go in one of a few different directions. Yes, I've learned to expect the unexpected, but generally my client will offer one of three scenarios: (1) not there (at the crime); (2) there (at the crime) but not involved; (3) there, but minimally and inadvertently involved.

Since this is a habeas case being reviewed as possibly a wrongful conviction, I must ignore what I might hope to hear or expect to hear. I force myself to listen objectively to his description of *what happened.*

Maybe I'm following up on someone else's belief that this is a wrongful conviction. I may be following up on someone else's wishful thinking. I might be listening to an innocent, yet inarticulate, man. By listening closely to *what happened* – compared with what I know from the investigation – I may begin questioning whether, or not, this really is a wrongful conviction. Or I may immediately start believing this person may be innocent.

One narrative I have encountered multiple times is the mistaken identity. If this was a case of mistaken identity connecting this defendant to the crime, I must carefully track the defendant's version of *what happened.* I want to track my client's moves for several days before, and several days after, the crime. I gather detail and verifiable information on the day and the hour of the crime. Given a claim of mistaken ID, I realize that knowing everything that happened at the crime scene will be crucial in knowing what facts and actions are relevant to my client's alibi and his veracity.

I expect my client to be a knowledgeable source. I track every possible connection this defendant might have to the crime, the crime scene, the victim, and any witness who has tied him to this crime. I want to Identify any potential connections between this "innocent" client and the witness, or the confidential informant, or whatever anonymous tip (i.e., Crime Stoppers, TIPS Hotline, etc.) led to his arrest and conviction.

If the police reports (Murder Memo) don't show an obvious connection between this client and the crime (i.e., no physical evidence), then one of my To Dos may be to prove such a connection *does not* exist. Such a scenario may indicate a *Mistaken ID*, or a *Malicious ID*, or a fabricated anonymous tip.

Another possibility is that the defendant offers a narrative showing knowledge of the crime, but minimal or no involvement in the actual crime. Maybe she was at the scene, or knew the victim, or maybe she claims to know exactly what happened. Instead of building an alibi, I may need to document her eyewitness account of the actual crime. She might have given a similar version of events to the police (or, lied to the police about her whereabouts). This information may or may not have found its way into a police report. Or the police did not believe this defendant after finding another witness to be more believable.

Once the police develop their theory (i.e., bias), they rarely believe the suspect's narrative, even if she claims to have been there, seen the crime, and can identify the actor. By then, it's too late.

If my client claims to have witnessed the crime, I still won't get too excited about her potential innocence. My job remains the same. I must gain verifiable facts, then go out and confirm them. Maybe this client is fabricating a narrative to bolster his innocence claim. Maybe the police are fabricating a scenario with a "cooperating witness" or a "confidential source." Maybe some witnesses gave the police a false narrative (which doesn't fit the crime scene, but no one has noticed). In the worst-case scenario, all three (client, police, and witness) are fabricating parts of their narrative. It's my job to discern the truth using facts. This is where a strong grasp of the crime scene is critical to discerning the truth.

My client may provide facts – verified by the crime scene reports – which the police overlooked or ignored. Once I start making those comparisons verifying her narrative, I might start getting excited.

If my client knew the victim, or the alternate suspect, or the state's witnesses who named him as the assailant, then he may know of other witnesses not mentioned in police reports. I must be resourceful. I must think of every possibility which may produce a third-party source. I ask this defendant specifically about his knowledge of the crime, the crime scene, and the witnesses. He may be able to fully identify witnesses partially mentioned in the police reports. He may be able to help locate some witnesses or identify relatives or friends of peripheral witnesses. In this case, my client, as a source, can clear up lots of unknowns and items on my Queries List. All, of course, still to be verified.

I have learned not to assume my client will freely volunteer everything he knows. In several cases, I found out much, much later in my investigation that the client knew something significant about the crime, the crime scene, or a witness.

"Why didn't you tell me this earlier?"

"You didn't ask."

A cautionary note pertaining to being resourceful and looking for witnesses: the defense team and the defendant must always assume all non-legal calls from jail or prison (by the client) are monitored and recorded – and anything said can and will be used against the defendant.

I always avoid inadvertently encouraging my client to reach out to witnesses, for any reason. In most cases I openly discourage him from contacting witnesses or discussing their case with anyone by phone. That said, I will use my client as a source to identify or gather whatever information they personally retain, without reaching out to anyone in "the free world."

I know of prison telephone conversations between the defendant and his acquaintances, where a *witness* was discussed casually. That recorded conversation was used against the defendant. In that case, the government claimed he was seeking to *harm* that witness.

I want my client to avoid even the appearance of any contact or any collusion or any stated interest with a crime scene witness or alibi witness.

Another scenario I have encountered in my first client interview speaks to the quality of his original defense counsel. I may begin interviewing this habeas client 20 years after the crime, and find I am discovering *new*, relevant, and verifiable information – all related to his innocence.

I have found useful facts easily gained from a new client that apparently were ignored by the original defense team, overlooked, or, worse, maybe the original defense team never asked. If they did ask, they didn't listen.

Either way, I find it frightening to discover new, valuable, and significant information from the client – now a wrongfully convicted felon – 20 years after the fact.

First Client Visit: Assessing the Defendant's Veracity ...?

In most of my habeas cases in which I developed a successful innocence claim, the client gave me a truthful narrative, which I was able to follow and eventually verify.

I have also experienced innocent habeas clients who were initially untruthful about their actions relevant to the crime. When assessing an innocence claim, it may be helpful to know why a habeas client may not be fully truthful.

An innocent client who was present, or somehow connected to the crime, or the victim, or the true assailants, might minimize his proximity, or his connections – no matter how innocent – to the point of lying. One jury already convicted him, based on at least some of those "facts." He wants to minimize his exposure to any more suspicion of guilt.

Making this work more difficult, a *guilty* habeas client (claiming innocence) may offer an elaborate story in which he was present but had minimal or no connection with the crime. He might lie about his movements, hoping to create – in my mind – reasonable doubt. He might fabricate an alibi. He may think he can fool his defense team – if he can just convince me, his fact investigator. He still believes he can eventually fool the courts.

Of course, a fact investigator, regardless of experience, will never know which one it might be. Not initially. And certainly not during that first visit.

Which is why I listen intently for verifiable facts. In my notes, I flag any activity or contact between this defendant and any other person, or animate object or verifiable event (i.e., a birthday, a sports event, a cellphone call, school, work, a TV show).

If my client starts rambling about the crime scene (or anything else relevant to the crime) I let her talk. I take good notes. I already have or I will have photos of the crime scene, if that becomes relevant. I have already visited, or I will soon visit, the crime scene. Through police reports and witnesses, my understanding of the crime scene will continue to expand and improve. If not during that first visit, I will soon be able to measure her credibility, her honesty, and her recall, by comparing her version of events with what is known – hard facts.

I *never* correct or challenge my client – as a witness.

If my habeas client says something I believe is inaccurate, or worse, untruthful, I let him keep talking.

If he is guilty, I let him minimize his role, or explain his actions, or justify the crime, or even ... confess. If innocent, he may not want to tell the truth, or maybe not the whole truth – not this first time. So, I get what I can. Sometimes his claim of innocence melts away. If his innocence claim is false, and I let him talk, he will eventually provide me with evidence of that guilt – or evidence that he is *not* innocent.

If he is innocent, he may offer me a narrative, which I believe is incorrect or untruthful. I still let him talk. My understanding may be based on the false claims of a state's witness, or "bad science," which I had just reviewed and summarized in my Murder Memo. I want to capture every scintilla of verifiable facts from his narrative, so I can start moving the boulders of false testimony used to bury him.

If he wasn't at the crime, then he was somewhere else. I must identify each and every verifiable fact connected to his alibi narrative. After he has offered what he knows, I must then dig deeper. Ask more questions. Gain more sources from this defendant. Sources who may be able to verify his narrative but had never been approached. Or sources who had never been approached the right way with the right questions.

A client reluctant to tell me much about his connection to the crime (i.e., per the police investigation) the first time around could be a bad sign, but not necessarily. A second visit might open that door a little wider – once he realizes my objectivity is sincere, not a ruse.

Likewise, when a habeas client offers a fluid story with lots of action, but short on detail and specifics; that *could* be a sign of innocence – but not necessarily.

If my client (or any witness) rattles off a long, rambling narrative, I never interrupt. I listen. I take notes. I flag all verifiable persons and events. If I see he is offering few verifiable facts, I start flagging each of his claims which needs clarification. Every activity he describes needs a follow-up: Who exactly? When exactly? Where exactly?

I listen closely, trying to determine if his narrative may be based on raw memory of an event, or from a memorized script, a scenario he fabricated. If I remain objective and listen closely, I can usually tell the difference. Actual memories are expandable – using recall. A fabricated scenario is more finite. Any additional facts must be added on-the-spot – created, not recalled.

I may also be listening to an honest yet confabulated "memory."

But the most important thing for me to do, especially this first visit, is let them talk until they are finished.

Every client I have ever met likes to be heard; for reasons which may be psychological or emotional, or just human. I have always found that a convicted defendant desperately wants to share his entire narrative and believe he has been heard. I often see a palpable sense of satisfaction after a habeas client is allowed to complete his entire narrative.

After offering his version, I go back over his story, line-by-line if necessary, and gain specifics. This is when I start to measure the narrative's veracity. Every real person has a name. If not a name, every person has a descriptor, some kind of identity. If my client doesn't know their name, then my client must be able to identify a person-in-common – someone who personally knows that person.

It is never a good sign when the client refuses to identify a relevant witness. He may claim the reason is for someone's safety, or someone's privacy, or to avoid someone's embarrassment. At that point, I will pause, look around at our surroundings, and ask the client if he is OK with his current status. Because his current status (i.e., incarceration) may represent the exchange he is making.

I believe these perceptions are based on my experience, not my cynicism: I generally discount narratives in which relevant persons do not have names (beyond a generic first name or street name), or any known identifiable relation to anyone else. I believe these zombie witnesses are probably imaginary characters in an imaginary narrative.

I have had experience with guilty clients, both pre-trial and habeas, who created fictitious alibi witnesses and eyewitnesses, who could never be identified, or located, or even verified. These witnesses, I was told, could prove *the client's innocence, if only I could find them. I am thinking of at least a half dozen Capital Murder cases where I was asked to identify and locate a key witness, who, I later determined, simply did not exist.*

Going back over my defendant's narrative, I continue gathering specifics. Every car identified in a narrative must have an occupant or an owner. Every house sits on a specific street. If the address is not known, then a nearby cross street must be identified. Every house sits on the left side or the right side of the street, facing toward or facing away from downtown. Every house has a porch, or it doesn't. Every house is made of wood or brick or stone. Every house has a color or is next door to a house with a distinct feature of some kind. All relevant facts and objects have shape and identities. If my client is recalling a true memory, I believe he should be able to describe that person or place from his memory. On which side of the street was the house? I will always ask, "Describe it."

Many people may not know east from west, or north from south. But most cities have remarkable landmarks, which are useful for geographic context. Everyone in St. Louis knows the placement of buildings relative to The Arch. Everyone in Kansas City knows their direction of travel relative to the Missouri River (whether they live to the north or south of it). "Facing the river, on which side of the street did she live?"

If his story remains full of nebulous, non-verifiable activities and events, I begin to consider the client may be fabricating. Depending on the facts of the case, I may wonder if the client has mental or cognitive issues.

A client with mental deficits, who offers a flimsy narrative, could still be innocent. It's not his job to know why or how he got convicted of a crime he did not commit. If a client simply cannot help me understand certain things, I still have facts to gather. My client is just one witness. I once proved innocence in a case where the client had already been executed. It can be done.

And be aware, a false confession is not necessarily a sign of mental deficits. I helped gain one pre-trial dismissal and one exoneration in two Capital Murder cases where the defendant had confessed to police during lengthy interrogations. Yes, the police used deceptive practices in each case to gain their "confessions." In each case, the defendant's confession was not, in any way, supported by the crime or crime scene facts.

And, in each case, the client gave me a very factual, verifiable alibi, which the police had not bothered to obtain or explore. Both of those client visits were especially satisfying and rewarding. During my first visit with both of those clients, I began gaining the narrative I needed to start dismantling the state's case.

I have also developed successful innocent claims for clients who could not offer a reasonable explanation as to *what happened* nor offer an airtight alibi. As challenging and equally satisfying were the innocent claims I developed for clients who minimized their (innocent) involvement, or fabricated events to protect themselves from further scrutiny.

One innocent client lied to me because he feared that even the suggestion of his involvement with the suspected guilty parties would cost him his defense team's support. Once these lies were discovered and openly discussed, the attorney/investigator/client relationship strengthened. Suddenly the innocent client realized the truth – the whole truth – was vitally important, even if he didn't think the truth favored him. That client was Ricky Kidd.

Ricky Kidd had made a business contact with the alternate suspects the day before and the day after the robbery and shooting death of George Bryant and Oscar Bridges.

Ricky had lied about that contact with his original defense attorney, reasoning it shouldn't matter – the police didn't know about it – so, why should his defense attorney? Besides, he thought, knowledge of that contact might create the appearance of guilt even though police never investigated his business contact with this other individual – now our alternate suspect.

As my investigation continued – the more I tried to piece together what happened – the more I realized we were missing something. I found that the gap in our understanding of what happened traced back to Ricky's narrative.

I've heard many a good defense attorney describe this scenario as their "come-to-Jesus meeting," when the client is confronted with facts – the undeniable truth – which doesn't mesh with the client's narrative. The attorney must convince her client that whatever we have learned, the state will surely learn. Whatever we have discovered, the state may already know and will be able to prove. It is at this meeting when the client must explain what really happened, present a truthful narrative the attorney can present, OR be willing to acknowledge his guilt, so the defense attorney (pre-trial) can deal with that as well.

After our "come-to-Jesus meeting" with Ricky, he explained in great detail his business associations and contacts with the alternate suspects. These contacts he described led to new evidence, which added to newly discovered evidence of his innocence. While trying to hide any suggestion of guilt, Ricky was actually hiding good and verifiable facts of his innocence from his habeas team.

Once Ricky saw we were able to look past the inference of guilt, he began trusting and respecting his defense team even more. He needed proof that his defense attorney and investigator would not abandon his case, after learning he was not perfect. Innocent – just not perfect.

I'm also always aware of a reason mentioned earlier, which can lead to a client's fabricated scenario. If this habeas client told the truth about his innocence and still got convicted, he may wonder if he needs a different narrative, a different explanation for his activities. I will always ask a client what he told his original defense team. I will review any statements he may have made to the police, with him.

If I sense any reluctance to be candid, I refer the defendant back to my introduction and my assurance that I will objectively consider his narrative versus the narrative that convicted him. I may tell him I understand why a person who told the truth and still got convicted might fabricate a scenario, which – in their mind – does *a better job* proving their innocence. I may understand, but I still need facts – verifiable facts – before I can help him.

Another issue in habeas cases, which is much harder to detect – I am aware of the possibility of "false memory." The clinical term is confabulation – creating a false memory of past events.

Being wrongfully convicted, then incarcerated, then threatened with an execution, or a slow, certain death behind bars, could certainly create a candidate for confabulating a narrative.

I don't believe I have ever encountered a true case of confabulation, which is considered a neuropsychiatric disorder. If I did, it would be an issue for the lawyer and a psych exam to evaluate.

I bring this up only because it is a plausible scenario in habeas cases.

A wrongful conviction can impact a person in ways I cannot imagine. When the state falsely proclaims this person committed a horrible crime, and his defense counsel can't convince a jury otherwise, what *should* be the normal reaction – after 10, 15, 20 years?

In habeas cases, I understand the possibility exists for considerable emotional and psychological issues. These are issues I am not qualified to address or diagnose, but, as a factfinder, they are issues I may need to acknowledge and work around.

Most of my habeas clients have been helpful, often valuable, witnesses in their own defense. I understand and am not surprised when I find habeas clients who really are dealing with a poor memory, an unreliable recall, a cognitive deficit. None of those issues are indications of guilt ... or of innocence.

I see my habeas client as my first witness. I have my Murder Memo, which has already exposed some concerns. My job is to investigate the investigation and investigate the crime. Find out *what happened*. Find those good facts – if they exist.

Now, discovering the *third reason* a habeas client may lie to me might only be found in my Murder Memo.

Sometimes, the police create the reason for a habeas client to fabricate his narrative. During questioning, homicide investigators may lie to a suspect, claiming the suspect's hair, or a fingerprint, or their DNA, was found at the crime scene. When, in fact, that evidence does not exist. Only a thorough review of all lab reports will disprove whatever false claim the police made decades earlier (and convince the client that "false" evidence does not exist).

Note to Reader

This is a questionable, yet legal, technique; unseemly and, I think, responsible for an unknown percentage of wrongful convictions – endorsed by the US Supreme Court.

Now understand, that whatever false claim may have been made by the police, it was never used by the prosecutor at trial (because it was a false claim). And doubtful, the jury ever heard about this false information used by police during interrogations and witness interviews. So, this fictitious "fact" was never openly challenged in court. It's even possible the defendant's trial lawyer did not know about this police ruse – especially if the police interviews were not recorded.

That false police claim may have led the suspect to fabricate his story in general, in order to defend against this false and probably confusing claim by police. My habeas client may still be explaining-away that "fact" 20 years later.

Having read scores of police interviews and suspect interrogations, I have seen, when the police tell a suspect something is true, many suspects believe them. I have seen how a long, stressful police interrogation can force suspects to believe anything is possible – even if they know such a "fact" is "impossible."

This issue of police fabrication can take on a life of its own. Homicide investigators may lie to a witness or lie to the suspect's girlfriend, offering this bogus, incriminating "fact," hoping to get a witness to cooperate.

I have seen this "suggestion of incriminating evidence" offered by police eventually spread through the community, confusing witnesses (or convincing them of a false narrative). I have seen enough cases like this to believe this method of poisoning the witness pool is reckless. I don't know if this is a conscious police technique. Nor do I know if this is a widespread technique.

I also believe that, if the police falsely "suggest" physical evidence ties a suspect to a crime scene, that could alter the thought process of any "witness."

I'm aware of police sharing false, incriminating evidence with an eyewitness. People associated with the victim, interviewed by police, will openly talk about what the police told them about the crime and the suspect. That includes any false evidence the police may mention. Eventually, a cooperating witness may come forward, willing to support the police theory.

So, I listen carefully to my client and his story. Although the above scenario is rare (I think), it is an example of the bizarre paths these cases can take. Some habeas clients have told me up front about their suspicions of police fabrications. I believe other clients kept quiet and ignored false claims made by police – maybe worrying the evidence actually existed.

And I guess there is one last inhibition I have encountered with habeas clients. The defendant claims innocence, yet refuses to offer much information about the crime or any information about the true assailants. The client still thinks his actual innocence should be enough to gain post-conviction relief.

In his world, passing along information about a crime is "snitching" – even if it's proof of his innocence and the key to his own freedom. The last thing he would do is pass along information which incriminates another person.

He certainly won't discuss this information with someone he does not trust. Race and demographics and basic survival may play into his thought process. This scenario will require more work in developing trust. And even trust might not be enough.

I have sat across from more than one convicted felon who knew the person whose time he was serving – but refused to identify that person.

I have met inmates – 20 years into their sentence for a crime they did not commit – still reluctant to tell the whole truth. I think they know who committed the crime. But they worry that identifying the true actor will get them killed in prison while waiting for the wheels of justice to correct their mistaken conviction. Resolving wrongful convictions is a slow, tedious process, especially without the cooperation of police or prosecutors. These inmates believe if their habeas petition names (or suggests) the actual killer, they could be labeled a snitch and killed.

Out here in the free world, it's difficult for me to tell a prison inmate with confidence, "that's crazy." I trust my client knows his world better than I will ever know it.

Given this scenario, I block out what the client refuses to share and focus on what parts of his truthful narrative may help me determine *what happened*.

Chapter 7

Time to Get Out: Visiting the Crime Scene

I'd be lying if I said I visited every crime scene of every criminal case I ever reviewed. That said, many of those cases in which I *did not* visit the crime scene became increasingly difficult to investigate and understand.

I have learned to embrace that general rule: visiting the crime scene will *almost always* improve my understanding of the case and enhance what is ultimately communicated to the Judge and the jury.

In most of my earlier cases, I skipped past visiting the crime scene, because I didn't think I had time. Other *To Dos* seemed more important. The defense team, unlike the prosecution, is always on a budget – either time or money, or both. I noticed in those early cases, when I didn't find time to visit the crime scene, the case often grew more confusing as my investigation moved forward. It became more challenging for me to determine exactly *what happened*.

(Understand, my investigative career began before Google Earth and Google Maps existed. I believe Google Earth is helpful, but not an absolute substitute for a physical visit.)

In 2008, I began reading the police reports and witness statements in Lamar Johnson's case, describing the 1994 murder of Marcus Boyd in a south St. Louis neighborhood. I noted, "The shooters ran up the gangway, … the shooters came through the gangway …."

What the hell is a gangway, I thought. I was unfamiliar with the term. At that time, I lived in Kansas City. This neighborhood in south St. Louis was unfamiliar to me – and 250 miles away.

On the evening of October 30, 1994, Marcus Boyd was shot and killed by two masked shooters as he sat on the top step of the small porch in front of his turn-of-the-century, brick, two-family flat. The police reports provided no map or diagram of the scene. Initially, I had no crime scene photos to view.

Where the shooters came from, and the direction in which they fled, were extremely relevant.

DOI: 10.4324/9781003543299-7

During my next visit to St. Louis, I visited the crime scene. What a revelation to view the front of the duplex, and the surrounding neighborhood. In just a few minutes, witness statements I had read months earlier started making more sense.

A year later, when I was able to interview the two actual assailants, it was very important that I had seen the crime scene and gained an understanding of the entire neighborhood. Because of my first-hand knowledge, I knew the actual assailant's narrative and their full admissions of guilt absolutely matched the physical crime scene.

(One of those shooters had already served his time for Boyd's murder in a plea deal. The other was serving a LWOP sentence on another crime. I gained their signatures on affidavits describing their role in the crime and excluding Lamar from any involvement or knowledge of Boyd's murder. More than 12 years later, in December 2022, a Judge finally read and ruled on the veracity of those affidavits.)

In a 1999 Murder I case – *Mo. v. James W. Boyd III*, filed in Clay County (Kansas City), Missouri – police reports included a crime scene diagram drawn on a blank 8.5″ × 11″ sheet of paper. This "not to scale" diagram indicated, in the top left corner of the paper, a path beginning at a paved parking lot, leading into a wooded brushy area, through a field, to the location where police found the victim's body in the bottom right corner of that piece of paper. Lost in translation was the fact that this crime scene covered 60 acres of raw, rough, hilly, open fields and densely wooded land.

When I visited that crime scene, I found the worn dirt path leading from the parking lot (described in the top left corner of the police diagram). This path began at the northwest corner of this parcel of land, before entering a densely wooded area. I walked this dirt path, as it continued in serpentine fashion through dense woods, up and down steep hills, curving into and through a large open field of wild brush, before turning back into more wooded, hilly terrain,

This path led to the far distant, southeastern corner of this 60-acre parcel, finally reaching the actual location of the murder. All this acreage and terrain became relevant to witness statements, alleged movements, witness activities, and, eventually, a successful defense.

For context and a layman's understanding, one acre is roughly the size of a football field. Imagine a rectangular piece of land, the size of 60 football fields covering rough, wooded hills and overgrown fields.

Neither the witnesses nor the crime scene tech provided any context in their statements or reports, other than, "... a field ... a wooded area ... from the parking lot we followed the path into the woods ... we were walking along the path, then I heard ...."

Compounding the problem, in this particular case, the witnesses in this horrific, teenager "thrill-kill" were interviewed by homicide detectives at police headquarters located downtown. Some of these "witnesses" interviewed downtown by police were later proven to be actual participants. The crime occurred in the Kansas City, Missouri jurisdiction, only in a different county (Clay), north of the river, miles from police headquarters downtown. These were, essentially, two distinct geographic and political entities. (Most of Kansas City, Missouri proper lies in Jackson Co., but also includes parts of Clay and Platte Counties.)

These initial witness interviews by police occurred just hours after the crime was discovered by Clay County authorities, but days after the actual crime. The KCMO PD homicide detectives (in downtown Kansas City) were seemingly unfamiliar with these 60 acres, or even where the body had been discovered within this 60-acre tract.

Based on the questions asked by police, evident in their interview reports, it appeared the homicide detectives were learning about the crime scene from the witnesses. This resulted in inaccurate and ambiguous witness statements. These macro-misunderstandings and inaccuracies affected the outcome of the first trial. Our client was convicted and sentenced to life without parole (LWOP).

A Missouri Appellate court reversed that conviction, granting a retrial. The new trial Judge agreed to the defense motion for an inspection of the crime scene by the judge and jury – to gain an appreciation of the terrain, comprising this 60-acre crime scene.

The terrain itself was a critical factor, impacting the credibility of the witness statements. The terrain also impacted the state's case against one of the defendants (our client), who exhibited several traits consistent with Asperger's Syndrome. His condition would have prevented him from navigating complicated environments like these 60 acres – on his own. His Asperger's symptoms prevented him from gaining a driver's license. At his community college, a student had been assigned to help him find his classrooms and navigate his way around the small campus.

In total, the defendant's diagnosed conditions raised serious doubt about his ability (not to mention his willingness) to navigate 60 acres of wooded terrain and murder the victim, an acquaintance – by himself – before leaving the wooded area – again, by himself.

The witness statements themselves (some by actors later proven to be involved) created a narrative which incriminated our client. The statements were taken to be incriminating, even though some details they offered contradicted the terrain and our client's physical abilities.

Visualizing a crime scene, merely by reading police reports, can be challenging. Often, my mental picture of the crime scene – based on police reports – simply *does not* match the actual crime scene. Sometimes the discrepancies are significant.

In habeas cases I have reviewed, I'm always glad to find crime scene photos in the legal file or included in Discovery. But even those original crime scene photos can have limited value. Crime scene photos often focus solely on the victim and not the surrounding area. Crime scene photos seldom contain "wide shots," offering the very context I'm looking for, the context I gain, from visiting the crime scene, years later.

I appreciate the analogy that watching TV cable news broadcasts (i.e., CNN) is like watching the world through a telescope, from 1,000 feet in the air. Just like viewing official crime scene photos – *what I don't see, what I can't see, is sometimes crucial to understanding what I can see.*

In a perfect world, police reports provided in Discovery include accurate diagrams and crime scene photos which are both contextual and specific – actual documentation of where the crime occurred. Relevant aerial shots can help, depending on the crime and the location. Too bad all homicide investigations are not documented and described in great detail.

Normally, in cases I am asked to review in which a wrongful conviction is suspected, that lack of detail may be an issue. I have found criminal cases which were poorly investigated are generally criminal cases even more difficult to re-investigate, especially if innocence is suspected. Often in those cases, the lack of detail begins with the crime scene.

The fact is, I normally don't find crime scene photos inside the legal files of the habeas cases I have been asked to review. In some of these habeas cases, we spent an inordinate amount of energy trying to locate lots of simple things – like crime scene photos. Police reports may reference crime scene photos; even document crime scene photos; identify photos in evidence inventories – yet these photos somehow disappeared or were never handed over to the defense. In my experience, crime scene photos are the most likely piece of evidence to be mishandled or misplaced, lost, or never obtained.

Pre-trial, it should be a simple Discovery issue. So, I don't know why I generally start out reviewing police reports without the benefit of crime scene photos. In most cases, for me, years later, it was just easier to visit the crime scene and take my own photos.

Most defense attorneys I have worked with pre-trial understand the value of official crime scene photos. Apparently, some defense attorneys don't. Some defense attorneys might dismiss the need for crime scene photos. Or maybe they were too busy to make that second Discovery request. That's a case some Wrongful Conviction team may be asked to review years later. And there won't be any crime scene photos in the box.

So, after reviewing a habeas case with or without crime scene photos, I visit the crime scene. I take pictures. I draw my own diagrams. That step always helps me eventually understand *what happened.*

But there are other important reasons for me to obtain my own photos from the crime scene: Whether the crime occurred one year or 25 years earlier – *most eyewitness* interviews I conduct will benefit from photos of the crime scene.

Experience has consistently shown me, any attempt to gain the best recall from an eyewitness should include an accurate diagram, or a wide-angle[1] photo of the crime scene. Sometimes, an aerial photo of the general area will enhance a witness' recall. It certainly makes it easier for the witness to communicate their recall.

Depending on the layout of the crime scene, I might create a panorama photo. When I visit an area which was once the scene of a crime – if I feel a panorama may be useful – I stand in place, taking several photos, to the left and to the right of my focal point at the crime scene. I print those photos, then tape them together to create a panorama. In past habeas cases, witnesses found these panoramas very useful. With my photos from the crime scene and surrounding area, a witness will sometimes recall other witnesses and where they were situated at the scene. Sometimes, they will recall witnesses no one else knew about.

My smartphone makes it easier to capture the same visual context. But a printed image may still be more useful. Witnesses like to point out where they were standing when they saw what happened. It may be legally relevant for me to document where that witness claims to have been located when they saw what they say they saw. Besides having these photos of the crime scene on my phone, having a photocopy with me allows a witness to mark on the photo for clarity – and evidence.

One night, in May of 1990, Recco Rogers was sitting on a neighbor's porch with friends, on the north side of St. Louis, when someone approached the group and began shooting. Twenty-two years later, I was asked to review the shooting and the conviction of Chris Dunn. The police reports took less than an hour to review. It was the thinnest report of a homicide investigation I had ever reviewed. There were no crime scene photos. The witness statements summarized in the police reports were brief and somewhat vague.

The crime scene report provided exact locations, directions, and measurements of where Recco fell when shot, before the teenager was taken away by EMTs and rushed to a nearby hospital – and died.

Two teenage boys, friends of Recco Rogers, had told police they saw Chris Dunn shoot their friend Recco that night. They told police what

1 "Wide-angle Shot" is a photojournalist's term in which the main subject is captured in the middle of the frame, showing considerable surroundings, thus providing "context."

Dunn was wearing and approximately where he was standing. Their investigation concluded the next day following Chris Dunn's arrest.

Generally, residential neighborhoods change very little. It can happen, but I expect to find today's neighborhood with useful similarities, if not the same layout, as 20 or 30 years earlier.

Sometime in 2012, I drove by the location where Recco Rogers was shot in 1990. I photographed the same house with the porch where Rogers was reportedly sitting with friends before the shooting. The house was smaller than I understood, and the front porch was closer to the sidewalk than I expected. None of those dimensions came across in police reports. This house and its front porch protruded from the row of houses on either side, standing much closer to the street and the sidewalk. I felt this might be a detail which could matter in understanding witness statements.

The shooter *allegedly*[2] came from the west side of the house and began shooting, either at Rogers, or in the direction of the entire group. I pictured a rectangular house with a porch centered and set back from the street. I pictured the front of the house to be consistent with all other houses on that side of the street. So, the location and proximity of the porch and porch steps Rogers sat on, compared with the first house to the west, was relevant to the activity described by witnesses.

Now standing across the street from this crime scene – due to the configuration of the porch – I saw that the shooter could have been standing anywhere to the west of that house and still have a clear line of sight at the boys sitting on those porch steps. I saw how the shooter's position could have been to the side of the victim and witnesses, or slightly in front of them, or slightly behind them, as they sat talking on the steps. The shooter could have been several steps to the west, or nearly 100 steps to the west, and have the same line of sight.

The space between the edge of the porch and the side of the house to the west was about 5 feet – not the 10 or 15 feet I envisioned from the reports and the witness statements.

After reviewing the police reports, I looked at some post-conviction witness interviews conducted by the defense. These witness statements suggested some witnesses may have been standing outside further to the west, several houses away, when shots were fired. These witness statements described their location as being, "up the hill." The street showed a slight incline to the west.

From the scene of the shooting, I drove up the hill and took panorama shots of the houses on each side of the street. I then assumed the point of view (POV) of anyone standing outside their house that night and, looking

2 I use the term *allegedly* as that was the state's theory.

down the hill, I took photos facing east, toward the crime scene near the end of the block on the left side of the street.

These photos showed the one lone, relevant streetlight, about 60 feet from the porch on the south side of the street. This streetlight was not mentioned in the police report. In fact, no ambient lighting was mentioned or described in this police report. The shooting occurred at just about midnight.

My investigation determined the weather conditions that night were warm (66 degrees) and dry, "cloudy" with a "waning crescent moon" rising at 2:29 a.m. So, there was no natural light from above, at the time of the shooting.

A few weeks after visiting this crime scene, I contacted a woman who had supposedly lived "up the hill" from the shooting, 20 years earlier. A defense team interview had suggested this woman might have come out of her house that night, looking for her nephew, when the shooting occurred. She had not been mentioned in any police reports.

When I approached this woman, she could not remember living on that block, in 1990, but said it was possible. She had lived in many different inner-city apartments on the north side. I showed her a photo of one of the few remaining houses still standing "up the hill." She immediately recognized the brick duplex in the photo. She said she had lived next door, in a similar turn-of-the-century, two-family flat – now a vacant lot. She knew her daughter gave birth to her grandson just a few days after the young boy, Recco Rogers, was shot. So, she was able to confirm to me that day, that yes, she was living on that street, in that building, in May of 1990.

Unfortunately, she was also positive she had *not* stepped outside the night Rogers was killed. She remembered hearing about his death the next day. She then told me the young boy who was shot lived next door to her, with his mom, in the two-family flat still standing – the one in my photograph.

Understanding this crime scene also helped me understand my interview a few years later with Eugene W. He was a witness to the shooting who had been on the porch with the others but had never spoken to the police about the shooting. Eugene confirmed the shots that killed Recco Rogers came out of the darkness, and no one could see or identify who shot at them. His affidavit and testimony supported the recantations already gained from the first two witnesses.

Following two evidentiary hearings, two different judges determined that the witnesses did not know, and could not identify, the shooter due to the conditions that existed that night. That evidence, coupled with the detailed alibi evidence I had initially gathered, helped Chris Dunn gain his release in 2024.

Over the years, I have seen many witnesses grow frustrated when they wanted to help, tried to help, but could not articulate, or accurately picture, the crime scene from memory. Photos of the crime scene offer a simple visual aid and a memory aid to a witness. Generally recalling the scene where a crime occurred is one thing. Accurately recalling that scene with clarity makes for a better witness.

I have seen witnesses show visceral excitement when I pull out a photo of the crime scene area. Every eyewitness I have ever interviewed appreciated seeing a wide-angle photo of the location where they stood, horrified, years earlier, witnessing the fatal shooting of another person. (Most eyewitnesses I have approached, and asked to describe a murder, seem motivated to get it right.)

I think viewing such a photo allows the witness to confirm her memory, helps her collect her thoughts, and probably improves her recall. Viewing a wide-angle photo of that scene may confirm a witness' belief in his memory, despite the time that has passed. Trauma can cloud one's recall. I think a simple photo allows the witness to concentrate on what he saw the day of the crime, without needing to guess where the doorway or the stairs were, or where the water fountain stood. I believe confusion forces the brain to work harder. And clarity helps.

On the afternoon of May 18, 2009, following a high-school graduation ceremony in Nashville, Tennessee, a young man leaving the event in a crowd of families and friends was shot at an exit door by another young man. All witnesses saw a shooter run up to the victim, shoot him in the torso with three or four shots, then flee the area. Sheer chaos ensued.

Two years later, I was hired by the defense attorney to prepare for trial in this shooting of Andres T. After reviewing police reports, I gained only a vague understanding of the physical crime scene. I learned that Andres was shot, in a crowd, near an exit door, following the high-school graduation at a large indoor arena at a local university in Nashville, Tennessee. The chaos and confusion caused by the shooting were evident through the police reports and their witness interviews. Every witness saw something slightly different. The victim was shot in a crowd, while exiting the building, then ran outside about 100 feet before tumbling down a steep hill. The victim was found at the bottom of the hill, where he died from gunshot wounds.

The shooter was seen by witnesses, following the shooting, running in a different direction, toward a crowded parking lot.

Police interviewed numerous witnesses at the scene. There were also numerous witnesses to the shooting not interviewed by police, who were contacted by me more than two years later.

The police reports contained no diagrams or floor plan. From the crime scene narrative, I could not determine the exact door the victim was exiting when he was shot.

The official crime scene photos were taken several hours after the shooting, after the crowd of 1,000+ people had cleared, and – I later learned – after the maintenance staff had moved all tables, chairs, and barricades out of the lobby area adjacent to the shooting.

No police photos existed showing the placement of these inanimate objects. The tables and temporary pedestrian barricades described in many witness statements indicating where they were standing, and where the shooter ran after the shooting – all critical information – all lost.

Nor did the crime scene photos show any wide-angle shots providing views of the lobby area.

No police photos showed the interior stairs in relation to the northwest exit, in relation to the trophy case, in relation to the northeast exit, in relation to the ticket booth windows. These were all "points of reference" used in witness' statements to police and in crime scene reports.

The police had no photos or diagrams to share with witnesses when they were interviewed. All police interviews conducted that day involved traumatized eyewitnesses trying to describe not only the shooting and the shooter, but the layout and floorplan of a place foreign to them. Nor did it appear the police were very familiar with this crime scene or the building's floor plan.

After reading the reports, I imagined a large, maybe oversized, high-school gym with one main entrance and exit. Many witness statements made little sense to me, with references to "upper level," and "ground floor."

After reviewing the reports and completing my Murder Memo, and before contacting any witnesses, I visited this crime scene.

I found a large, world-class, multi-purpose center, designed for basketball on the main floor, surrounded by facilities designed for full indoor-track and field competition. The main arena seats 9,000+ people on three levels. Events related to this crime and witness locations related to this shooting covered all three levels from the main arena above, to the exit door on the building's north side, two floors below, where the young man was shot.

This high-school graduation ceremony, attended by 3,000 friends and family, was still dwarfed by this structure. Technically, this entire indoor arena was part of the crime scene. Every witness used some element of this building to describe where they were – and whom they were with – when they heard shots, or heard screams, or saw something, or saw someone, of relevance. Literally, "location" in this building became a part of every person's perspective and part of every suspect's alibi.

I saw the value of having photographs of the main floor showing which end contained the stage where the graduates received their diploma, and which doors the graduates used to exit. All the parents and friends knew where they were in relation to the stage, and where they saw the graduates exit. Otherwise, these witnesses were *lost* in a building most had never visited before that day.

During my visit to this crime scene, I started upstairs in the main arena. Suddenly "the upper level," described in police reports, made sense to me, as did the witness descriptions of steps descending the two levels to the lobby. I walked the path taken by these witnesses. I viewed the location of the shooting, at the bottom of the stairwell, near the first door, in a row of six exit doors. This row of doors sat immediately to the right, as victim and witnesses walked down the stairs, exiting the building that day. Witnesses I interviewed helped me identify visual markers in my photos, which then gave other witnesses a reference point.

In the ground-floor lobby, I stepped back and took my layman's panorama shot of the lobby, left to right, from the main arena entrance, moving right to the restrooms, the water fountain, the bank of northwest exit doors, the descending steps, the trophy case, to the bank of six northeast exit doors, and, finally, the ticket booth. (I stood in the center of the building's lobby, facing north.)

With the aid of these photos, the witnesses I contacted were able to tell me exactly where they were standing when they heard that first shot – the one they will never forget. The photos helped them remember distinctly their reaction when the gunshot grabbed their attention and, sometimes, they remembered who was standing next to them.

Witnesses I contacted were able to show me the placement of the tables and the temporary pedestrian barricades, since all these objects had been removed before the "official" crime scene photos were taken. I eventually had photos marked with those barricades which had been removed, as well as the permanent points of reference, a structural column, a trophy case, a restroom entrance, a water fountain. These photos showed a center handrail on the descending steps – forgotten by many witnesses but, once they had seen it in the photo, they could recall on which side of the handrail they had stood when the shots were fired. That handrail placement provided witnesses (and me) their exact proximity to the shooter and the shooting.

Virtually every witness I contacted was grateful that they could refer to interior, exterior, and aerial photos, to determine where they were standing or sitting, relevant to the shooting they had unexpectedly witnessed.

During trial in Nashville, Tennessee, the Federal Judge asked to retain my panorama of the crime scene. My amateurish "panorama" offered a much better aid for the witnesses (and the Judge) than anything the government (prosecution) had provided.

Chapter 8

Identifying and Finding My Witnesses

Most homicide investigations will identify anywhere between 10 and 100 witnesses, various people related to the crime or the investigation leading to their suspect. Add to that list my client, his family, and anyone he has mentioned relevant to his alibi, his narrative, and his innocence claims.

I want to locate and contact many of these individuals, but which ones? Where do I start? What is my strategy?

It's a simple step.

I reviewed the police reports and created a searchable Murder Memo. I built a People List including everybody I could identify who was possibly relevant to this crime, relevant to the defendant, the victim, or significant witnesses. I created a list of my questions and concerns with the state's case and the police investigation leading to my client. I visited with the defendant and gained his narrative supporting his claim of innocence. I visited the crime scene and noted anything about it which looked or felt inconsistent with incriminating witness statements. My list of Queries and Needs and To Dos grew after visiting the crime scene and the client.

Each of these steps, and collectively, *all* of these steps, help me identify the witnesses I would like to interview.

My client's claim of innocence and his narrative provide a subset of witnesses to contact. Maybe the client provided two distinct sets of witnesses – those who may help verify his narrative surrounding the crime and those who may confirm his alibi. Each of those witnesses may help verify my client's veracity in general.

If the client's narrative of innocence is to be believed – if I'm able to verify – then witnesses who gave "incriminating statements" suddenly become suspect. In that case, the accuracy of those incriminating witness statements to police must be confirmed. Or the accuracy of the police reports themselves must be verified. If certain incriminating witnesses can no longer be believed, I begin looking for witnesses to those witnesses.

At this point, the "Bio" notes on my People List help me ID witnesses who can tell me about certain other witnesses.

DOI: 10.4324/9781003543299-8

Long before the Innocence Project developed their list of "Contributing Factors," I had already learned from my habeas work – if the client's narrative and claim of innocence are *true*, then the state's theory must be based on certain *falsehoods*. The conviction must be based on a *false identification*, or a *false informant*, or some element of *bad (faulty) science*, or a *false confession*. The *only* other possibility I and the Innocence Projects have encountered is that *no crime* was committed (i.e., a suicide or accidental death ruled a homicide, a faked kidnapping, a fraudulent claim of sexual assault, etc.).

Each possible factor defines its own set of potential witnesses, and the possibility of additional witnesses, witnesses I have not yet even thought of, whom I will need to contact.

If my client's narrative is unhelpful (and that can happen for a variety of reasons), I am left with the simplified goal of determining *what happened* related to the crime. I begin to identify witnesses who can help me run a *stress test* on the state's conviction.

If my defendant can only offer that he wasn't there, didn't do it, and was passed out on a couch somewhere, I still have the crime and the investigation to investigate. In determining *what happened*, maybe all I can do is attempt to confirm and verify the state's case – the original police investigation. If my client is truthful, then one of those other factors exists. Or my client is not being truthful.

I look for persons who may have witnessed the crime but were never interviewed by police. I look for any witness who was interviewed by police, and reportedly provided a narrative supporting my defendant's guilt, but who was not asked to testify. (Generally, prosecutors put everybody with incriminating testimony on their list of witnesses, but they may or may not testify. They may not testify for several innocent reasons. They also may not testify because their story changed, or the police report was in error.)

This is an exciting stage of my investigation – when I start identifying witnesses who may help verify facts relevant to the crime and facts relevant to my client's guilt or innocence.

If Witness X saw my client flee the crime scene with a gun in his hand, but Witness HH was talking to my client at the same time – at a gas station miles away – someone is mistaken.

A witness observation (based on police interviews) might be mistaken, or the police report itself might be mistaken. In one of my cases, the police reports themselves were found to be fabricated.

There are several plausible scenarios.

A witness interview by police can be poorly conducted. A witness may be uncooperative or untruthful to the police. The homicide investigator may not ask the right question. The witness may have told that investigator what she thought the investigator wanted to hear.

Witnesses can be pressured by the police, or the victim's family, or some other persuasive force, to provide false information.

In the scenario described above, I would start with Witness HH to verify my client's alibi narrative – at the gas station miles away. (And then start the verification process for everything that witness tells me.)

Oftentimes, I'm not looking for *the* witness who can prove a wrongful conviction. I'm looking for witnesses who might help me assess the veracity of the police investigation, or the veracity of the client (i.e., the stress test). Sometimes a third-party witness, not an eyewitness, helps me confirm the veracity of her police interview report.

If a police report indicates a witness saw my client commit the crime, obviously that witness needs to be contacted to confirm that police report.

I am not so cynical as to think all homicide reports are false, or all witness interviews by police must be questioned – until I find verifiable evidence challenging the state's theory. Once I find a "Witness HH" who is willing to cooperate, and swears he was with my client at the time of the crime, miles away, then all reports become suspect. (And verification of Witness HH begins.)

If a police report indicates a witness was unclear as to what they saw, or whom they saw commit the crime, that witness needs to be contacted to confirm that police report. Was she unclear? Or did she tell police she knew the assailant was definitely not my client, but otherwise was unable to ID anybody else? And *that particular* claim was not expressed in the report.

I have found it helpful in habeas cases, where I am evaluating an innocence claim, that assessing the client's credibility, early on, is always a good thing. Once credibility is established, the real work can begin. If my client's veracity comes up short, finding out earlier, is better. A wrongful conviction may still be possible. But it's time for that client *meeting*, discussed in Chapter 6.

So, with a strategy in mind, I begin selecting witnesses for contact.

Normally I classify this witness list in some type of order, either geographical or by priority. I may first designate the witnesses whom I want to approach to assess my client's credibility. I'll often start with alibi witnesses, or anyone from the client's narrative who can verify his version of events.

I generally save any witness I deem *sensitive* or *critical* until later in the investigation. The more I know about a case, the better I will be able to conduct a witness interview with the more sensitive, maybe the more knowledgeable, maybe the more critical witness.

I don't believe there is any magic in the way witnesses are prioritized. I always discuss these decisions with the lead attorney. If I am left to devise my own strategy, I may consider time, budget, geography, and availability. The main objective is to *get started.*

Oftentimes, I organize my witnesses into priority groups, let's say "A," "B," and "C" witnesses.

"A" witnesses impress me as being critical in what they may know and can verify, or I think they may know more about what happened than is reflected in their police reports. I will also start here with the witnesses who can verify my client's narrative (i.e., innocence claims), including his alibi.

"B" witnesses are more routine witnesses. These will be eyewitnesses who appear to incriminate my client, but I still want to verify their narrative, per their police reports. This group may also include some witnesses I want to approach and ask about the veracity of other state witnesses. These may all be "stress test" witnesses.

"C" witnesses, initially, are all the rest of the witnesses I have identified who may be able to answer a question I have about the crime or fill a gap in my understanding of *what happened.* They may have been peripheral eyewitnesses who reportedly did not see or hear much. They could be third-party witnesses who may know about other witnesses. They don't appear to be knowledgeable of any crucial information, but they are associated with the victim or the crime or the defendant, and I don't want to skip them. I simply won't know what they know, until I locate, contact, and ask them. Also, if I am talking to "C" witnesses, that means several witnesses have already verified aspects of my client's innocence.

Experience has taught me that many "B" and "C" witnesses should have been placed on my "A" list. I just had no way of knowing that before our interview.

Now with a finite list of witnesses to approach, I edit my People List, placing an "F" next to the names of any witness I need to locate. My "F," quite simply, means FIND. If this person is not fully identified, I add "ID," as in: I need to IDENTIFY this person, before I can attempt to FIND her (i.e., "ID/F").

If I already have a location on a witness I want to contact, I designate that witness in the margin with "O." "O" tells me this person has been located, and I need to contact and interview her.

Now my People List names (at least the "A" and "B" names) are labeled "F" and "ID/F" and "O." If I'm not interested in finding or contacting them at this time, I leave a neutral mark ("*" or "-").

I'll start my interviews somewhere on that list.

After I have interviewed a witness on this list, the "O" is changed to a "/".

My Shorthand:

D	=	Deceased
Dob	=	Date of birth
DOD	=	Date of death
F	=	Find
ID	=	Need to more fully IDENTIFY
LKA	=	Last known address
NKA	=	Now known as (helps w/married name changes and businesses)
O	=	NEED to Contact/Interview
POE	=	Place of employment
Res	=	Residence
YOB	=	Year of birth
/	=	I have Contacted/Interviewed

Oklahoma v. Willard O'Neal

What follows are the first few pages of my initial People List in Willard O'Neal's case in Tulsa, Oklahoma. I was still in the initial stage of identifying witnesses based on my Murder Memo, my Queries List, and following my first visit with Willard O'Neal and the crime scene.

O'NEAL PEOPLE

[Updated 3/3/14]

[Re: The 2:55 a.m. 12/23/01 (Sunday a.m.) shooting death of Bruce Chamberlain, and shooting of Gildardo Rueda in front of Trapeze Lounge and Omega Laundry, near 3100 S 101st East Ave., Tulsa, OK]

F (A) **Robert G A[redacted]** – [Bouncer at Trapeze. Reported assoc of Sandra H[redacted]. Reportedly heard Sandy H[redacted] tell Bruce Chamberlain that Charity was looking for someone to rob Trapeze. SEE H[redacted].]

Dob: [redacted] (52 in 2001) Age 66
SS# [redacted]

F (B) **Shawna (Shonna) A[redacted]**?– [G.F. to Misty B[redacted]. Called Misty B about 10 a.m. 12/23/01, left a message about Chamberlain's death, Shawna had heard all about from a 2:40 a.m. voice mail message from Mary S[redacted], per Misty B's statement. Confirmed by her 2001 phone#.]

Dob: [redacted]
SS# [redacted]
LKA: **918-902-**[redacted] In Trailer Park behind K-Mart on Admiral, Tulsa, OK (per Misty B)

F (A) Alejandro "Alex" A[redacted] **Aka:** [redacted] – [Heather's friend/roommate. Never Interviewed by Police??? Occupant of Paul B's apt. where Alex, Heather, Stephanie and Kevin spent night of 12/22–12/23. Boyfriend to Charity [redacted] 2000–2004, per Marsha F. Arrested for Feb 2013 kidnapping? Currently lives w/Heather M[redacted] (?) per Marsha F. A GD, per O'Neal. Too Fat, sez Rueda.]

Dob: [redacted] (5′7″ 300 lbs per Prison 2003 … Lt brown skin, per photo)
Okl DOC: [redacted] – [5′9″ + 250 lbs per DOC 4/26/01]
BOP# [redacted]

F (B) Lorraine "Kitty" B[redacted] – [Dancer at Trapeze 12/22–12/23. Danced w/2 b/m guys at club. Left bar really drunk about 1:45 a.m. w/Marsha F. and Danny C[redacted] to go home. At home ([redacted] Apts, 1 blk west of Trapeze) she heard multiple gunshots.]

Dob: [redacted]
SS# [redacted]
LKA: [redacted] E 31st St. #30[redacted], ([redacted] Apts. 31st & Mingo) Tulsa, OK (per Tulsa PD 1/02).

ID/F (B) Darren B[redacted] – [State's Witness, never testified. Knows what? Jail Inmate?]

Dob:
LKA:

ID/F (B) Jason B[redacted] – [To Trapeze after 2:30 a.m. 12/23/01 to give Marsie C and Karen W[redacted] a ride home, per Marsie C[redacted].]

Dob:

PROBABLE ID:

Jason Lee B[redacted]
Dob: [redacted]
SS# [redacted]
Res: (9/13) [redacted] E 3rd St., Del Rio, TX
NO RELATIVES IN OKLAHOMA

O (A) **Paul [redacted] B[redacted]** – [Leased apt in which Alex A[redacted], Heather M., Stephanie K, and Kevin L partied 12/22–12/23. Confirms Alex and Heather stayed with him, Dec. '01. And that Stephanie and Kevin stayed w/him Jan '02. Can't recall specifics of 12/22/01. 1993 Grand Am – WHAT COLOR?]

Dob: [redacted] w/m
SS# [redacted]
Res: ('08–1/17) [redacted] E 78th Pl, Tulsa, OK
Res: (12/23/01) [redacted] S 105th E #4, Tulsa, OK (61st and Garnett) [South Port Apts.]
POE: ('15) Huddleston [redacted], [redacted] S 127th East Ave., Broken Arrow, OK 74011 (918-451-[redacted])
POE: [redacted] [redacted] (918-857-[redacted])

* **Benjamin** B[redacted] – [O'Neal friend/assoc convicted in robberies in which O'Neal was charged and acquitted. B[redacted] possibly committed robberies with Bonnie F[redacted](?). B[redacted] and O'Neal had "danced" together.]

Dob:

* **Melvin Ray** B[redacted] – [Cloud 9 [redacted] on 12/23/01. Knew of W O'Neal's contact w/police 12/23 re: alleged car break-ins. Melvin B normally escorted dancers/girls to their cars. Claims he did not see O'Neal between 1:55 a.m. and 2:15 a.m. on Cloud 9 property.]

Dob:
LKA: [redacted] Pryor Dr., Missouri City, Tx

O (C) **Eguana J B[redacted]** – [Friend of Rueda. Discussed shooting w/Rueda after the fact. No new facts? He told police he knew nothing about the actual crime. CAN HE CONFIRM RUEDA'S APPARENT CLAIM THAT

O'NEAL WASN'T THE SHOOTER – THAT THE PHYSICAL HE GAVE POLICE WAS ACCURATE?]

Dob: [redacted]
SS# [redacted]
Res: ('06–'13) [redacted] S Holmes Ave. #C, St Louis, Mo

/ **Jason** B[redacted] – [Reportedly with Charity O[redacted] in Bartlesville, OK night of 12/22/01. SEE Gobble Intvw.]

Dob:
RES: [redacted] N Wallace St., Sapulpa, OK (918-693-[redacted])

O (A) Misty Michelle B[redacted] NKA; [redacted] – [X-Dancer (?) Reportedly knows (along w/Stephanie K[redacted]) who robbed Bruce/Trapeze in Nov 2001, per Donna H[redacted]. On 12/22, loaned her car to Stephanie and Kevin L[redacted] for the evening. They at Alex A[redacted]'s apt that night. No knowledge of 12/23 robbery. Writes statement which appears to claim W O'Neal admitted committing the 11/14/01 robbery of Bruce C. Lived in Apt complex across (?) from Trapeze 12/01, per O'Neal. O'Neal swears he never laid a hand on B[redacted], nor threaten her. ID SPARKLES??? Any misgivings about Kevin L[redacted] and the murder? **ID Delila?**]

Dob: [redacted]
SS# [redacted]
Vehicle: Blue 1998 Pontiac Sunfire Ok LP: TPE-[redacted]
LKA: (12/23/01) [redacted] ~~S Birmingham Ave, Tulsa, OK~~
Res: (12/13–12/14) [redacted] Harrison St. Pawnee, OK 74058
Mom: Lynnda [redacted], [redacted] Denver, Pawnee, OK (918-762-[redacted])

Finding the Witness: The History of Database Searches

I have used web-based database searches to locate witnesses since their inception in the early 1990s. These were primarily Social Security number (SS#)-oriented databases, coupled with public records and sometimes not so public records (i.e., information from Credit Reports, known as "credit headers" was originally used in the mix of database searches before privacy laws began to catch up with this new technology). Federal privacy laws began restricting the types of raw data commercially collected and maintained. As technology and laws evolved, database wholesalers refined their data gathering and sorting, and the available ways (for users like me) to manipulate my search for specific data.

The number of ways data may be searched – the starting point – has probably advanced farthest, in this evolution of harvested data and database information. Advancements in the sorting and manipulation of data now allow for successful searches, requiring fewer specific identifiers. A person can now be identified and located using more anecdotal information (i.e., prior address, approximate age, known relatives, spouses, even associates).

Federal laws began restricting public access to our SS#s and dates of birth (DOBs) due to a series of high-profile stalking incidents in the late 1990s.

Following 9/11 (of 2001), these database searches remained SS#-driven, since that is still the most accurate identifier of people in the United States. However, these identifiers (DOB and SS#) were now offered as redacted information to all non-law enforcement database users. Eventually – post 9/11 – access to this "redacted" information became even more restricted depending on the requestor's status as an end user (civilian versus government/law enforcement versus commercial).

Currently, a legal reason for conducting a search (i.e., pertaining to a civil or criminal court case) must be documented before one may use the better SS#-driven database searches. A (State Bar) Law License or a state-issued Private Investigator license are two of the many credentials accepted by a reputable data wholesaler before they will share (sell) any identifying information. This wholesaler must request my legal purpose for each search and may randomly audit my searches to satisfy government oversight. (Other acceptable industries and credentials include insurance, banking, credit, real estate, etc.)

I use Accurint®, owned by LexisNexis®. I believe most data wholesalers rely on the same or similar raw data comprised of public records. How they market and price and package the user's access to this data creates the main differences between the more reputable database wholesalers. For instance, some may charge a monthly fee for blanket access, or a smaller "access" fee with an à la carte, pay-as-you-go search fee. One wholesaler's à la carte menu might be priced differently, or one wholesaler might offer different levels of information at different prices.

Mainly, I search individuals, for residential-history only – for $2 or less.

I ignore the online offers to search and conduct backgrounds on people with costs ranging from $10 to $50. (These offers often follow any search engine request for records of information on an individual.) Although not scams, these may be high-priced retail outlets who upsell you on information – costing them pennies – information which you don't need (i.e., Do they have a boat registered in Florida? Or a concealed carry permit in California?)

I won't offer a tutorial here on the best way to conduct database searches. Every service offers its own tutorial, and I recommend any novice to sit through one.

Years ago, I began characterizing these database searches as being like "reading tea leaves." I have never read tea leaves and really don't know what that cliché means. But it still seems to fit. When searching for witnesses, I won't always get a simple answer (i.e., current residence) to a simple query, especially with the more transient, less settled witnesses.

I have learned to experiment with the various databases and database tools available. I know to be creative and resourceful in searching for available data. I prefer a surgical, short list of probable residences, compared with a 30-page report of irrelevant data.

I look at these database searches as a large radar screen. Any routine lifestyle places a person somewhere on that radar screen, throughout their adult life. This is not Big Brother. This "radar screen" analogy simply documents our whereabouts based on public activity and public records.

These databases are composed of public records, not necessarily one's daily and personal activities. This collected data helps me determine where someone is living, or where they were most recently living. Just because I can probably find a witness (any witness actually), doesn't mean I can look into his banking practices or his educational background, or find out anything else about a person, beyond what he may share on social media. Conducting a database search just means I will probably be able to approach the right door, when I go out to contact that witness. That's all I want. That's all I need.

Finding the Witness: Pre-Database Searches

Before search engines like Google, there were libraries and reference books, the Dewey Decimal system and other tools used to conduct research.

Likewise, before database searches on the Internet, there were more primitive, albeit effective ways of locating people. I think understanding the older system and the older methods may help develop a better thought process using today's seemingly "automatic" tools.

During the 1980s, I was a news and general assignments reporter for the *Houston Chronicle*, and then the *Houston Post*. Reporters had to find people all the time. There were thick phone books – the White Pages – for residential listings. The names were in alphabetical order, with the specific street address and the home phone number (landline). Most listings used the first name only (Robert Shapiro), sometimes just initials were listed (J.B. Smith), and sometimes an entire name (James Patrick Sharp). (We were not afraid to let everyone know our phone number and where we lived.)

The phone book was not an absolute list, nor was it necessarily current. The telephone company published this phonebook once a year. By the time it arrived, some people had already moved.

For people who wanted more privacy, they could pay the phone company for a "non-published" number, meaning those people were not listed in the phone book, nor would the telephone operator (Dial: 4-1-1) provide that person's information. And for those who wanted only some privacy, there were "un-listed" numbers for people who were not listed in the phone book, but by calling 4-1-1 the operator would still provide their address and phone number.

"I'm looking for a James Sharp on Lawndale ..."

"In Houston, I have three Sharp residences on Lawndale, none of them are James."

"Do you have a Sharp Residence in the 2000 or 2100 block?"

"I have a J.P. Sharp at 2107 Lawndale."

"Yes, that number please. Thank you, operator."

"OK. You're welcome. Have a good day. Please hold for that number ...."

If I was looking for someone in Houston and I only knew the name (i.e., "Fred Jones" or "Maria Garcia"), without an address, I would be clearly out of luck. Even with an address, I might never find the right Fred Jones, or Maria Garcia. Not in the Houston phone book. The phone book represented about 90–95 percent of all the area's residences. This was before cell phones, but not before poverty, wealth, and privacy concerns. Some poor people simply did not have a home phone. Some people lived with someone else who had a phone, but it was only listed in that other person's name. If the "Fred Jones" I wanted fell into that 5–10 percent pool of people who had no phone, I could waste a lot of time looking in the large pool of people (95 percent of residents) who had phones and some level of phone listings, including F. Jones.

Reporters and other professions used another tool, which narrowed that 5–10 percent gap. For several decades, most large to mid-sized cities had *City Directories*, or some equivalent, which offered a "Criss-Cross Directory" and a "reverse phone number" search. With Houston's voluminous City Directory, I could search by street and house number and identify who was living at a specific address (2107 Lawndale = J.P. Sharp). In the back of the book, I could find a phone number from the long columns of sequential numbers and see who had been assigned that landline phone

(862-2972) = J.P. Sharp). This information had been gathered between 1 and 18 months earlier, but was still valuable.

As a reporter trying to locate a source, these tools were normally all I needed. Using both tools, I could normally "work the phones" and find my subject.

The next best source for locating people was the County Courthouse. The County Courthouse then, and now, continues to be where people register to vote, apply for a marriage license, file for divorce, get charged with misdemeanors and felonies and traffic violations. Various Courthouse clerks in various departments maintain lists of names, all public records. Anyone who owns personal property is on the tax rolls, so they can pay personal property taxes and renew their vehicle's state license plates.

Anyone who files a civil complaint, or is named in a lawsuit, has their name listed on the Court Docket. All deed records related to mortgage papers and other real property records are recorded in the Courthouse. There is a list of people named in tax liens, for being delinquent.

So that each person is properly identified (better than "Fred Jones"), these recorded names will likely include a current residence, and probably a middle name or middle initial, possibly an age, or a date of birth, maybe a phone number, maybe a state Driver's License number, maybe even a SS#. (Certain identifying numbers will probably be redacted for public viewing.) These are all public records.

The Courthouse is where the rich uncle filed his will and recorded the inventory of his estate, naming all of his nephews and nieces and maybe some cousins. Courthouse records exist of individuals who legally changed their name; individuals committed for mental health care; individuals named in protective orders related to stalking or domestic abuse; and individuals who filed their military discharge papers.

The Courthouse may be a place many people wish to avoid, but in terms of searching for people in the community – the Courthouse records represent a wide net. As reporters, we knew a wide net cast over the Courthouse could reach beyond Southwestern Bell's White Pages, in both substance and detail.

I knew if I could not find a person in the phone book, or somewhere in the Courthouse, that person was either homeless, or hiding, or lived somewhere else.

It is my understanding that these records (public records from the Courthouse) comprise much of the raw data today's database wholesalers gather and update throughout the year. These database wholesalers harvest this information electronically, allowing me to search by name or phone number or address, by city, by county, by state or zip code, until I find exactly who I am seeking. The more identifiers I know – such as LKAs, age, date of birth, SS#, driver's license number, relatives' names – the easier I can narrow my search.

That – I believe – is how today's database searches work.

Note to Reader

The following caveat means less and less with each passing year: if all I have is a name and a last known address from many years ago, the most accurate residential history data begins between 1985 and 1988. That's when our world (United States and beyond) began going "digital." During that time period in the late 1980s "records," kept in books and on index cards, began morphing into "digital" computerized data. This 1987 rule of thumb might change in the future, but the line between paper records and computerized data appears to be drawn about 1987.

Finding the Witness: Beginning the Database Search

When conducting database searches, my first step is to identify the pool (of people) I wish to search. By "pool" I mean the geographic location, the city, town, county, or even state, where I believe my witness lives or had once lived.

My second step is to be sure that I have fully identified the person I want to find. I must know *exactly* who I am looking for. That may sound overly simplistic, but I must know some distinctive or distinguishing fact about that person before I can find her.

If I am asked to find Anna Smith in Kansas City, Missouri, I don't know who I am looking for. If I conducted a web-based database search, I would at least need to know her approximate age. But being told she is "about 40ish" will not distinguish which of the several Anna Smiths I may find with a residential history in Kansas City.

If I knew that this Anna Smith had a local criminal record, I could search a court records index and maybe find an Anna Smith with a few misdemeanor convictions, with a YOB putting her age in her early fifties. But I would not know if that was the right Anna Smith.

Without an obvious identifier like a DOB, or SS#, or Mo DL#, I would not know *which* Anna Smith I sought. A very useful secondary identifier would be a last known address (LKA), or the name of a relative, like her sister or mother or father. A database search could identify members of a Smith family who lived at that LKA in the 1990s. I find that one of those Smiths is named Maria Smith, another is named Lillian. If I knew the mother's name might be Lillian, that would confirm that the Anna Smith I'm looking for belongs to this family, who lived at that address in the 1990s.

The database tells me Lillian Smith is now deceased. Lillian's relatives include a Maria A. Smith, now 53 years old.

A closer look at Maria A. Smith indicates her middle name is Anna. And her DOB matches the local court records of the Anna Smith with the three misdemeanor convictions. So, I now know those two "Anna Smiths" are one and the same person.

Being asked to find Anna Smith did not preclude the possibility that Anna was the name she goes by, and not her given name. Beling told anecdotally that this Anna Smith is about fortyish was apparently someone's guess, and not a documented identifier.

Finding an LKA from the 1990s was the key identifier, since that address was based on some documentation. Knowing the mother's name became helpful corroboration. All of which led to the very distinctive identity of Maria Anna Smith, born 53 years earlier, with a few misdemeanor convictions in Jackson County, Missouri, who formerly lived at that residence with her family, including her mom, Lillian Smith.

It cannot be overstated: Before I find someone, I need to know who I am looking for.

Looking for Sherri or Sherry or Sheryl or Cheryl WHO?

The following is from my People List in the Karl Fontenot Case:

F/ID **Sherry? Sheryl? Cheryl? (Aka: Shannon?) Kiel Aka: KEEL?** – [DEF WIT. Fontenot Alibi witness. Sez he was making out on couch with this woman at Janette's night of 4/28/84, until Karl passed out. Both woke up at 4 a.m. when a friend knocked on Karl's door. She drove a hideous orange station wagon. About 5'5", chunky, large breasts, red hair, no freckles.]

Dob: (1960–1968) [She was old enough to drive]
LKA: maybe Sherry D Kiel (dob: 10/xx/74) [redacted] Royal Ln, OKC, OK 73135 (or [redacted] Sylvester) (405-732-[redacted]) Moved to Tulsa, OK?
LKA: Sherry (Kiel) Wheeler) Dob: 8/xx/55 (NOT) [redacted] ~~Admiral Blvd, Tulsa, OK 74127)~~

I first began working on the Karl Fontenot case in 2012. Early on, I was given a list of witness names gathered by Oklahoma City University students with the Oklahoma Innocence Project. This witness list represented people who had reportedly attended a keg party in Ada, Oklahoma on April 28, 1984. One of those very important alibi witnesses was someone who reportedly had the name "Sherry Kiehl."

Initially, I thought I was looking for the same Sherry Kiel a previous investigator had once traced to Oklahoma City. I thought Ms. Kiel needed to be found again. Then I read notes indicating students had contacted that person (Sherry Kiel), and she adamantly claimed no knowledge of our client, the defendant in this case, and knew nothing about any keg party in Ada, Oklahoma, back in April of 1984.

Students and lawyers thought this woman was being uncooperative. They hoped I could approach her and gain her cooperation.

Then I asked the attorney how she knew this was the person at the party at 515 S Townsend, Ada, Oklahoma on April 28, 1984. I got a blank stare.

"Her name is Sherry Kiehl." A previous lawyer or his investigator had found her in an Oklahoma database search. She had the right name and approximately the right age with a residential history in Ada, Oklahoma.

There may not be two names with more potential spellings then Sherry (aka Cheryl, Sheryl, Cherie, Sharon, Sherie, Cher, Sherilyn, etc.) and Kiel (aka Kiehl, Keel, Kill, Kehl, etc.). And the spelling of the name only matters if Sherry/Cherie (sp?) is her given name, and not an informal moniker, or her true middle name.

The more I reviewed existing notes, the only absolute ID was that of a woman reportedly using a name with that phonetic spelling, who showed up at this party, with a person or persons unknown and allegedly spent some romantic time on a couch that night with our client.

Everything else was a guess; pure assumption. The "Sherry Kiel" whom students found was presumed to be the witness ... just ... because. I had to explain to the lead attorney that that *Sherry Kiehl was probably being honest when she denied knowledge of that keg party. That Sherry was likely unrelated to the witness they sought.*

When I was able to talk to the client during a prison visit, we talked about this witness. I asked questions which gained much more specific information. But like most of us who have been to a keg party, the client never asked the woman whom he was kissing on the couch to see her ID.

He only knew her by the name she gave: "Sherry Kiel." The spelling of her name was a phonetic guess. Karl was able to describe her physical appearance, which could help if we found another witness who knew anything about this "Sherry Kiel" person. He described her as "pretty, with red hair, no freckles, large breasts, slightly overweight, but not fat, and about his age or a little younger (18 to 22 in 1984)."

He was able to describe (not identify) two persons he saw with "Sherry Kiel" the next day – a man and a woman – both of whom seemed to know this person, "Sherry Kiel."

Just in case I still thought I could take anything for granted, several months later in this investigation I contacted a key witness on the west coast. This key witness, Bruce D., had attended that April 28, 1984 keg party. I knew his name and identifiers from a police report. Toward the end of my interview with Bruce, I asked if he knew another person from that party we were seeking – unsuccessfully – by the name of Bruce Self. He looked at me and smiled. "Bruce Self" was the name he had used and given to Karl that night, at that party. Bruce D. for whatever reason was not offering his true name to anyone at that party, so he made up the name "Bruce Self" – on the spot. That explained why we couldn't find Bruce Self, about the same age as the rest of the partiers, from any pool of Oklahoma residents we searched.

And no, Bruce could not help us identify "Sherry Kiehl."

So how do I find out if Sherry Kiel is Cheryl Kiehl's real name? I don't. Or I can't until I find someone else from that party who knew that person. And I didn't.

The odds of finding the wrong person when searching for a witness with a common name are always higher than I would guess. I have found the number of people with similar names and similar identifiers is almost illogical, until I start searching a database and see how many people about the same age share a common name in a medium-sized population pool. The more common the name, the greater the need for a fool-proof identifier (i.e., DOB, SS#, home address).

Of course, searching for a person with an uncommon name (like Grothaus), I can broaden my search, sometimes even statewide, with a good probability of identifying the right person. Knowing any additional identifiers – besides the name – will help confirm my findings.

While drafting this book, I came across a story in USA Today *about the projected benefit of palm scanners to be used commercially for quick, accurate identification in places like hospital maternity wards.*

An example was given in this article for this palm scanner's benefit in a hospital setting, where multiple patients may have the same name. The news article referred to a hospital system in the Houston area, which maintained a database of 3.5 million patients. That database included 2,488 women named "Maria Garcia." Of those named "Maria Garcia" in this database, "231 of them had the same date of birth." (I think that sounds statistically improbable, but that is what the article said.[1]

---

1 *USA Today*, November 25, 2012, reported by Brian Shane.

The next most important variable in my witness search phase involves the exactness of my People List information.

As with our search for "Sherry Kiel," it is important to recognize what is *known* versus what somebody has *speculated* about someone's name, or where that person lives or once lived.

To me, *factual information* is information documented by some sort of official record. *Anecdotal information* is information generally passed along, or "someone heard that ..." Either could be accurate – or inaccurate. But I prefer to go with factual, documented identifiers first. If it's anecdotal, the investigator needs to know that.

A police report identifying an address in Kansas City, Missouri is documentation. Police normally rely on some form of ID when identifying a witness in a report.

In a *trial transcript*, a witness may testify during a deposition given on the west coast that he "lived in Kansas City." Without a follow-up question for clarification, that could be the generic "Kansas City area." If the witness had been asked to state exactly where he lived, he might answer, "Overland Park, Kansas (a suburb of Kansas City, Missouri). People often confuse their suburban residence with the main metro area in which they live. Suddenly, that information transforms from anecdotal to factual.

In anecdotal terms, "about 30" might not be much help as the approximate age for someone with a common name. But it's better than no age at all. When I get an approximate age, I still go with +/– 5 years and I'm not surprised to find the witness is +/– 10 years off of someone's "best guess."

Random Attorney Call

While writing the original draft of this chapter – I kid you not – a lawyer called me late one Friday afternoon, asking for help in finding a witness in Lexington, Kentucky. "This is a really important mitigation witness. We need to talk to him this weekend."

She gave me the name: "Richard Stephenson ... born between 1970 and 1972 ... of Lexington, Kentucky." Then I started asking questions.

She wasn't sure of the spelling of his last name, or of his age, or if the person actually lived *in Lexington, Kentucky. I had to ask questions several different ways to convince the attorney that she did not know who her defense team was trying to locate. She was willing to send investigators out to find all individuals with that name in the Lexington area.*

I held off starting any database searches. I kept asking her what she knew about this witness, "Richard Stephenson."

She said her client (facing an execution date) was reluctant to identify this person. This witness had lived with the client and the client's aunt sometime during the client's high school years. She "thinks" the last name is "Ste-P-H-E-nson" and not "Ste-V-E-nson." The lawyer "thinks" this person might still live in Lexington, or nearby.

When told that searching for this person with that information was a waste of time, she insisted, "Just find anyone that fits that description. This is a really important witness."

I persisted with my questions. This attorney was not familiar with the ways and means to find witnesses. She finally agreed to tell me where the client had lived when he was in high school. I conducted a database search using that address. I learned the specific street name she gave me (Brown Street) did not exist in Lexington, Kentucky. I pressed the attorney again and convinced her to give me the aunt's name and SS#.

Using the aunt's full ID, including her SS#, my database search identified the residence where the aunt and this lawyer's client lived during his high school years. The actual street name where the aunt and nephew had lived was Brownstone Street, not Brown Street.

Around 1988, this witness (Richard Stephenson?) reportedly lived with the attorney's client and his mom in his aunt's house. The client had identified this person using the name Richard Stephenson. The attorney was guessing *that this important mitigation witness was about the same age as her client.*

I ignored the fact that this lawyer did not know who she was looking for, despite her insistence that she did. I continued asking several pointed questions until I learned that most of this identifying information was anecdotal (name) and presumption (age and current residence). Eventually I gained what was factual (the aunt's residence).

The database search identified an adult male, associated with the aunt's residence in 1987 – Richard Englehart, born in 1965. I was able to identify Richard, and provided his current address – not in Lexington, Kentucky, but in a different city and state. This apparently was "the very important mitigation witness" they needed to find that weekend.

The attorney was – surprised – to learn she might have been looking for the wrong person.

Database Search TIP #1

When trying to find younger witnesses (under age 30) I have found they may continue to use their parents' or grandparents' address as their official residence. I may find an extensive residential history for a younger, transient witness, all outdated locations, along with one long-standing or recurring residence. I may ask the database to search "occupants" of that recurring address, and I will often find several people with the same last name as my witness. I may find what appears to be two or more generations of this family, associated with that address. For lack of a better term, I call this my witness' "homestead" address.

I often find such a homestead address may be the long-time residence of an older family member, a grandparent, an uncle, or the parent. If I can't find a current residence for a young witness, I approach the homestead residence knowing I'm likely to encounter a big sister, an aunt, maybe a cousin, or a grandparent of the witness I wish to contact. Sometimes that's the best I can do. Sometimes, the witness I am seeking will answer the door.

Database Search TIP #2

An alternative to finding a homestead address for a young transient witness is not finding any current residential associations at all. I have come to expect that these missing witnesses are likely living with a friend or acquaintance, unknown to me. When the utilities, the lease, all the identifiable public records are in the roommate's name, or the girlfriend's or boyfriend's name, and my witness is just passing through, I won't be able to find them. If this witness never uses that temporary address on any document or public record, that witness remains "invisible" (or "off the radar."). That person will remain off the radar until he or she begins using that residence as their pseudo official residence, in their daily life.

Related is the fact that my database searches will lag one to three months before catching up with someone who recently moved. That's about how long it takes for the data to be collected, to begin "associating" my witness with their new address.

I have learned, from searching for others, if I ever wanted to hide out, exist off the database radar screen, I simply need to find a friend's couch for an extended period. But even then, all my LKAs would still be visible. And, at some point, every witness will need to use a current address to do something official, like renew a driver's license or register to vote, or secure a bond after last night's arrest.

The better I have become at "reading the tea leaves," the easier I have been able to determine, through database searches, if my witness is very transient, recently moved ("misplaced"), or consciously hiding.

One more caveat pertaining to identifying and finding witnesses: although rare, I have read police reports in which investigators misspelled the witness names in a homicide investigation. These happened to be critical witnesses. I know it can happen.

A database search of a person's last *known* address, if provided, is a good way to verify the spelling of a first name or a family name. However, if a witness is mentioned in passing, without identifiers ...

Missouri v. Lamar Johnson

While investigating the 1994 homicide of Marcus Boyd, and Lamar Johnson's innocence claim, my work was delayed for months while I tried to identify a witness described in police reports as "Christine Sherman, age 28." No address was noted in the police report.

"Christine" was a casual acquaintance and co-worker of another witness – Dawn B. – whom police had accurately identified in their interview report (... with name, age, residence). Police had interviewed Dawn B. and Christine S. together at St. Louis PD HQ.

Christine was on my "B" list of witnesses to contact.

When I contacted and interviewed Dawn, she could not help me with my attempts to identify her casual acquaintance. Dawn knew her as Christine; that was it. Nor did Dawn know exactly where "Christine" had lived before she stayed a few months with Dawn, 15 years earlier.

Police interviewed "Christine," because Christine was friends with Dawn, and because she knew the suspect (Lamar Johnson). The police report described an incriminating conversation "Christine" reportedly had with Lamar, about 20 hours before the shooting death of Marcus Boyd.

I could not find this witness.

In St. Louis, I did find and contact three women, all the right age, all named Chris, or Christy, or Christine Sherman. (In each case, Sherman had been their maiden name before getting married.). All three had lived on the south side of St. Louis at some point in their lives, not far from where Christine had lived temporarily with her friend Dawn in 1994. None of these women knew anything about this case, or what I was asking them about.

I was almost out of ideas.

I again contacted the one-time roommate, Dawn, and obtained a physical description of Christine from when Dawn last saw her in 1994. She described Christine as being 5′4″, 120 lbs, blonde hair, blue eyes, and about 28 years old.

I had considered that age might be a variable, given the report merely offered her age, not her DOB. Then I considered the accuracy of her name. "Sherman" can be spelled with two Rs or two Ns or an "A" instead of an "E." And I wondered if "Chris" could be "Kris."

I contacted the Missouri Motor Vehicle Dept. and, in a few minutes, I had identified "Kristine Sharman" living in a St. Louis suburb. Her height and weight, and her eyes and hair color matched. Her DOB was consistent with the age on the police report. I requested a copy of her DL photo, scanned it, and forwarded a digital copy to her former roommate. Dawn confirmed I had found the woman police interviewed in 1994 in the Marcus Boyd homicide case.

Both the first and last name had been misspelled in the police report.

After locating this witness, I shared the police report with her describing that interview. After reviewing and discussing that police report, she signed a statement affirming that police had fabricated their report. The police report claimed "Christine" and Lamar had discussed Marcus Boyd (in an incriminating way) prior to Boyd's murder.

Kristine's first reaction to my questions was, "Who is Lamar?" Her affidavit supported other affidavits I obtained, suggesting the police fabricated several witness reports describing incriminating statements reportedly made about Lamar, which the witnesses swore they did not say.

I also got lucky looking for another of my "B" witnesses in the Marcus Boyd homicide case. The police report described witness "E. N-I-E-ger," whose name, I learned, was actually spelled "E. N-E-I-ger." The report provided only his misspelled name, his age, and fortunately his 1994 residence. In that case, the database search helped me out.

I contacted witness E. Neiger. He also signed an affidavit affirming that police fabricated his police report, claiming Neiger had knowledge of animosity between Lamar Johnson and victim Marcus Boyd, when, in fact, Neiger said he knew nothing about those two individuals or their relationship.

From Neiger's affidavit:

> *I read through my interview in this police report describing what I told police, in which facts and information were attributed to me. My interview started on page 1, of CRN 94-166120. I was surprised to read several paragraphs of this police report, which attributed facts and observations to me, which I did not say, or facts I knew to be false, or facts about which I had no knowledge. I also noticed this police report had my last name misspelled as "Nieger." My name is correctly spelled: Neiger.*

Finding the Witness: When the Database Fails to Locate ... Other Sources for Locating Witnesses

Over the years, I have needed to locate witnesses who, for different reasons, were hiding or at least making some effort to stay *off the database radar*. Their reasons for hiding never had anything to do with the case I was reviewing. These people had every right to hide. And they were not hiding from me. Nevertheless, I needed to find them, contact them, give them a chance to offer up their recall of events for the sake of my client. Just because they were hiding from a bill collector, or a drug dealer, or an old relationship, that didn't reduce their relevance in my case. Several wrongfully convicted defendants would still be locked up, some executed, if I had simply stopped looking for someone I could not easily locate.

I have contacted witnesses in wrongful convictions who initially acted upset that I found them. After a few minutes discussing the situation, they expressed gratitude that I was looking into that case – a case which had always bothered them. The first few minutes of that contact, they were nothing but belligerent. By the end of the interview, they thanked me for my efforts. That is the nature of the business.

On those rare occasions when my database searches fail to locate my witness, or, after knocking on a few doors I realize this witness was just out there somewhere, off the grid – I take a step back. It's time to be creative, get resourceful, and return to basic records searches.

If I am sure I have this person identified but they appear to be "off the grid," they may be incarcerated.

Prison and Jail and Criminal Records

Sometimes, someone at the homestead residence claims that "Rashaad is locked up." Asked where, this relative may not know, just, "he got locked up last summer. Haven't seen him since...."

From experience, I know most families keep track of where their extended family members are incarcerated – some do not.

Many people cannot distinguish between county jail, state prison and federal prison, or some type of municipal incarceration. Is my witness awaiting trial, or is he convicted and serving his sentence? To persons outside the criminal justice system, "locked up" is locked up. While still at the homestead, I try to determine the jurisdiction, the crime, or the severity of the crime. That information can save time searching the right court records or searching through several jurisdictions for jail inmate websites. Most states provide a website for state prison or their Dept. of Corrections inmate searches (i.e., doc.mo.gov). A search of the Federal Bureau of Prisons (i.e., BOP.gov) requires the inmate's BOP# or an exact name match, and offers only an inmate's age, rather than a DOB for confirmation.

In the greater Kansas City area, a comment that "Rashaad is locked up" could mean he was sitting in one of six county jails, or two state prison systems, or in federal prison, or the federal holding facility in nearby Lansing, Kansas, or in one of a dozen municipal jails.

However, if I have no homestead residence to help with Rashaad's whereabouts, I must consider incarceration on my own as the next pool for me to explore while looking for my "missing" witness. I start checking state prison and local county jail websites, looking for Rashaad.

If that fails, I start searching online court records in the jurisdiction where my witness was last known to live. In jurisdictions where court records are accessible online, those records offer far less information than what's available by inspecting that case file in-person.

If I have time, if the courthouse is local, and the witness can't be found, that may be my next stop. Online, or in person, I search for any recently filed, or current, pending criminal charges.

If the case is pending, or has been recently disposed, that criminal court case file contains considerable personal information. That file will offer the defendant's emergency contacts, relatives' contact information, as well as the final judgment: dismissal, acquittal, conviction, sentencing, incarceration, or probation, including conditions of probation.

Finding the Witness: Searching Courthouse Records

Note to Reader

Most of you will not be familiar with the records available in a courthouse. I have discussed these records in general, but I thought you may find value in being offered a simple walk through of a typical county courthouse. These local government departments contain a wealth of Open and Public Records. These records describe the legal and sometimes illegal acts of community members. These records describe acts of commerce, items to be taxed, and records of events, recognized by our government. All of these records reflect the day-to-day ebb and flow of a civilized society.

I started searching courthouse records as a journalist long before I started criminal defense work. All Civil, Criminal, Probate, and Domestic Courts I have visited in the United States use the same or a similar index system. Before computers, all courts used large, hefty index books with an alpha index in the front half for Plaintiffs and in the back for Defendants. I would search KOMINSKY, JAKE under the Ks for plaintiff (civil), defendant (civil), and defendant (criminal). I would conduct the same search in the Probate index, the Domestic or Family Court index (if separate from Civil), and in the Deeds office for grantor/grantee (seller/buyer).

The time period covered by a court Index Book depended on the size and population of the county. An index book may represent one year, or several years, of activity.

Some rural county courthouses still use these large index books. If working on a habeas case, I may need to go back in time and request physical access to these books, depending on the time period of my case and the age of the witnesses I am researching.

Every court uses a "Party Index." Sometimes, court clerks have told me they only have a "judgment index." Not true. All courts (to my knowledge) maintain an alphabetical index of parties who have filed cases in their court, or an index of the parties who have been named in lawsuits in that court (civil or criminal). All courts maintain an index for their *Plaintiff* (the person filing, which is the State in criminal cases) and the *Defendant* (persons being filed against or charged in criminal cases). In every courthouse I have ever visited, that is how the clerks track these cases.

The courts in the United States, by statute, must maintain an accurate index of these cases, and an accurate record of the disposition of these cases. It bothers me when I hear people discussing court records as being "open records." Court records (the judicial branch) are generally not part of any state's open records laws. I consider court records to be more sacrosanct than say, police records, which seem to always be in the middle of any "open records" dispute.

Court records are intended to be an accurate record of the court's actions. The courts in the United States are always open to the public (with very rare exceptions), and the court records I seek are meant to "speak for the court."

Any courthouse search for a missing witness should include all recent civil or criminal cases naming that witness as a party. I have always found criminal and civil court case files to contain abundant and relevant information, for both background research and attempts to locate a person.

Long before the Internet, I spent many hours as a criminal defense investigator in the cramped and stuffy Harris County Courts' archives building in downtown Houston. I sometimes spent days at a time reviewing stacks of civil and criminal cases, researching witnesses for background or for identification and location. In those archives, I discovered what I called, "the good stuff" – readily available in those civil and criminal case files. I sometimes found valuable information written on a sticky note attached to the inside of the manila case folder. I might find that a court clerk wrote anecdotal information about a witness in the margins of a court document. These notes would never be found in a digital, online scan of the case file.

I believe that "good stuff" still exists in today's case files, in the courthouse, for anyone who takes the time to look.

I learned not to ignore older cases. Civil (and domestic) lawsuits may drag on for years. In ten-year-old cases, I have found recent, sometimes current, *garnishment* activity or some other court action, identifying a residence, or a place of employment (POE) for my missing witness.

In civil suits naming my missing witness, I am looking for individuals or businesses who had a commercial relationship with that witness. These parties are highly motivated to know where he lives or works. Looking through that case file allows me to "go to school" on their research.

In a criminal file, I may find accurate residential information listed in applications for a public defender, or in applications for a bail bondsman. The criminal courts, the probation officers, and the bonding agencies are highly motivated to know exactly where their defendant – my missing witness – lives and works. (This is how I have found my missing witness living with a friend.) If I am still lacking identifiers on my missing witness, a criminal file naming her as a defendant will provide me with an exact date of birth and other useful identifiers.

Some state courts have a separate index for *Domestic Cases*. The index for domestic cases may include divorce, paternity, child custody disputes, child-support issues, plus adult protective orders pertaining to stalking or spousal and adult abuse cases. Some jurisdictions may restrict public access to these files or restrict access to parts of the index protecting the privacy of victims or complainants. However, if my missing witness was recently accused of abuse or stalking, that protective order, if accessible, will be a rich source for location information.

An older divorce case naming my missing witness as a party may be worth my time to review. If the divorce involved child support or some other ongoing financial obligation or dispute, an older divorce case might still be active. I have found current residential and employment information in a 15-year-old divorce case, due to child-support issues.

Other locations to check in the courthouse are the court clerks who handle Traffic Offenses, Small Claims cases, and the smaller (by dollar amount) Civil Lawsuits. (Different states have different court structures for these lessor criminal and civil matters.) If I am simply trying to locate a missing witness, I will search any of these recent cases for useful, somewhat current information (i.e., a current traffic case may contain the handwritten police ticket).

Overall, a personal review of these civil and criminal and domestic case files, although tedious and time consuming, offers far richer information than any online database. A review of the court's paper file will likely include information not normally "harvested" by database wholesalers. These files contain an exclusive level of raw data.

I consider it an advantage that I spent so much time in courthouses before online access existed.

Currently, depending on the jurisdiction, the following records discussed here may be found on a county government website, or a state website, or, these records may *only* be available in person, at the courthouse.

Marriage Records

Marriage records are generally available at the county courthouse, either through the County Clerk's office, or the Recorder of Deeds' office. All marriage indexes I've seen use an alpha list for the groom, and an alpha list for the bride (by maiden name). Most states provide open-records access to both the marriage license and the marriage application (redacted), which provides valuable identifier information. Marriage records may be used to confirm one's age or DOB. Locating a woman's maiden name may confirm that she is the witness I am seeking.

(States' organization of records varies state to state. Some states allow or require marriage records searches only at the state level. Some states allow searches at both the state and local (County) level.)

Today's SS#-driven database searches are pretty good at cross-referencing married and maiden names since about 1985. But these database searches are not perfect. Reviewing the actual marriage records – especially for woman – can help identify and locate a female witness. In a habeas case, any woman married prior to 1985–87 might not be found in database searches if I only know her family name, or her maiden name.

If my witness was Joann Roberts, who graduated from high school in 1983, and possibly married before 1988, chances are I will not find her today by conducting a database search of "Joann Roberts." (Although I will find lots of other people named Joan and Joann Roberts.) It may help to review county marriage records for Joann Roberts, with an approximate YOB of 1965. If I find a record showing *Joann Lee Roberts* married *William Ray Jenkins* in 1986, I now have her DOB and full married name. I can now conduct a new database search for *Joann Lee (Roberts) Jenkins.*

Property Tax Records

The County Assessor enforces the tax rate and maintains an inventory of all property for taxing purposes. There are usually three, sometimes four, types of property tax indexes.

Each county generally has an index for *real property* (i.e., a house, raw land, or any rental property). This category represents "real property," or land-based property.

Depending on the state, the local tax assessor may maintain an index for everyone's "Personal Property," listing the owners of all motorized vehicles, boats, motorcycles, airplanes, jet skis, snowmobiles, or any other significant item the local or state government wants to tax.

The listing of these properties (both real and personal) should provide a physical address (the physical location of the property) and an address for the mailing of the tax bill. Either one might provide an address previously unknown to me. If I have a missing witness, it always helps to locate a different address for the tax bill, or a lake house (real property), or the location of a boat, or an airplane locker.

Rural counties may have a separate property tax index for mineral rights (i.e., the value of what might be underground, such as oil, gas, and minerals).

And some rural areas might have a separate tax index for livestock or agricultural equipment. Either of these indexes could identify locations of real property (farmhouse), or property deed records, which could lead to a previously unknown "tax address" for my missing witness.

Deed Records

Most county governments (varying from state to state) have a *Recorder of Deeds*, or some equivalent. Some states assign this task to the County Clerk. What is recorded in this office might also vary from state to state. Here is a list of what I commonly find in one or the other of those offices:

Deed records: A grantor/grantee (seller/buyer) index organizes all documents pertaining to the buying and selling of land. Those Deeds describe loans, collateral, liens, and lien releases. (Sometimes marriage records will be found in this same grantor/grantee index.)

Liens: This grantor/seller and grantee/buyer index lists liens recorded against persons and property. This list of liens probably includes state and federal tax liens and mechanic's liens, filed against a person or against a person's real property.

Assumed Name Companies: An individual might declare his ownership of a simple business using a "Doing Business As" (DBA), or an "Assumed Name Company" application. This DBA or company status might be filed with the County or with the Secretary of State.

Voter's Registration: The county voter's rolls have always been public records. They could contain current information not necessarily evident in the database searches. However, I feel most database searches use the raw data contained in Voter's Registration Records. The only question is how often this information is updated.

Occupational Records: Many states and local jurisdictions require various certifications before one can be employed in a certain profession or in operating a particular business. These records might also be maintained at City Hall, rather than the county government.

Examples of specific occupational license records might include barber, manicurist, beautician, physical therapist, etc. These occupations could stretch from the arcane "blacksmith" to the contemporary "tattooist."

Other categories which may require a specific license or some registration with a specific government department include: a Food Handler's License; an Alcohol Liquor Server License; or an Adult Entertainment Card.

Additionally, some states have a long list of professional and skilled occupations, which require some type of license or registration. These license applications may be registered with the Secretary of State. Often, I will find, online, some variation of a "Professional License Registry" at the state level.

Uniform Commercial Code (UCC): These are generally commercial liens reflecting commercial loans or a commercial line of credit. UCCs are sometimes filed at the county level, and sometimes at the state level.

Military Discharge Papers: These are generally filed in the county where the individual is physically discharged from his or her branch of the military. My understanding is that military personnel are free to file these papers in whatever county they want, as long as they remember where they are filed. I was not in the military. I suspect these papers may become more valuable later in life, if documentation of military service becomes an issue.

Corporations: Corporate papers are normally filed at the state level with the Secretary of State; however, I have seen some states where paperwork for the corporation, including Limited Liability Company (LLC) and Assumed Name Companies (DBAs for Doing Business As), are filed at the county level. These corporate papers will provide an official address for both the Incorporators or Organizers, or Owners, as well as the entities' Registered Agent.

U.S. District Court Records

Located in a different courthouse from state courts, these federal court files are also valuable to review in person, whenever possible.

Federal court records are generally accessible online through an excellent court records system known as PACER (Public Access to Court Electronic Records) at https://pacer.login.uscourts.gov/.

This website allows me to search nationwide, or by state, or by federal district, for parties named in civil, or criminal, or bankruptcy cases. The public has access to the docket sheet for these cases. Access to court documents and filings will vary from case to case. Older files (pre-1990) will likely require a personal visit.

I can cross-reference online federal criminal court records with federal BOP inmate information, found on the Bureau of Prisons website. With a little extra research, I can identify the federal court district in which a federal inmate was convicted, based on the inmate's BOP ID#. When I search for a witness in federal prison, if I only know their name and where they were convicted (i.e., St. Louis, Nashville, Miami, etc.), I can still ID and locate that inmate using the code built into their BOP ID#.

For instance, Jamal Shakir, convicted in the Middle District of Tennessee, has BOP# #####-075. Kurt Wallace, convicted in the Eastern Missouri District, has BOP# #####-044.

These federal court records are always part of any "wide net" search either for witness location or witness background research.

Driver's License Records

I keep thinking a state document such as a driver's license, which most of us only renew or update every four to six years, is not very helpful in locating current information on a witness. I'm constantly surprised at how often the state driver's license data helps me locate a missing witness.

Between 1995 and 2003, states began placing restrictions on public access to driver's license information. As a result, most (probably all) states limit public access to un-redacted driver's license data. Only certain licensed individuals and businesses sworn to uphold privacy laws, with a legal reason to request this information, are eligible to access these records. It is cumbersome, but apparently a necessary restriction. Those eligible must create an account with the state agency responsible for driver's license data. Any factfinder in criminal defense will want legal access to this pool of public record data.

In most (or all) states, the same department which issues the driver's license issues the non-driver's state ID. Both provide similar ID information, and both require the same level of security clearance, before I may obtain this information.

At one time, I had that security clearance for both Kansas and Missouri drivers' and motor vehicle records. In other states, in the past, I have relied on someone local who had security clearance for that state's drivers' and motor vehicle records.

More recently, my security clearance (as a licensed PI) allows me to gather this unofficial information through a database, essentially a wholesaler of the state's drivers' and motor vehicle records.

A Word About Dealing with Records Clerks ...

I have dealt with hundreds of courthouse clerks over the years, in scores of courthouses in a majority of our 50 states. As a rule, these women and men are very knowledgeable of what records they control and how those records are organized and maintained. They are generally competent, like librarians, and helpful like true public servants. Most clerks spend many years in their job, growing more professional and knowledgeable each year.

With the proliferation of online records, it's possible that personal requests for public records in local court houses have decreased. That is both good and bad news. These clerks now deal with fewer records requests. But they tell me they now see fewer professionals who know how to search records.

Every court clerk I've ever met is happy to help a novice understand their system.

I have always treated these court clerks and records clerks with great respect. As part of my respectful attitude, I always try to learn their system in their jurisdiction, if I am able. That always helps my research, on their turf, go smoothly.

Also, I consider it my job to know the Open Records laws in whatever state I am working. Sometimes a clerk who is poorly trained might be unwilling to grant access to what should be a public record. By knowing the law, I may be able to make my case and gain access to a needed record without causing a scene.

When confronted with "No," I have always found knowing the open records laws got me to a supervisor more easily, with better results – as long as I knew the law and found a supervisor who agreed.

Chapter 9

The Witness Interview (Part 1): Approaching the Witness

In 1993, I interviewed my first significant witness in a wrongful conviction. Her clear recall strongly contradicted the state's theory. Before that witness, I had interviewed hundreds of witnesses to hundreds of events – as a journalist. Yet, the significance of interviewing Wilma Amos felt different, because it was different. That interview and the affidavit she signed two days later helped save the life of Death Row inmate Gary Graham – for the time being.

Some of my cohorts in the criminal defense business suggested that defendant Gary Graham and witness Wilma Amos represented a "career case" – a once in a lifetime opportunity to right a wrong.

Not so.

The next year, in the fall of 1994, I was asked to work on the criminal defense of a teenage boy, charged in Houston with Capital Murder. The state was threatening to certify him as an adult, making him eligible for the Death Penalty.

The case was *Texas v. Leroy P.* (fictional name).

Note to Reader

The following passage includes my actual notes with summaries from the original case file. For privacy concerns, I used all fictitious names.

The defense attorney created a detailed, 25-page memo based on his review of the police reports and evidence introduced at the preliminary hearing. After reading his memo and meeting with the defense attorney, I understood the following:

DOI: 10.4324/9781003543299-9

From the Police Investigation

At about 8:30 p.m. on June 29, 1994, the surviving witness, Josh Boyd, and his friend Billy Jenks (both white males), drove to the 6800 block of Ridgeway in a southeast Houston subdivision. They intended to purchase crack cocaine. Boyd drove his Ford pickup truck. Jenks sat in the passenger seat. After stopping at the curb in the 6800 block, Boyd told police he saw three black males approach the passenger side of the truck and then attempt to rob his friend Jenks. As Boyd started to pull away, one of the black males shot Jenks one time in his right arm. Boyd drove to a business less than a mile away, where police responded and found Jenks dead in the passenger seat, from the gunshot wound.

Boyd told police he did not normally buy drugs on this street. This drug purchase was his friend's idea. Boyd did not know the three Black males who approached the passenger side of the vehicle. Boyd described one of the three as having a gold tooth. He could describe the barrel of the gun. But otherwise, Boyd could only confirm seeing, "three young Black male teenagers."

Police spoke to two young neighborhood boys, ages 11 and 8, who witnessed parts of the shooting. The police report claims they saw "several" older boys who were apparently involved in the shooting of the man in the pickup truck. The two boys could not ID any of the other boys, but knew these other boys hung out at the neighborhood basketball court a few blocks away. These two young witnesses did not know any names, nor could they describe the clothing of any of the older boys.

Two days after the shooting, on July 1, police found a witness who reportedly overheard a conversation the day before, about the shooting. This witness reportedly heard Leroy P. describe the shooting and the shooter in a way which the witness thought incriminated Leroy P., or at least suggested Leroy was a witness.

Leroy P. was arrested July 1, 1994 and charged with Capital Murder.

Based on police reports, Leroy told police that on June 29, he was walking along Ridgeway with an individual he knew only as "Duke." Leroy and Duke were with another teen who became the shooter. The three of them walked up to a pickup truck, which had stopped at the curb. Leroy told police that "Duke" would confirm that this other teen, the shooter – on his own – approached the truck, asked for money, and then spontaneously shot the victim.

Houston homicide detectives began looking for "Duke," the teenager who reportedly witnessed the fatal shooting of Boyd.

A few days later, police found and interviewed Derek "Duke" Williams, a 15-year-old from that neighborhood. Sometime later, Williams reportedly told the grand jury he saw Leroy P. standing with the shooter alongside the pickup truck, participating in the robbery/shooting of Billy Jenks.

That was the sum total of what I knew about this case and the witness claims of Derek "Duke" Williams. Leroy P., age 16, was being held without bond, which is typical for Capital Murder defendants awaiting trial. I knew that Leroy's version of events (per his attorney and per police reports) was different from the official narrative attributed to Derek "Duke" Williams.

On the afternoon of November 13, 1994, I knocked on Duke Williams' apartment door about 4 p.m., hoping he would be home from school, and that his mom might also be there.

When Derek Williams opened the door, I confirmed he was "Duke" before introducing myself as an investigator with Leroy P.'s criminal defense team. Derek was 15 years old. He looked nervous, maybe scared. He certainly looked overwhelmed, as any 15-year-old would be, dealing with adults – strangers – imposing their will on him. I asked about his mother and, fortunately, his mom was inside the apartment. I invited her outside to join us. I discovered during this interview that the mom was hearing about a lot of this for the first time.

My written report from this witness interview:

Derek "Duke" Williams (born 10/xx/79) was interviewed on tape 11/13/94 in front of his apartment at 6xxx Waltrip, Houston, Tx in the presence of his mother, Katherine Williams (born 5/xx/63). They have no phone.

Derek and his mother appeared nervous but were willing to cooperate. He recalled police coming to his residence sometime in July asking him about the shooting at Plainview and Ridgeway on 6/29/94. "I said I didn't know nothing," he said, he told police, and the police left.

Derek said he was over on Plainview all day on 6/29/94 hanging out with "Daleon and Leroy and the two Darryl's and La Duc." Derek said he left the Plainview area about 8:30 p.m. just prior to the shooting. When Derek left, he had no reason to suspect anything was about to happen, he said. The reason he left was because his sister's current boyfriend, Kirk J, came by and said to Duke (Derek), "let's go home." Derek said he had just decided to walk home (about 4 blocks) with his sister's boyfriend, Kirk.

Derek said he does not recall hearing anyone, especially Daleon or Leroy, claiming that they "were going to jack somebody," earlier that day. Derek doesn't remember seeing Daleon or anyone with a gun and has no recollection of any conversation or boasts or threats that anybody was going to get robbed or shot.

Derek identified the "Duke" who was at the shooting with Daleon and Leroy and Darryl Robinson. as being "La Duc Gravois" who lives on Dawnview Rd.

About a month after the police first stopped by and asked Derek about this shooting, the police came back. Derek said the police detectives did not know his name, just his nickname, "Duke." The police said Leroy P. had told them where they could find him (Derek). The police told Derek they wanted him to testify before the Grand Jury about what he saw of the shooting (on 6/29/94).

"If I didn't admit I was there, they said they would lock me up for lying to the Grand Jury," Derek said. "They said if you don't testify, they would have me certified as an adult and charge me with being an accessory to murder."

Before they left Derek's apartment to go to the police station to be interviewed, the police asked Derek, "Are you gonna run?" Derek said when he did not respond, they handcuffed him and put him in the car.

Derek said that both he and his mother tried to explain to the police that they had the wrong "DUKE," and that Derek did not witness any shooting on 6/29/94. Derek and his mother said the police ignored this information and claimed that Derek was lying and that he had been present at the shooting.

"Police wanted me to say, I saw Daleon kill the dude," Derek said. "They (the police) said I was standing 50 feet away on Plainview (when the shooting occurred)."

The police drew up a statement, which Derek said he signed "Because I was scared … I tried to tell them about the other DUKE," he said.

Derek does not recall the names of any police or investigators involved in these interviews.

"They (police) told me, 'You was there – now tell the truth,'" Derek said. "I tried to tell the truth and tell them I wasn't there, but they wouldn't let me."

This investigator (Grothaus) attempted to gain more specifics about what the police told Derek, that he had witnessed at this shooting. Derek was reluctant to describe more specifics or could not recall what exactly they told him. Then Derek volunteered that he had heard about Mister's (aka: Leroy P.) involvement in the shooting. He was asked about what he had heard happened at the shooting.

Derek said he had heard afterwards that Daleon had run up to the pickup truck to talk to those guys. Then Mister (Leroy) ran up to the truck, pretending to have some crack/rocks to sell and told the guys in the truck, "I got the crack." Daleon then pulled his gun, said, "give me your money." Daleon then shot the passenger and grabbed his money.

The validity of this story was not questioned. But Derek was asked where he had heard this story … who had told him that that is what happened? Derek whispered, "the police."

"I heard that from the police," Derek said. "That's where I got most all of my information (about the shooting)."

Derek was asked about when he got this information about the shooting, which he admittedly did not witness. "I got most of that story right before I went in (to testify before the grand jury). He (the homicide investigator) was telling me what had happened at the shooting."

Derek was asked if he repeated that story to the Grand Jury and he said that he did, that that was what the police had told him had happened.

DJG

A few days later, I located and interviewed "La Duc," the real "Duke," who actually witnessed the June 29, 1994 shooting of Jenks. I interviewed La Duc in the presence of his stepfather in their living room. By simply asking what happened, I gained La Duc's version of events, which was consistent with Duke's honest understanding of events and identical to Leroy P.'s version, which Leroy had initially offered to police.

La Duc told me how he and Leroy followed Daleon as he walked up to the truck. La Duc and Leroy then saw Daleon suddenly pull out a revolver and shoot the man in the pickup truck. Both La Duc and Leroy and another witness began running from the pickup truck before the shot was fired. They had no prior knowledge and no reason to believe that Daleon was going to rob and shoot this man.

In March of 1995, Leroy P.'s defense attorney, George "Mac" Secrest Jr. wrote to tell me that the State of Texas "ultimately dismissed the case (against Leroy P.) … but not before (the police) accused me of bribing a witness."

Witness Apprehension – the Unannounced Cold Call …

After knocking on strangers' doors for 40 years – first as a journalist, then as a criminal defense investigator – I have strong feelings about how to do this successfully.

When I approach a stranger, hoping to resolve a wrongful conviction, a few thoughts come to mind.

First, I understand that this witness won't be sitting around, waiting for me. Anecdotally, I believe most, maybe almost all, of the witnesses I have contacted in habeas work would rather I hadn't knocked on their door – preferring that I had never contacted them.

So, I quickly learned to lose my ego. I understood that I was a stranger to them as they were to me. I was probably in an unfamiliar neighborhood, standing on this stranger's front porch. The person living there did not care who I was, my station in life, or my honorable objectives in this case. Depending on the witness, she likely did not know or care about my client.

What mostly concerned this person, and rightly so, is how her day was going. She may be thinking about her job, her problems, her bills, her kids, her boyfriend's car problems, any number of things which did not include me or my client.

It was my job to introduce myself in a way which got past this apprehension, past this personal drama, and elevated my client's situation to at least a temporary priority. Knowing this stranger – this potential witness – had no obligation, no moral imperative, to cooperate.

All of which led me to approach these witnesses, "hat-in-hand," asking for a favor, without ego.

Second, I realized that it mattered what this person inside sees when he looks out, after being startled by a knock on his door. We now live in a world where people won't answer a phone call from an unknown number. Most people prefer a text message to a ringing phone. A knock on the door … it better be important.

I expect my witness to look outside at a stranger on her doorstep and ask herself, "is it safe for me to open my door?" I know that I mean no harm. But I must convey that in silence and convey that instantly. If my mere presence sets off alarms inside the head of the person I hope to interview, this potential witness may not hear a word I say – not until I convince her she is safe.

That's why I assume I have mere seconds to convince this person that I mean no harm. I have maybe 20 seconds to introduce myself, my credentials, and my reason for standing there. My dress and appearance are all I have to initially gain a stranger's trust, long enough to hear me out.

The flip side is also true. The wrong appearance can sabotage this one chance.

Looking for a Friend ...

Just as the right mindset helps me approach a wrongful conviction case objectively, I know the right mindset helps me approach witnesses, successfully.

Years ago, I was trying to describe to an old friend from college what I did for a living. I remember acknowledging that I had somehow become comfortable approaching strangers, gaining their trust at their front door, then engaging them in conversation about a years-old criminal case they had long forgotten. She astutely pointed out what I was *really* doing – I was going out, looking for friends.

Without realizing it, that had become my mindset. Working in the field, some days I'd feel lucky if I found one "friend." Some days I found lots of "friends." That simple mindset of "looking for a friend" – someone who will take the time to help me understand *what happened* years ago – helps me approach a stranger's door with the right attitude.

Whether the witness knows nothing about this case or knows a lot, whether I spend five minutes or an hour with this person – if I make a new friend, if he at least sees me as a friendly person, it was a successful contact. Otherwise, why would this stranger talk to me? I believe that's the right attitude for a successful interview.

A third thing I learned is to expect this person to have a life. Before knocking on her door, I may have spent six months reviewing this criminal case, which may be a wrongful conviction. This stranger, this eyewitness from 15 years earlier, is not losing sleep over this case – she is not even thinking about this case.

There could be a dozen reasons why she has forgotten about the crime she witnessed. I must expect that and understand it is my job to work around her schedule and her current distractions. I expect her to be busy. If she has time to talk to me, great. I ask politely for her time and if she agrees, I let my appreciation show.

This work requires respect, which is why having the "right mindset" is critical. If I have any hope of gaining this stranger's trust and cooperation, I must appear respectful and genuine. If I foolishly think I can bluff this witness with false sincerity, well ... good luck.

Remember, I am standing outside *his* front door. I *need* his trust. Being honest and genuine is the only way I know of to gain that trust.

Another way I have seen false sincerity fail is *pandering*. Maybe I'm splitting hairs here. There may be a fine line between being polite and respectful during a cold call, and pandering.

But I have seen pandering. And I think it offends the potential witness.

I suggest the best antidote to pandering might be professionalism.

I do not find "making friends" and "acting professional" to be mutually exclusive.

When approaching strangers (i.e., witnesses), I find "acting professional" helps me navigate many tricky, sensitive, unpredictable, emotion-laden witness interviews.

Being professional allows me to ask sensitive questions in a straightforward manner. No doubt, being a journalist taught me the art of acting professional during interviews. But acting professional is a learnable skill. Professionalism helps me cut to the chase when it's time. Acting professional allows me to steer the interview in a productive direction at just the right time. Professional, to me, means non-judgmental. Acting professional demands a solid *poker face*. I cannot show my emotions and expect a witness to continue sharing deep, dark secrets. "OMG" is not professional.

While acting professional, I often find myself in the role of *confidant*, like the Rabbi, or the Imam, or the Priest, listening to a confession.

The only other reaction I have found appropriate in a witness interview is compassion – in limited doses.

One time I was asked to work with a professional mitigation investigator on a case in Wichita Falls, Texas. The first day we worked together in the field, I let her take the lead, conducting our witness cold calls.

When the first witness opened her door to us, this investigator skipped over any greeting or introduction and began apologizing to this witness. The investigator apologized for our interruption of her day, she apologized for our presence on her porch, and apologized for our desire to review this crime, which had torn apart their community years earlier. Her excessive apologies continued with each witness contact that day, costing us access to otherwise approachable witnesses.

Her apologetic, pandering demeanor only added to the skepticism and reluctance to cooperate, these witnesses were already feeling. Her apologies even made me *uncomfortable, which is hard to do.*

The (In-Person) Cold Call Recommended …

I guess I didn't explain why I am standing on a stranger's porch in the first place. Why not use my cellphone? I could call that witness from where I was more comfortable – at my desk ready to take notes? I could call when it was most convenient for me.

Remember my *thoughts* one, two, and three, about witnesses having a life, bills, kids, work, personal problems, things to do? And the part about gaining a stranger's trust. And the fact that this witness may not know or care about my client, or the crime I have been reviewing for months. If this potential witness thinks about this crime at all, he probably thinks the police already took care of it: "The system works ... The guy got convicted ... They must have had plenty of evidence ... Case closed."

If I called that stranger on the phone, I could expect this to happen (if he even answers):

Who are you?
I don't have time right now.
I have a lot to do.
I can't remember that far back.
This is not a good time.
I've got to get going ... I need to pick up my kids ... I'm heading out to work ... can you call back some other time?

Or his response could be much, much worse: "I don't have anything to say... I don't want to get involved, so I'd rather not talk to you about this again ... ever. Don't call back (click)."

And I still haven't made eye contact.

Maybe phone conversations between business associates, family members, lovers, can be productive. Phone calls between strangers – unless I am making a dinner reservation – often fall short of a productive conversation.

To clarify: due to geography and budget constraints, I have probably conducted a hundred or more witness interviews by phone. It *is* possible for two strangers, during a phone call, to exchange meaningful information.

But the most productive phone interviews of a witness will never be as effective as a personal, face-to-face contact – if I can pull it off. My best phone interview with a significant witness still required a personal, follow-up interview. A good phone interview, rather than replace an in-person interview, often confirms the need for a face-to-face interview.

Following a face-to-face interview, it is much easier (and productive) to follow-up with a phone conversation. Some level of trust has been established. A *connection* has been made. The witness *knows* who I am.

The Witness Answers the Door ... Now What?

Much of this may be intuitive – *common sense* material.

However, I have seen so many well-educated and accomplished people, so many good-hearted and well-intentioned people, stumble all over themselves trying to approach a stranger about a 20-year-old homicide. There must be a lot about this task that is not so intuitive.

I was working with a new student/intern with the Oklahoma Innocence Project, one day. We were approaching a reluctant witness. This witness, at her front door, asked the student why this group was questioning who had shot her son (who survived) 12 years earlier.

The student wasn't ready for that question: "That man (convicted of shooting her son) wrote us a letter claiming his innocence. It is our civic duty to review this case."

Note to Reader

Wrong answer.

That student was no stranger to pressure or stress. Prior to college, she had seen combat with the US Army in Afghanistan. This mother's son had survived being shot years earlier. Contacting her was a sensitive and stressful event.

I saw another student forget her own name, when introducing herself at the front door of a potential witness, transposing the witness' name with her own.

The learning curve for this necessary task is steep.

My idea of how to approach a stranger at her front door, unannounced:

I dress business casual. I do not dress up or down for the neighborhoods I'll be visiting. I dress business casual – period.

I ring the doorbell or knock on the door, loud enough to be heard, but showing respect and restraint. The physical knock actually telegraphs my temperament. I stand several steps away from the door, holding my business card in both hands.

The door opens.

"Hi … Ms. Wilson? … my name is Dan Grothaus. I'm a private investigator. I am working with attorney Sean O'Brien (Or … a group, a school, an innocence project) and we are looking into the homicides of George Bryant and Oscar Bridges over on Monroe back in 1996. Ricky Kidd was convicted of that crime, and we are trying to determine if the state got it right.

"I'm wondering, if you have a minute, if I could ask you a question about some things you saw that day?"

I think most of us who have done this will agree, unannounced witness contacts can be stressful. I am approaching a stranger in an unfamiliar environment. She might hold the key to my client's freedom. She may, instead, offer evidence confirming my client's guilt.

I can only *hope* she will talk to me.

Every witness cold call I have ever made is a dive into the unknown.

It is reasonable to expect this process to be stressful. Over time, with experience, it may become less stressful – maybe.

Again, having the right mindset helps.

And it always helps that I am prepared, because that's about all I can control.

I must know exactly who this witness is and why I wish to talk to this person. I must be able to explain quickly and succinctly why I am standing at her door.

Oklahoma v. Willard O'Neal

I worked with student Tiffany Gobble on Willard O'Neal's case in the field for a couple of years. We both worked under the attorney and Oklahoma Innocence Project Director, Prof. Tiffany Murphy. Student Tiffany Gobble became very adept at approaching witnesses. She will also confirm the stress involved in that work. Here is an example of a cold call we made on a witness in Willard O'Neal's case:

TG: *Hi, I'm Tiffany Gobble, I'm a student with the Oklahoma Innocence Project. We are reviewing the 2001 homicide of Bruce Chamberlain, the man shot outside the Trapeze Lounge. Do you remember that?*

Witness: *Oh yes. That poor guy. I knew his family. They caught that fella who did it didn't they?*

TG: *Well, they did catch someone. We are reviewing the case to make sure they got it right. A man was convicted. We are going back over the case to make sure they convicted the right person. I was hoping I could ask you a few questions about what you recall from that night.*

Tiffany had learned to immediately introduce herself and state the reason why she was standing on this man's porch. The man's response told Tiffany he was willing to engage in a discussion of the case.

Because that's our next task – engage this witness in our investigation of the investigation.

Many witnesses will claim they can't help:

I'm afraid I don't know anything that can help you.
I didn't see much.
I'm sure I've forgotten everything about that night.
That was a chapter in my life that I'd rather not revisit.
That was such a long time ago, how do you expect to find out anything now?
Oh, I'm sure the police got it right, they wouldn't convict someone if they didn't have evidence ... would they?

Many witnesses don't realize the significance of what they know. An important witness might know nothing about the crime itself but have critical knowledge about another witness. If a person is willing, I prefer to cut right to my reason for being there. A witness at his front door might not have much patience – or time. I tell this stranger/witness exactly what aspect of this case I wish to ask about.

"I know you weren't at the Trapeze Lounge the night Bruce was killed – at least I don't think you were there that night, based on police reports – but did you know Charity, one of the waitresses who worked there back then?"

We want to walk this witness back in time to the year Bruce Chamberlain was killed outside his business. We aren't sure if we know the names of all the people who worked at the club that night. (We only knew what we found in police reports). So, Tiffany asked him what waitresses he remembered. I threw out the names of some customers to help him think back to December of 2001, and his times at the Trapeze Lounge. I asked him if he knew, or how well he knew, the victim, Bruce, the owner of the club.

When we engage the witness in our investigation, get him talking about the Trapeze Lounge, get him thinking about some of the people he knew from that Lounge, from that time, maybe other memories will surface. At this point, I wanted to keep the witness talking: what he knew about the victim, if he knew a witness, if he recalled the day or the time he first heard the news about that tragic crime. As long as he is talking and thinking about that incident, he might recall something else about "Charity," the waitress, or something relevant to this crime.

This witness did not help us directly determine *what happened*. But this witness knew the waitress, Charity. We understood Charity to be the main source police used to convict Willard O'Neal. We already had reason to suspect Charity's story wasn't entirely truthful.

Eventually, we learned that this witness knew things about Charity and her boyfriend that the police didn't know and had not investigated.

Obviously, some witnesses are easier to engage than others. Once I learn a witness has knowledge about a significant aspect of a case, I let him know I find that information very helpful. Most witnesses are thrilled to think they know something helpful. Who doesn't like to be appreciated?

Without sharing too much, I am always willing to play on a witness' curiosity. I may tap into their sense of humor. I call out and compliment them on their sense of fairness. All along, I am assessing this witness for credibility issues. I do that by letting them talk … and talk and talk. Eventually, this witness will make a statement about something I know, or about something three other witnesses have told me. His statement is either accurate and truthful, or not.

With this witness, by knowing the case, knowing the names of the night club's employees and patrons, we were able to share information (names), which prompted his sharing. This witness added to our information and greatly expanded our knowledge of these individuals (i.e., employees, customers, other witnesses).

When interviewing a witness, I never go into the state's theory, or the defense theory, or any alternate theories. This is never the time to retry a case, unless the witness just wants to talk about the trial or the case. If that happens, I let the witness do all the talking.

That way, my job remains simple. All my questions are about *what happened*. Only with this witness Tiffany and I interviewed, our questions were about the people who had given police their version of *what happened*. Their version, it turned out, led to Willard O'Neal's wrongful conviction. This witness answered a lot of questions about the people who falsely claimed to know *what happened*. And he did most of the talking ... once Tiffany Gobble got him engaged.

The Witness: Why Didn't You Call First? This Is Not a Good Time

"Why didn't you call first?"

That's a fair question. I am always ready to answer, calmly.

But, first, let me explain. Meeting a witness face to face is the best way to establish trust and gain a candid conversation. Making that contact unannounced is my best chance to gain their cooperation.

I consider showing up at a person's front door to be a sign of respect. I consider this witness to be so important that a personal visit is warranted. That's also my mindset. I believe that. Seldom will I lead with that reason for my visit. But I will let that mindset show through.

Knowing it is on me to gain this stranger's trust as quickly as possible, I now have a unique opportunity to do just that.

Certainly, I apologize for the imposition (... realizing the only way to approach someone is to approach someone). I explain to the witness (truthfully) that I was in their neighborhood and believe they may be a valuable witness in my investigation of this case. There are several witnesses I hope to approach and interview that day, so, I could easily come back at a more convenient time. If I sense further explanation might help, I suggest that "discussing this case in person" is considered the best practice (i.e., being professional).

From experience, I understand that no matter how offended this witness might claim to be, he will probably make time to answer, "a few questions," as long as I act professional and respectful of his time. Probably 95 percent of my cold-call attempts result in a completed interview, right there, on the spot – even if I need to apologize and explain why I've just shown up unannounced, on their doorstep.

And no matter what they might say about being surprised and slightly offended by the intrusion, this witness is far more likely to discuss this case, face to face, during a cold call, than talk to a stranger (me) over the phone. It's true that a cooperative witness might benefit from a scheduled appointment – giving him time to reflect on this 20-year-old crime. But I never know who is cooperative until my first unannounced visit. And the recall of any witness, willing to engage in conversation during an unannounced visit, will likely catch up, in time. Some witnesses might need a second visit, or a follow-up interview by phone. A phone call interview is now possible, after this face-to-face visit established some trust and familiarity.

It is also true that many witnesses – stressed out by the crime they witnessed or stressed by any involvement in the process – might panic if they had three days to anticipate a scheduled meeting with an investigator. The unannounced approach avoids that stress – for the witness.

Now, there is one more possible scenario during a cold call when the witness asks why I didn't call first. Some witnesses simply want to control the situation. I say, let 'em. They may refuse to talk at that time, under those circumstances. I must quickly determine if their reluctance calls for my "Hail Mary question" (see below), or a scheduled appointment.

If I sense this witness just needs to control the situation, I take a step back and allow him to call the shots, set the time, the date, the place, whatever is reasonable. I let him know he can absolutely pick a time convenient for him, and I will accommodate. Once this witness realizes he can dictate the terms, he may be more likely to cooperate. (I also leave my card with him and ask for his phone number in case something comes up.)

One alternative I will try to avoid at all costs is the scheduled phone call. If the witness asks me to call her later that afternoon, I will instead, try to schedule a convenient face-to-face meeting later that day or the next day. The farther into the future this person tries to set up a visit, the more likely she is trying to create an appointment she has no intention of keeping. When I sense that, I usually pull out my "Hail Mary question" (again, see below).

I also understand that these personality traits, these quirks, these various levels of cooperation, have very little to do with the potential value of what that witness may know. I have reluctantly accommodated controlling witnesses, who it turned out, had breath-taking, game-changing, valuable facts to offer. I have also accommodated control freaks who, I later learned, knew nothing – really nothing – about the crime.

The Witness Answers the Door … Listens to My Introduction … and Begins to Close the Door. Now What?

It's going to happen. Over the years, I've stopped worrying about what the witness might say or do. I'm mostly concerned that a witness might not say anything.

As a journalist, I hated "no comment." I never let that stop me. I always found someone else who *would* comment, sometimes to the chagrin of the "no-comment" official.

But I'm no longer a journalist, and these aren't government officials. These are witnesses that I need to engage to find out *what happened*. These are witnesses who might help confirm a wrongful conviction.

It has always been my policy that once a potential witness asks me to leave their property, once they declare they do not want to talk to me, they don't want to discuss this case, I'm done. I leave. I can't return, at least not directly. I have no authority. Beyond a final plea, I have never challenged a stranger's refusal to cooperate.

Confronting a witness will only lead to problems for that investigation. Even the suggestion or allegation that I was "harassing a witness" can scuttle a habeas investigation.

So, what can I do if the witness starts to close the door as I'm finishing my 15-second introduction?

Any time I approach a potential fact witness, I always have what I call a "Hail Mary question" ready to ask.

In this example, I've read the police reports and completed my Murder Memo. This witness – based on the police report of her interview – was standing nearby when she heard shots, looked up, and saw a late-model sedan speeding away from the scene. It's unclear from the report how many people she saw in the car. It's even unclear if she saw the actual shooting. The original defense team never contacted her.

The state charged and convicted a man with an alibi, who drove a ten-year-old, crème-colored 4-door Oldsmobile.

Two other witnesses I had already interviewed saw the shooters flee in a dark-colored, four-door sedan. The alternate suspect drove a dark blue Honda Accord.

From the police reports, I noticed a pattern of witness interviews where the description of the car seen fleeing the crime scene appeared to have been "influenced" by police or not mentioned at all.

At this woman's front door, I had already introduced myself as an investigator with the Midwest Innocence Project and explained that we were reviewing the 1998 shooting death of Christian Byrd outside his house on Michigan Ave.

As this witness began closing her door, claiming she didn't want to get involved, I blurt out my "Hail Mary question": "It's unclear in the police report. After you heard gun shots, did you see a car drive away?"

I was asking for a simple yes or no. Either answer called for a follow-up question. She answered "Yes."

Calmly, I asked, "Do you recall the color of the car, was it light or dark?" I was asking for another one-word answer.

She said, "Dark."

Again, calmly, I stated, "The police report claims you saw the shooter flee in an Oldsmobile. Do you recall seeing a white Oldsmobile involved in that shooting?"

Her front door is still open, but only about 3 inches. I can't see her face. I haven't even identified this person. I'm still hoping this is the witness identified in the police report, who I traced to this address.

Out of the darkness, behind the closed screen door, she said, "I heard shots and looked out my window. I saw two men getting into a dark-colored Honda and drive away, south on Michigan, then the car turned right on 59th St. That's what I told police."

Over the years, I've experienced this same scenario dozens of times. I have interviewed many a witness through a partially open door for five minutes, sometimes more than 30 minutes. I continue asking non-threatening questions in a calm, non-threatening way. The witness keeps answering.

I slowly weave my dilemma into the conversation. The witness learns that I am looking at police reports, apparently containing false, or ambiguous, information about the assailants, attributed to this witness. In simple terms, I'm looking at a case where the driver of a crème-colored Oldsmobile, who has a good alibi, was convicted of this homicide, apparently committed by the driver or occupants of a dark-colored Honda. The witness starts to understand.

But this witness still doesn't want to get involved. She doesn't ask, but I can guess what she is probably thinking. I'm careful not to suggest that this witness will need to get involved sometime in the future. I don't mention that she may be asked to walk into court some day and tell a judge what she just told me. That's a conversation for another day.

But I just gained some valuable facts from an important fact witness. I gained that information by being calm and professional and assertive. And I believe the key was having that one question ready to go as the door was closing: "After you heard gunshots, did you see a car drive away?"

And, at this stage, I still don't know if that witness was reluctant to get involved, or just reluctant to trust the stranger on her front porch.

Approaching a Witness: Avoid the Agenda ...

Normally, I look forward to every assignment I'm given. Not just because I'm a professional, but because every potential innocence investigation gives me an opportunity to discover *what happened* and possibly learn something no one else has yet discovered.

As a journalist, I had the same attitude. Each new assignment was a new adventure. Working as a reporter in Houston, I learned that "fact really is stranger than fiction." No matter how dark or bizarre the story, nothing was more compelling – to me – than finding out "what really happened." Telling the story was a secondary challenge.

But, occasionally, in criminal defense work, I have been asked to conduct an interview, or pursue an investigation, which made me uncomfortable. I'm thinking of one assignment from several years ago. I found myself pushing that attorney's request to the side. For some reason, her request was creating a strange sense of trepidation.

It took me a while to figure out why her request, and others like it, caused my concern.

Turns out, in each of these cases, the lawyer was asking me to "prove something." In this particular habeas case, the lawyer wanted me to confirm that a group of health care workers had collectively lied about what they heard the client say one day, while incarcerated. As in each of these other troublesome assignments, the lawyer had a theory. And she wanted me to prove that theory. I was being asked to "build a case?" The lawyer had an agenda.

As a reporter in Houston, the only time I did not enjoy my work was the rare occasion when an editor asked me to look into a story, and then he described what he expected me to find. I recall one *Houston Post* editor had already written the headline for the Sunday feature he wanted me to research. All I had to do was find and write the story, which matched his headline.

That's not how good journalism – or any good investigation – works.

In this troublesome habeas assignment, the attorney had asked me to prove that two professionals – one in corrections and one in psychotherapy – had lied about an outburst they attributed to our client. The state had interpreted this outburst as an incriminating admission.

The fact that this "admission" had been made, years earlier, by a traumatized juvenile on the one-month anniversary of his mother's death, was ignored.

This 15-year-old woke up early one morning to the smell of smoke. He raced through their small home and found his mother, dead on her bedroom floor, covered with bedding ablaze. Confused and stunned, he ran to a neighbor's house to ask for help and grab their garden hose, hoping it would reach into his mom's bedroom. The next few hours were chaotic. The Sheriff arrived. The 15-year-old boy was taken away in handcuffs. That afternoon in the Sheriff's office, a bogus "Lie Detector Machine"[1] was used as "proof," confirming that the boy had killed his mom.

Rather than being asked to find out *what happened* that day, one month later, I was asked to "prove" these women, and their associates, had lied at the boy's trial. (We already had compelling physical evidence, suggesting our client was innocent.)

A year earlier, I was told, law students had approached these same witnesses. These witnesses reportedly refused to discuss this case with the students. The attorney told me *what* she wanted me to gain from these witnesses, four women who had already expressed their reluctance to cooperate.

The lawyer told me she believed these witnesses were lying. And the lawyer was sure (i.e., she had a hunch), based on rumors, that one of the witnesses had been pressured by the state to change her initial recall of those events and the client's outburst. Based on the client's version of events, the lawyer believed these witnesses were lying. Of course, proof of that would certainly help his case.

This lawyer did not want to deal with the false admission of a vulnerable 15-year-old, made under incredible duress. She was not interested in documenting these ideal conditions for a false admission. Instead, she wanted me to "get them to admit they were lying."

Before I set out on this assignment, I took a step back and created a mini-*Incident Memo*. Based on police reports and written witness statements, my Incident Memo (like my Murder Memos) described the *who, what, when, where* of the alleged incident. I summarized the witness statements and arranged them in their investigative sequence. That exercise allowed me to change my mindset from the lawyer's request: "... prove they lied" – to my own assignment: "find out *what happened.*"

Once I created my new assignment (and my new mindset), it became easier to approach these witnesses objectively and gain their confidence. During my unannounced visits, each of the witnesses cooperated fully – once they understood I was not there to challenge them or question what they thought they heard. I showed them their handwritten statements from the date of the incident. I told them I was simply there to confirm these reports and see what additional information they might offer. And they offered a lot.

1 In this case, the juvenile suspect was wired to a computer and given a Voice Stress Analysis test. He was then told that the computer confirmed he was lying and that he had, in fact, killed his mother.

If their reports (and testimony) had been embellished or falsified in any way, I'm sure at least one of the four would have volunteered that fact – as part of "what happened."

Each of the four witnesses who heard the client's outburst was willing to candidly share their recall of that day. None of these witnesses took this boy's outburst as an admission, or *proof* of his guilt. But they all knew what they heard, and they heard the words described in their reports. All four told the same story, and their stories matched up consistently with their statements given 15 years earlier.

As a bonus, each witness added significant and consistent evidence regarding the video camera system and the protocol for retaining and storing the daily security tapes, at that state facility, from that time. This was relevant, considering the state had "misplaced" the security tapes from *that* facility for *that* day. The absence of security tapes from that day, documenting an incident described in several written incident reports – raised red flags.

From my interview reports, the habeas team learned *what happened* on that day. Each of these witnesses agreed to cooperate in the future. The False Confession Expert would need these witnesses' recall to gain the context of this outburst and the juvenile's underlying mental state. The expert would need these witnesses' observations to describe what happens when a vulnerable, traumatized juvenile – hours after discovering his mom's body ablaze – is told by the Sheriff that the computer he is wired to (i.e., Voice Stress Analysis) *proves* he killed his mother.

That is part of what happened. And, one month later, this teenager was overheard repeating what the adult authorities had told him. That too, is what happened.

I'm pretty sure the reason the students were not able to gain the cooperation of these witnesses a year earlier had a lot to do with their approach, and their mindset. The lawyer/law professor had apparently told her students that these witnesses must have lied, and it was their job to prove it.

Final Thoughts: Honesty versus Deception

> Let your cunning lie in your lack of cunning.
>
> – *Baltasar Gracian (a seventeenth-century Jesuit philosopher)*

Early in my criminal defense investigative career, some defense lawyers and other private investigators suggested *deception* was a necessary tool in this business. Later, while working with students involved in various innocence project investigations, I noticed a tendency for some students to also think that deception was necessary to gain the truth. As if they were pretending to be TV detectives, and thought their role was to trick people into telling the truth.

I will admit, on some very rare occasion, a ruse and a tape recorder might gain information from someone who was otherwise determined to lie about what they saw, or what they knew.

However, after conducting investigations for the defense in more than 100 murder cases, I still haven't seen any evidence gained through deception used in court. I have testified as to what a witness told me (absent any ruse), which contradicted what that witness had previously told the court. But I have never gained any useful evidence or information, by deception, which was later used in court.

The problem is getting the ruse into court as evidence.

If I am trying to prove a person is a liar, I've found plenty of effective strategies, resulting in real evidence – that are trial ready.

In *Missouri v. Lamar Johnson*, a crucial state's witness was a "jailhouse snitch." William Mock claimed to have heard incriminating statements made by Lamar Johnson and others in a holding cell. We were able to challenge whether it was physically possible that Mock had heard any statements. We were able to establish Mock's prior roles in other cases as a jailhouse snitch. We were able to document his lengthy criminal history, either not known or, if known, not shared by the state.

As important, I had gained from my investigation and interviews several affidavits signed by immediate family and close associates of William Mock, all swearing he was a dishonest person who should never be trusted in a courtroom to tell the truth about anything. I found no one who knew William Mock, who thought he could be truthful. None of those interviews involved a ruse.

In *Missouri v. Greg Breeden*, I was asked to investigate the veracity of a jailhouse snitch who was the state's key witness. I gained helpful affidavits from this person's mom, his dad, and his ex-wife. I then interviewed the local Sheriff in his rural hometown who was very familiar with this person, from multiple arrests, over the years. The Sheriff also signed an affidavit, swearing that this witness against defendant Breeden could not be trusted to tell the truth – ever – about anything. No ruse was necessary. The Capital Murder charges against Breeden were dismissed before trial.

So, as tempting, or enticing, or sexy as it may sound to some, after 35 years, I am still waiting for that case, or that situation, or that witness where deception was the only way to find out *what happened*. I'm not saying there is *never* a reason to use deception, I just haven't found one yet.

For Students: Three's a Crowd? ...

Once I approached a witness in South Carolina with two lawyers (a man and a woman). I was with my client's lawyer who had invited a co-defendant's lawyer to tag along. That did not go well.

Working in the field with Jennifer, my client's attorney, we were a perfect pair. When we knocked on a stranger's door, we were outwardly friendly, professional, and non-threatening. We never failed to engage our witnesses.

During this unannounced witness visit in South Carolina, the other attorney (a loud, pushy male) had promised to stay in the background, stand behind us, and listen quietly as we spoke to this potential witness.

After the woman opened her door and listened to my introduction, attorney #2 jumped in, began asking pointed questions, and then challenged her answers. This poor woman never opened her door more than ten inches. This second attorney's approach would have failed even if he had been alone. As a threesome, we never had a chance. Jennifer and I could not overcome the other attorney's brash behavior. Not surprisingly, the witness declined to answer any more questions, told us to never return, and closed her door.

If an intrusive knock on a stranger's door creates anxiety, what happens when the witness opens her door and sees several strangers standing there? Is she feeling friendly and talkative? Maybe not so much. I think the old cliché "three's a crowd" applies here.

For students trying to gain experience, working on a wrongful conviction case, this may be tricky, but I strongly suggest the witness be approached by only two students, not three, not four, or more. And no matter what the gender of the witness, I strongly suggest the student teams be male/female.

Note to Reader

I'm using "gender" here as how you present. Biology doesn't matter here. Only the perception of this perspective witness matters.

A team of male Homicide Detectives can pair up because they have badges and credentials. They can quickly and easily establish their credibility. Two male students may not be able do that, not as easily.

And homicide detectives aren't asking for a "favor." They have authority.

If any of this sounds petty, or even sexist, please remember there are three people to consider in this dynamic, and in this order:

- the client/defendant who may be innocent
- the prospective witness
- the investigator (i.e., the student, or students, and their supervisor/instructor).

The students' main objective should be to approach this witness in a way that maximizes his willingness to cooperate. One way to do that is to approach this stranger/witness in the least threatening way possible.

I understand from experience that students can be engaging, based solely on their youth and enthusiasm. But not all students, not all witnesses, and not all cases are the same. I'm suggesting general rules here.

Certainly, one unknown male on the front porch isn't necessarily threatening, depending on his appearance, his dress, his age, his demeanor, his posture. I honestly believe all these things matter ... if a stranger appears at my door, asking for ... what? My time? I will decide in seconds whether I want to engage.

If the stranger knocking on my door is a female, I (a man) will probably perceive a lesser threat, depending – to a lesser extent – on her dress, appearance, age, demeanor, and posture.

If there are two strangers contacting a witness (which I recommend for students or any group of novices), I believe two women will create the least threatening appearance. The next least threatening would be a male/female duo. Two unknown males on a stranger's porch could create some anxiety to some people. Can that anxiety be overcome in 15 seconds of conversation? Maybe – as long as these two men (students) appear professional, confident, and deferential.

If there must be three or more individuals contacting witnesses, I make the following suggestion:

> Let one person, and only one person, do all the talking. At least until the comfort level of this witness is palpable.

Always an exception: On a case, in St. Charles, Missouri, I went out with sets of two and three male law students, making cold calls on witnesses for a Midwest Innocence Project case. We engaged with all of our witnesses, mainly because two of the male students were visibly young, non-threatening, collegiate-looking, and our witnesses were all males only a few years older than the students. I made sure only one male student stood at the door knocking while the other two, or three, stood several steps back, off the front porch.

Once, as a precaution, I had the third student sit in the car parked at the curb. As soon as our witness stepped out and agreed to talk on his front porch, the third student ambled up and joined in the conversation. By then, the witness had become comfortable with the first two students and me and easily engaged with all of us, offering his recollections of the crime and our client.

Two of these witness interviews proved critical in our assessment of that client's innocence claim.

Note to Reader

I wrote my first draft of this chapter long before Stand-Your-Ground issues became real and topical in the United States. However, I had these concerns long before innocents (like me) faced occasional hostilities at a stranger's front door. Years ago, anticipating people's anxiety, I began the practice of keeping my business card in both hands, after knocking on a door, so that both of my hands remained visible to anyone looking out at me.

I have (almost) always worked alone. I have never owned or carried a handgun.

The only other rule of thumb for me is to never approach a stranger's door past sunset, or anytime in darkness, or before 9 a.m.

I never knowingly approach an alternate suspect, unless they are incarcerated.

Beginning as a reporter in Houston, I have always been hyperaware of my surroundings, especially in unfamiliar neighborhoods. I learned not to confuse poverty and impoverished neighborhoods with unsafe conditions. That said, I avoid isolated and abandoned properties, normally found in impoverished neighborhoods.

Beyond that, it would be impossible for me to gauge safety concerns in general, for neighborhoods, situations, and dynamics unknown. No situation is the same.

Chapter 10

The Witness Interview (Part 2): The Interview and the Report

In Nashville, Tennessee, I believe a wrongful conviction occurred in the brazen shooting of a young man in front of dozens of witnesses who were leaving a high-school graduation. I was asked to assist the defense – pretrial – as the criminal defense investigator.

Based on police reports, many of the crime scene facts in this case were well documented in terms of *what*, *when*, and *where*. When contacting the eyewitnesses, I felt free to provide certain uncontested facts, so all they had to think about was where they were standing when they heard gunshots, and what did they see of the actual shooting.

The prosecutor had charged one man with this shooting. Based on police interview reports, most of the nearby witnesses could not identify the shooter. Only one teenage girl at the scene identified the defendant as the shooter. (In this case it was relevant that the teenage witness was White, and the defendant, the victim, and all other witnesses were Black.)

As with any chaotic crime scene, lots of witnesses recalled slightly different facts and individuals and movements. One investigative theory pursued by the police suggested relatives of the shooter may have accompanied or assisted the shooter. That theory did not match this defendant.

On my People List, a woman not related by blood, but familiar with the alleged shooter's family, was also a potential eyewitness. She had been interviewed by police and was unable to help them ID the shooter.

(For various reasons, I have fictionalized these names.)

I had already contacted several eyewitnesses. During my initial contact with this eyewitness (Faye Young), and after gaining her cooperation, she confirmed her attendance at the graduation, two years earlier.

As with all these witnesses, I avoided suggesting any contested facts, nor did I identify the alleged shooter. I started by asking Faye where she sat during the graduation. (Having visited the graduation site, a large indoor college sports center, I shared photos of the venue.) Faye pointed out where she sat during the ceremonies, on the upper-level bleachers. She was there to see her nephew graduate.

DOI: 10.4324/9781003543299-10

I saw Faye relax as she described the non-traumatic events of that day. That was a happy occasion, a fun time, a family event.

Now that she was (mentally) back in time at the graduation ceremony, I asked her how she left the arena, what path she took. I then asked what the next thing was she recalled happening that day. With that question, her visceral reaction told me we had hit a wall. Faye literally and figuratively walked back into a bad memory. I had asked her to describe her steps leading to the shooting homicide, which had unfolded right in front of her.

From my report of that interview:

Ms. Y. easily recalled that she was on the third step up from the lobby floor when the shots were fired to her right. She saw that the shooter, was the same young black male who had just "bumped by us" further up the stairs.

She later clarified that the shooter "touched or bumped me" as he rushed by her down the stairs, moments before the shooting. Ms. Y. is 5′4″. She said this person was "a little taller than me." She described his body weight as "not big or medium." She said his body weight was difficult to guess, but he wasn't big and bulky.

Ms. Y. saw that the man who was shot was inside the door, and then went outside the door after he was shot. (The door on the west side of the lobby.) She saw that the shooter then turned and ran toward her left – toward the exit doors to the east.

Ms. Y. said all the people in that immediate area of the shooting immediately spread out in all directions.

Ms. Y. said she never saw the person's face from the front, (the shooter) who brushed by her. She saw him from the side, and the back. She was pretty sure this shooter had on a white shirt, with bright horizontal stripes, "yellow and orange ..." She thinks he was wearing a short-sleeved polo shirt.

Ms. Y. said she only saw one person who she thought was involved in this shooting. She said the victim was standing just inside the first glass door to her right, as she came down the stairs. "Shooter was not with anyone when he passed us (Ms. Y. and her family). He was by himself."

Ms. Y. still can recall the loudness of the "pow, pow, pow." This was followed by hollering and screaming.

Asked, Ms. Y. said it appeared to her that "all the young guys at the graduation had dreads." (This was relevant because this was a descriptive used to ID the shooter.)

With the police on June 30, Ms. Y. recalled being shown one photo spread. She did not ID either of these men as being the shooter. She said the police did not suggest anyone or suggest that the shooter was possibly in that set of photo spreads.

Ms. Y. said she probably could not ID the shooter at this time but thinks she could still ID the shirt because the colors were so brilliant. (The colors she kept repeating were yellow and orange.) "If they had video of people leaving the building, I could still ID the person wearing that shirt. It was that distinctive."

Ms. Y. initialed a diagram showing her on the third step up, on the west side (shooter's side) of the middle handrail. The diagram placed the shooter just to her right on the main floor, and the victim further to her right, in front of the column and the first glass door.

At no time did I mention the defendant's name. She never asked whom I represented. I had explained to her that I was a federal court-appointed investigator working for the defense, representing the individual who had been charged with this shooting. I did not want to influence her by naming the suspect. I wasn't sure if she knew the shooter, or knew the suspect, nor did I know if an objective ID of the shooter by this witness was still possible.

I initially shared with Ms. Y. some uncontested information about the shooting so she could more easily recall that traumatic event.

A few days later, I returned to Faye's house, hoping to speak to her daughter. I felt I had already gained her clear recall of the crime.

My report from that second meeting with Ms. Y.:

On December 18, Gladys (the daughter) was not home. During small talk with Faye Y., I mentioned the name, [redacted], as being the suspect in this shooting. At that point, Ms. Y.'s jaw dropped, and her eyes opened wide. She was clearly, sincerely, astonished to hear that anyone thinks [redacted] was the shooter she saw that day at the high-school graduation.

Ms. Y. said she knew [redacted], had known him since he was a little boy. She knows his mom and his grandmother, who just passed away. They (Faye Y. and Jasmine) are not friends. Ms. Y. clarified that she and Jasmine grew up in the projects together, and she knows Jasmine's friends, like she knows lots of other women from the projects and their children. Jasmine and Faye are 14 months apart in age.

Ms. Y. became very emotional in her disbelief that [redacted] had been charged with this shooting. Ms. Y. was right there, and knew that the shooter, the person who brushed by her on the stairs, was not [redacted]. It was a person she did not know. Ms. Y. said she would have ID'd [redacted] if he had been the shooter. She recalled seeing his picture on the photo spread she was shown and simply passed on [redacted] because he was not the shooter. She did not mention that to the police, and the police did not ask her specifically about [redacted] being the shooter. If they had, she said, she would have told them that the shooter was definitely not [redacted].

Asked if she would testify to that, I saw Ms. Y. become scared and nervous. She thought she might be willing to testify but would like some help (she requested a female attorney), although she said she was comfortable with me.

Ms. Y. agreed to sign the following declaration:

I, Faye Y., hereby state the following facts:

On [redacted], I attended [redacted] High School graduation at [redacted] campus. After graduation I was walking down the stairs to the lobby when a young man rushed by me. Moments later, while I was on the third step from the lobby floor, I saw this young man shoot another man in front of the first glass door.

I just learned today that the man charged with this shooting is [redacted]. I know [redacted] and [redacted] was not the shooter on [redacted] in [redacted]

Signed 12/18/[redacted]
Faye Y.

Interviewing the Fact Witness ...

So, I am standing on this stranger's front porch. I have introduced myself and explained why I am standing there, and this witness remains willing to talk. Maybe she just leaves the door open inviting my first questions, or maybe she invites me into her living room and asks me to sit down.

I understand this person to be a "fact witness." Let the interview begin.

At this point I need to *know* the case, all the facts, know the crime scene, and know all that this witness has previously claimed to be true. Every hour I have spent reviewing this case may pay off with this witness.

This is not a deposition. I want to engage this person in conversation about this crime. I am friendly and professional, with the mindset that I am there hoping to make a friend. Because I know this case so well, I can start a conversation about these events. I can relax and "think on my feet," as I would in any conversation about a familiar subject. My preparation allows me to be ready and able to ask my next question based on her last answer. I don't need a list of questions, or a script.

The more relaxed I am, the more relaxed and candid this conversation will go. The more relaxed the setting, the more agreeable this witness may be, trying to remember this event. The more knowledgeable I am of the crime scene, the more relaxed I will appear, discussing the crime.

Friendships are often based on common ground and shared experiences. My knowledge of this crime is vicarious, but heavy on detail. My knowledge may be enough to establish some common ground and shared experience with this person. Many times, I have seen my knowledge of the crime help me engage the witness into recalling their personal knowledge of the same event. My goal is to help her relax. That alone may help her grasp the greatest detail from her memory.

One key is for me to let her talk. It is generally understood (or it should be) that our best friends are the ones who let us talk. No one likes to be asked about a shared event, then be interrupted by the other person's recollections. No one.

In my mind, I really am in her living room, hoping to establish a friendship, however fleeting.

To clarify: a fact witness, to me, is any witness with first-hand knowledge of facts relevant to guilt or innocence. An eyewitness, for instance, is a fact witness who actually witnessed (saw or heard) at least part of the crime.

A fact witness may also be someone who has first-hand knowledge of what someone said or did before or after the crime, which may be relevant to guilt or innocence.

Most fact witnesses will recall the crime and the crime scene (or the alibi or their witness contacts) at least in general terms. They may be hazy on various details. The day of the week may not be as important as the event itself. The time of the event may only be important to my investigation, if the actual time of the crime remains unknown. Details about the crime, maybe where the crime occurred, may be known or still unknown, at this point. (The state's theory, which led to a wrongful conviction, may have speculated on some parts of *what happened*.)

To what extent can this fact witness fill in those gaps?

A witness might need some help remembering elements of the crime or need some assistance with established facts about the event. How much help should I offer? Is it wrong for me to suggest what might have happened, or when, or where it happened? What information can I offer, without being suggestive?

After 35 years' experience with roughly 100 cases, I can say definitively, no crimes, no crime scenes, no witness recollections are the same.

As I learn the crime scene – before ever contacting a fact witness – I mentally inventory what I consider to be uncontested facts about the crime. Sometimes this is an easy list to create. Sometimes the list of unknowns – or contested facts – is far greater than the state wants to admit. Sometimes the state will base its theory on *assumed* facts. Prosecutors have been known to create the logic to support their assumptions at trial, much like a magician creates an illusion.

A consensus of witness comments indicating shots were heard around 10 p.m. ("just as the TV news was coming on …"), and a documented string of calls to 9-1-1 ("shots fired …") beginning at 10:02 p.m., would suggest the *time of the shooting* is uncontested; unless additional evidence suggests the victim found in the alley might have been shot hours earlier, meaning the shots heard about 10 p.m. could be irrelevant to this crime. I try to never assume anything.

In Karl Fontenot's case (the 1984 abduction and murder of convenience store clerk Donna Denice Haraway in Ada, Oklahoma), an anecdotal eyewitness statement claimed the young woman he saw leaving the store with a young man about her age, acted casual. They were "arm in arm." Police showed this witness at the scene the driver's license photo of the missing store clerk and asked if the woman he saw could have been the store clerk. "I guess it could have been her, now that I think about it …"

That witness statement, "I guess it could have been her …," became uncontested evidence of the actual abduction of the store clerk, which immediately led to the suspect ID, the suspect vehicle, the time of the abduction, the entire case.

Not included in the report were facts that the witness was sitting in his truck about 50 feet from the entrance, that he had only a side view of the woman for three seconds, that it was dark, with backlight streaming out of the store's glass door, under overhead neon lighting from the gas pumps 30 feet beyond the entrance. Besides, he really wasn't paying much attention to this young man and woman as he watched them get into the passenger side of a pickup truck and drive off. He thought they appeared to be laughing and talking.

Yet, this: "could have been her ...," which established the time of the abduction and identity of the suspect, went uncontested through two trials, and a couple of habeas appeals. This assumption led to two convictions, and a Death Sentence (reduced to Life Without Parole). This assumption went uncontested for nearly three decades – until the Oklahoma Innocence Project investigation identified, located, and contacted witnesses who had walked into the same store earlier that same night and found it empty. No clerk.

So, when I say I make a list of *uncontested facts* about the crime and the crime scene (i.e., who, what, when, and where), I must make sure these really are uncontested, irrefutable facts (i.e., time-date stamped 9-1-1 calls).

The more uncontested facts of this crime I can share with this witness, the easier she may recall her observations. I have obtained many relevant observations from an eyewitness which did not get into the police report; however, the clarity of their recall was evident years later.

A cooperative witness wants to get it right. He wants to help. The more facts I can share with him, facts about the what, when, and where of the crime, the more energy he can devote to additional recall. He may volunteer an observation which really matters, something which adds to my *what happened* picture.

The downside of sharing much about the crime or crime scene is the possibility that I might hinder this witness with "assumptions" made by the state. If my witness recalls facts in conflict with the state's theory, she may be reluctant to share those facts with me. She may doubt her own memory, she may wonder if she is imagining things. She may be afraid, or just reluctant to offer conflicting facts. I believe most people are comfortable letting the *officials* decide what happened, even if the officials are wrong. Few people want to be the witness who rocks that boat and contradicts *the official version.*

Mentioned earlier, another real danger of sharing information occurs when police influence witnesses with false information or false theories during their initial investigation. This false information may have hindered the witness from telling what he saw or heard during the original investigation, because he knows it contradicted what police were claiming to be true. Contacting that witness years later, I need to be sensitive to that possibility and somehow open my interview to all possibilities. There have been times when I needed to literally ask the witness what he recalls seeing or experiencing firsthand, not what he was told.

The Background Witness ...

In Ricky Kidd's case, my Murder Memo prompted this entry on my Query List:

- Marcus [redacted] (convicted co-defendant to Ricky Kidd) had told police that the last week in Jan. he was staying with a friend, Eugene [redacted], who lived at [redacted] Myrtle, KCMO. It does not appear police ever contacted Eugene [redacted].

A *background witness* might have arrived at the scene soon after the crime, left the crime scene just before the crime, or had some type of personal relationship with an eyewitness, or assailant. A background witness might have some useful information about the crime, or the victim, or about the credibility of a witness. He may recall what a witness shared immediately after the crime or, in this case, what the assailant said and did before and after the crime.

Eugene had come to my attention in 2006. Not until 2007 did I put Eugene on my list of witnesses to locate. Here is my interview report from my initial contact with this background witness in 2009:

Eugene [redacted]

Eugene [redacted] was contacted 5/27/09 and interviewed at his mom's house, [redacted] Drury, KCMO. The home phone for Ms. Dorothy [redacted] (secondary contact# for Eugene [redacted]) is 816- 920-[redacted]. Eugene's cell phone# is 816- 278-[redacted].

After contacting Ms. [redacted] on 5/20/09 and asking to contact her son, Eugene, He called me on Memorial Day and agreed to meet at his mom's house on 5/27/09.

Eugene was at first reluctant to discuss candidly his understanding of events on 2/6/96. He said he still believed that Marcus [redacted] was innocent of his charged crimes. After reviewing the affidavit signed by Marcus [redacted] on 12/8/08, and hearing about the status of the state's case against Ricky Kidd and Marcus [redacted], Eugene appeared to relax and agreed to answer questions about Marcus and the [redacted]

Eugene had been friends with Marcus since high school. They were in the drug business together and were doing well, he said. That business may have included some "Licks" or dope house robberies. No one ever got hurt.

Eugene knew George Bryant, and had been to his house with Marcus and [redacted] and [redacted]. Eugene had known the [redacted] for a long time and was aware that Marcus and [redacted] "were family."

[NOTE: Eugene claims to have gotten out of all illegal business activity in 1997 when his first child was born. He currently works [redacted] and said he has held that job for 10 years. He said he now has 5 children, and at least three of them stay with his mom on Drury (from personal observation). He appears to be a very loving and devoted father.]

Eugene said he and Marcus and [redacted] were at George's house a few weeks before his death, "kicking back." Asked if it was possible he was over there that Saturday, two days before George's death, Eugene thinks it was earlier.

Eugene recalled the time period around George's death, when Marcus came to town. Marcus stayed with Eugene. He recalled that during that time, one morning, about 10 am or 10:30 am, the [redacted] came over to his house on Myrtle and picked up Marcus. Eugene knew they were going to rob someone, but he didn't know who. He knew that Marcus had been pressured by [redacted] to accompany them on this robbery. Eugene was sure that Marcus did not expect this robbery to go any different than any other robbery run by [redacted]; and that no one would get hurt.

Eugene recalled that on that day, [redacted] had a .45 cal handgun, which he said actually belonged to both he and Marcus. He described it as a "military style" weapon which had a gun barrel which could be replaced. He said he never saw that weapon again after that day. Eugene claimed to know that [redacted] had a .38 which belonged to Marcus, and that Marcus left the house with a 9mm which belonged to Marcus.

Sometime later that morning, but before any robbery took place, Eugene said Marcus called him apparently on a cell phone and discussed with Eugene the fact that he was uncomfortable with the robbery that [redacted] had planned. Eugene said Marcus did not tell him who was to be robbed, and Eugene does not know if Marcus knew who was to be robbed. Eugene only knows that Marcus called him and let him know he was having reservations about participating in this robbery. Eugene told Marcus to get out if he wasn't comfortable with the situation.

After Eugene mentioned seeing TV news stories describing the death of George Bryant, Eugene was asked if it was possible that the [redacted] had picked Marcus up from his house on Myrtle earlier that same day, and Eugene acknowledged it was probably the same day.

Eugene speculated that [redacted] was still upset with George for sleeping with [redacted] x-wife, and that this robbery might have been a charade for [redacted] to gain access to George and hurt George.

Eugene could not think of any reason why [redacted] would want to rob George. And Eugene was certain that Marcus would have had no motive to rob George, since George sometime supplied drugs for sale and because George's daughter knew Marcus by face.

Eugene said he spent time with Marcus and took Marcus to the airport later that week. Eugene said he never discussed this robbery or murder with Marcus and Marcus never discussed this crime with Eugene.

[NOTE: It was clear and evident that Eugene knew [redacted] and Marcus had robbed and killed George without any need to discuss details.]

Shown a picture of Ricky Kidd, Eugene immediately recognized Kidd [redacted] This was apparently Eugene's only encounter with Ricky Kidd.

Asked later, and Eugene said he had no knowledge of Ricky Kidd being involved in the robbery or murder of George Bryant or his friend.

Asked repeatedly about his knowledge of what Marcus knew prior to this crime and Eugene was certain that to his knowledge, Marcus did not know who [redacted] wanted to rob that day. Eugene is also certain that Marcus left the house without any intention of robbing George or killing anyone that day. Nor, Eugene said, did Marcus have any reason to expect that anyone was about to get hurt or killed, based on [redacted] history of robbing people but not killing them.

Eugene said he would be willing to discuss what he knows with the attorney representing Ricky Kidd and/or the attorney representing

Marcus [redacted]. He said he would like to be able to help Marcus with his truthful testimony but was willing to testify truthfully either way.

Eugene seemed to understand that Marcus had been wasting his time, thinking he was protecting the [redacted] all this time.

Eugene was made aware that a federal court hearing has been scheduled in this case for 6/22/09. However, he was told that the next step would be contact from one or both of the attorneys, if they thought his testimony was relevant and useful.

DJG

I have had good results approaching a friend, or relative, or acquaintance of a significant fact witness during my habeas investigations.

In Ricky Kidd's case, Eugene was apparently a friend of Marcus, the convicted co-defendant who had signed an affidavit affirming that Ricky Kidd was not involved in the double murder/robbery of George Bryant and Oscar Bridges.

Such a background witness may help measure the credibility of that fact witness. A fact witness might have shared relevant information, tales of police coercion, or threats, or some admission that they testified falsely.

It can be helpful to know the current relationship between a background witness and the eyewitness, in terms of how to approach someone. I may be approaching an ex-wife, or a high school friend, a former college roommate, or a former neighbor. Are they still friends? Are they still in touch?

The dynamics of these relationships – then and now – can help me make a more intelligent approach.

I've learned not to rule out who might be willing to talk to me, based on speculation, or even logic. I have had immediate family (of a witness or co-defendant) give me extremely candid, negative, or incriminating information about their brother or sister, son, or daughter. I have also found lots of family members who will protect their own and offer no useful information as a background witness.

The same goes for the ex-wife, or the ex-boyfriend. Sometimes an ex may offer an honest, candid answer, sometimes not.

Before approaching a background witness, I want to know everything the eyewitness offered the police, the prosecutor, or the trial court.

Without feeding that information to my background witness, I want to learn what he recalls, about what his former girlfriend told him about the crime. If I offer what the witness (ex-girlfriend) told police, the background witness will likely just confirm that version and bid me farewell.

If the background witness can't recall exactly, or is reluctant to "quote" what his friend may have said – "Don't' quote me, but ..." – I'll ask the background witness for his best recall. I'll explain that this is just for background anyway. (And it is.)

If the witness is not sure, or is reluctant to be specific, it may help if I "step down" my question. Based on their reluctance to respond, I may then ask what was their "understanding" about what she knew, or saw, or believed happened (i.e., "Do you remember if she claimed to *recognize* the shooter, or did she claim to *not know* the shooter? What was your *understanding* of what she claimed to know about the crime?").

Since I may be asking this witness to go back ten, even twenty years in time, it is reasonable for a witness to avoid trying to quote a conversation verbatim.

However ...

"Was it your understanding that she was able to identify the shooters?"
"Was it your understanding that she told the police she knew who shot Bruce?"
"Was it your understanding that she personally *knew* the shooter?"

These are all big picture questions. They are important, but very broad. I am asking this witness for something much easier to remember – their understanding of what was said, or her understanding of what happened. That is an easier question to address than asking, "exactly what do you recall Sarah telling you, when she came home that day (17 years earlier)?"

The Interview ... Listening ...

When I approached Eugene in Ricky Kidd's case, all I knew was what I wrote on my Query List. I had no expectations that Eugene would know anything relevant about this crime or Ricky's claim of innocence. What a surprise. Eugene became valuable in corroborating much of what we already knew and hoped to prove.

My interview of Eugene was a perfect example of everything I have learned about conducting interviews and everything I have discussed here. I knew the case so well I was able to have a conversation with Eugene. And I listened.

When I approach a witness with the right mindset and knowledge of the case, the next most important trait is being an *active listener*. I am not there to run down a list of questions. I am there to engage this person in a conversation. A conversation requires active listening. When I hear something that I wasn't expecting, I respond with a question, eventually.

If the witness is a talker, I let him talk, all the way through. I make notes. Then I ask clarifying questions – after he is done. To me, that is listening – active listening.

Some witnesses prefer responding directly to questions. In that case, I walk the witness through the day, or the event, or the time period, in chronological order. I ask open-ended questions as I create a narrative in my mind based on his recall. If the witness allows, I ask my questions in an order, which helps me construct his narrative, like a timeline. All the while, I am actively listening for specific details.

Some witnesses are scattered in their recall, or in the way they retrieve their memories. In those cases, I let the witness get to her recollection any way she wants. It's more important that she relax and feel comfortable while retrieving her memories. It's my job to put her scattered thoughts in order.

I've seen witnesses retrieve their memories like one might retrieve a photo from a pile in a drawer, pulling out one, then another, and then another. There may be no obvious, logical sequence to her recall, only vivid snapshots, retrieved from the top of the pile.

Having asked more than a thousand people to recall an event, I can say, at least anecdotally, we don't all think the same. We are all wired differently. I respect that. I have learned to work with the large variety of witnesses I have encountered.

That is why – before I knock on that stranger's door – I need to know *everything* about the crime, and specifically what this witness reportedly told the police. This is when my complete knowledge of the case is necessary.

This witness may force me to look at physical facts in this case, in a different light. I may contact a witness whose recall fits the physical facts of the crime scene but contradicts the state's theory – thus, the makings of a wrongful conviction.

Knowing the case makes me a better listener. Knowing the case allows me to engage the witness in a conversation. Knowing the case is the difference between a successful interview and a waste of time.

That is my contribution to a successful witness interview.

Along with being an active listener, it is as important that I be careful how I ask my questions. I like to start out with generic queries. It is important to show this witness I am open to him knowing more than was included in his police report or, in some cases, he may know *less* than was included in the police report.

As often as possible, without sharing the facts, I prefer asking, "What do you remember from that day?"

Or, "What first drew your attention to this incident? What did you first hear, or see, which got your attention?"

Some police are good at asking open-ended questions. Other police – by their questions – tell the witness what answers they expect. No surprise, many wrongful convictions involve the latter.

Once we have a starting point (to their recall of this incident), I'll follow up with, "What do you remember doing next? ... What did you hear next? ... See next?"

At the right time, I might ask, "Who else was there? ... Then what?"

I am offering to take this witness by the hand and walk her through that day – if she will let me. But I must consciously keep my questions open ended and not ask any question which anticipates an answer.

The Alibi Witness ...

When contacting an *alibi witness*, I treat the recall of that witness like I'm evaluating a crime scene. All facts recalled about that day are extremely relevant. I want to determine *what happened*, in a universe parallel to the crime.

In Willard O'Neal's wrongful conviction case in Tulsa, students working with the Oklahoma Innocence Project helped confirm Willard's alibi. In his case, the corroboration involved several third-party witnesses, and one cousin. Student Intern, Tiffany Gobble, wrote this report:

Lois [redacted] Interview

Lois [redacted]'s residence
[redacted] N Frankfort Place
Tulsa, OK 74106
(918) 955-[redacted]

Tiffany Gobble and Abby M[redacted] conducted an interview with Lois [redacted]("Lois") at her residence on January 23, 2013 RE: the 2:52 a.m., 12/23/01 shooting murder of Bruce Chamberlain outside the Trapeze Lounge, 3113 S 101st E Ave., Tulsa.

After arriving at Lois [redacted]'s residence, and identifying ourselves, Lois was happy to come on the porch and freely talked to us about O'Neal and the case.

Willard's Alibi

Lois said that on 12/23/01, she had a full house because Christmas was two days away. According to Lois, Bonnie, Bonnie's mother, brother, Lincoln [redacted], Carl [redacted], her, and O'Neal were at her house on December 23, 2001, and they spent Christmas together. Lois confirmed that in Dec. 2001, she lived at [redacted] E 44th St. N., in Tulsa. (approx. 12 miles or a 15 min. drive from Trapeze Lounge).

Lois explained O'Neal asked her to take Bonnie [redacted] ("[redacted]") to work at a strip club across the street from Wal-Mart on Admiral earlier that night (12/22/01). Gobble inquired about why Lois took her to work instead of O'Neal. Lois said O'Neal's car was messed up and he along with Carl and Lincoln were in the driveway trying to fix his front tire. Lois also remembered she had a fridge delivered, and O'Neal helped get the fridge inside the house and installed it for her. Asked, Lois could not remember where she purchased the fridge.

Later that evening, Lois said O'Neal picked Bonnie [redacted] up from work, and they got home around 2:30 a.m. (12/23/01). [redacted] stated O'Neal and Bonnie were fighting at 2:35 a.m. and woke her up. [redacted]'s children were also woken up by the fighting. Lois tended to her children and went back to sleep.

The Case

Lois said two men (Police) later approached both her and Carl. Lois expressed she was never asked to testify and was sent a letter from the Tulsa Police Department saying, "Sorry for the inconvenience." Lois said she was never harassed or threatened. Lois also never heard anything about the statement in reference to Carl's incompetency. Lois stated she would help as much as she could because she does not see O'Neal as a killer.

Miscellaneous

Lois described her relationship with Carl; they had been together for five years and had ended their relationship [redacted]. Lois also stated [redacted]. Lois said their relationship was so serious that she got a tattoo of his name above her breast.

Lois called after the interview to tell OIP that there is a sign-in sheet at Cloud 9, and to look into that to verify that O'Neal was there.

It is my opinion Lois is beneficial to O'Neal's case. Most important, she can verify his alibi. This interview leads the investigation to interviewing the other people in the house that evening further to verify O'Neal's whereabouts at the time of the crime.

With alibi witnesses, I am attempting to document an exculpatory event which the police never attempted to explore at the time of their investigation. In a wrongful conviction, the original defense team probably spent little time investigating the alibi. If the defense even acknowledged the alibi, they may not have committed any resources to corroborate the narrative. At best, the original defense may have put a witness on the stand to testify – without corroboration.

The good news: the alibi witness is generally cooperative. She will often be an acquaintance, a friend, maybe a blood relative. Even if the alibi witness is not related, or not even associated with the defendant, once a person understands the defendant could not have committed the crime while the two were together, they generally agree to engage.

So, the interview of the alibi witness and all the secondary witnesses used to corroborate these facts becomes its very own investigation. I am looking for a story which can be verified or corroborated in any way possible. Proving innocence will require several layers of corroboration.

Defining the alibi and proving the alibi can require creative and resourceful work.

I look at an alibi as being like a latent print found at the scene. Fingerprint experts generally require eight to twelve points of similarity before declaring a latent *match*. Alibis seldom have eight points of corroboration. But the more points of corroboration – like photos, video, phone calls, cellphone records, third-party witnesses, newsworthy events, televised shows/events, professional contacts, official notes, etc. – the better.

Let's say my client claims he was sleeping on his sister's boyfriend's couch at the time of the crime. I probably won't find a smartphone video as corroboration (although I might, and I need to ask all parties). But a neighbor may have seen my client sleeping on the couch at 1 p.m. and again at 3 p.m., so he could have been sleeping on that couch at 2 p.m. Maybe a delivery was made, which can be documented. What if my client was sleeping on that couch while baby-sitting because someone was rushed to the hospital in an emergency, or to give birth. I'll want the medical records.

I am aware, once the state believes my client committed this crime, even video of him sleeping on that couch at the time of the crime will only *help* prove his innocence. But it will be a start.

Looking over the 30 cases of innocence (including acquittals, dismissals, and wrongful convictions) I developed, I found fewer than 20 involved alibis. These alibis were fully developed and added to their innocence claim. However, in none of those cases was the alibi alone enough to gain relief. (In the other cases, an alibi was simply not relevant due to the crime or the defense.)

Each one of those alibi narratives was challenged by the state. Despite strong supporting evidence, physical evidence, documented evidence, anecdotal and witness evidence, each of these alibis was attacked by the Prosecutor as untrustworthy and unreliable. And yet, these were the alibis of defendants eventually acquitted or exonerated.

Here is the affidavit provided to the courts, used to corroborate Willard's alibi, based on that one witness interview (see Figure 10.1).

AFFIDAVIT

State of Texas)
)
)
County of Gregg)

I, Lois [redacted], first being duly sworn, on my oath state the following facts:

In December 2001, I ~~lived~~ stayed at [redacted] East 44th Street North, Tulsa, Ok, 74126. Willard Eugene O'Neal, Bonnie [redacted], and Carl [redacted] also lived with me.

On December 23, 2001, I woke up around 2:30am when Bonnie and Willard got to my house. I remember this evening because it was two days before Christmas. I remember Bonnie and Willard fighting. The argument also woke my children up around 2:35 am.

Two Tulsa police officers approached me one time about Willard O'Neal's alibi on December 23, 2001. I told the police officers Willard arrived at my house around 2:30am after picking up Bonnie from work, and that the couple fought, which woke my children and I up. He did not leave again after arriving.

Willard's defense attorney never spoke to me about his alibi on December 23, 2001. I was never asked to testify at Willard's trial.

I have read this affidavit consisting of 1 page(s) and make this statement of my own free will without promise or threat. Further affiant saith not.

Lois [redacted]
Lois [redacted]

Subscribed and sworn to before me this 17 day of April, 2015.

Notary Public in and for
The State of Texas

NOTARY PUBLIC STATE OF TEXAS
BRANDEN D JOHNSON
My Commission Expires
August 16, 2015

Figure 10.1 A witness affidavit submitted to the courts in Willard O'Neal's habeas case

If the Witness Cannot Remember ...

Unfortunately, not all witnesses are as helpful and cooperative as the witnesses in these examples. Sometimes, a witness may claim they can't remember. I generally prod a little. If the witness remains uncooperative or unable to recall, I remain friendly. I try to determine if their memory lapse is permanent or passing. Do they not want to remember, or are they having a difficult time remembering that event, at this time?

Do I need to do a better job calming the witness? Sometimes, I'll change the subject and ask him about something going on in his life. I think of fear and anxiety as one big wet blanket covering their recall. If I can distract his anxiety, maybe I can help the witness recover some useful memories of the crime hiding under that mental blanket.

I try to gain an understanding of what this witness does recall, try to walk him back in time and see if he can get that memory door open. Exactly what *does* he remember? Does he remember hearing gunshots? How many? Does he recall what he was doing, or where he was standing or sitting when he heard these shots? Does he remember getting up and looking out the window, or did he move to a back room? Of did he just sit there? Did he go outside after the police arrived? Did he talk to anyone while standing outside?

A witness who can't remember the crime might be a witness who needs some assistance. I will ask some open-ended questions, some fact questions, and maybe one random, off-subject query before I determine this witness simply has no recall.

Sometimes, I think I simply wear down some witnesses who claim no memory but eventually *remember*. And I'm pretty sure some witnesses just needed to feel comfortable with me before deciding to share their recall. The more time I spend with a stranger/witness on a cold call, the more time he has to assess me and size me up. He might be measuring my sincerity, or my trustworthiness. Am I who I say I am?

For that reason, I practice patience. I never want to be too quick to write off a potential witness as uncooperative. I must give her a chance to trust me, to know me, to engage with me. I also am a stranger here, asking her about a significant event. Maybe this crime was a life-changing event for this witness, along with the victim, their family, the accused, and all others who wondered whether the state got it right.

For me, to do my part, I may need to muddle through a few "I can't remembers" before I gain the trust of a valuable witness.

Of course, on the flip side of "I can't remember" is the *talker*. Some witnesses really, really want to help. When I meet a talker, I let them talk. I let them run through their narrative at their pace.

As they bounce around from topic to topic, person to person, events out of order, I listen and jot down notes for follow-up questions. I note every person's name, or event, or topic unfamiliar to me and my understanding of the case. These may be important nuggets, or irrelevant tidbits. I will find out later.

Letting the witness talk through the scene at his own pace (I think) helps him relax and work through his memory bank.

I never forget I am asking someone to recall an event 10, maybe 20 years old. I want to give each witness a chance to walk back in time.

Various Witness Types ...

It has always struck me that each person appears to think about significant events, recall these events, commit these events to memory – differently. I've not studied the science of cognitive skills. I am not educated in the ways in which a witness recalls significant memories. Nor am I trained to understand how the brain processes memory and recall. I only know the memory of each witness is relevant to my mission. And my decades of asking indicate we are all unique in that process of recall.

That is why I let each witness "seek their own level," so to speak.

After I introduce a witness to the reason for my visit, some will calmly invite me into their living room, sit down, and politely ask what I would like to know. This witness appears to have an organized thought process. This witness can call up that specific memory, on demand, without anxiety.

Another witness may start blurting out everything he knows, all at once, like a gushing hydrant. After he finishes, maybe gaining some cathartic relief, maybe gaining some calm, he can then handle specific questions about this event and offer answers more calmly.

Some witnesses are reluctant to retrieve the memory I'm requesting. They don't want to get involved, or they don't want to revisit the trauma. For reasons unknown to me, they have closed the door on that memory. By gentle prodding, I may discover this witness was originally disrespected by the police or maybe the defense team. Their narrative surrounding the crime was discounted. They moved on.

It's now my job to find a way to motivate this witness, to re-engage her as a witness. Maybe, simply, I can offer to value her observations and memories.

I may be approaching a potential witness who has never been contacted – *by anybody* – about a crime they witnessed months, years, decades earlier.

Police reports or Defense Team notes may suggest this person was an obvious witness contact, but I could never find a report. Maybe they were interviewed by someone ... maybe not? That is why I am knocking on their door.

After all these years, they would be justified in believing that whatever they know (or knew) is irrelevant. No one ever asked them what they saw or knew. What else should they conclude? That may lead them to believe or claim they don't know anything relevant to the crime. They may feel disrespected by the system. They may even be upset with the legal system which overlooked their knowledge of the case. Or, they may trust the system, and assume the system got it right – without needing them.

I have met witnesses in this category who possessed game-changing information once I convinced them to cooperate with me.

Another take-away is my realization that most people will not go out of their way to share what they know about a crime. They will wait for someone to come and ask them. And they will wait ... and wait ... and wait.

Some witnesses may be reluctant to cooperate for entirely different reasons. Maybe they were friends with the defendant. They believe that what they know about the defendant and the crime only further incriminates their friend, and for that reason they don't want to answer any of my questions. I often explain to reluctant witnesses: "I am interested in both the good news and the bad news."

I may continue, "We (the defense team) are trying to determine what happened. We are looking for all relevant evidence. Evidence of innocence and evidence of guilt. Either way, we want to know what happened."

Note to Reader

That may sound counter-intuitive, considering my role, but please, read on.

That request for "good and bad" often gets a witness to share what they think is incriminating information. It may, in fact, be incriminating. But I've gathered lots of so-called "incriminating information," which was not the least bit incriminating. Ambiguous at best. And sometimes this "incriminating information" led to exculpatory evidence. I never know until I ask. And if I hadn't asked for both the "good and the bad," they would have kept that information from me.

A witness may be reluctant to cooperate because they *believe* the defendant is guilty based on what they heard on the streets or based simply (and justifiably) on the jury's verdict. Some witnesses received false information from the police, who were making false claims about a defendant in an effort to gain incriminating witness evidence.

As previously noted, homicide investigators may lie to a witness, for instance, claiming the defendant's DNA was found at the scene (when it wasn't), just to encourage this witness to share what they know about the suspect's guilt. The Supreme Court thinks it is acceptable for police to lie in order to solve crimes. But the actual result of that practice is the spread of misinformation through the community, eliminating any doubt of a person's alleged involvement.

Or, a witness may not like the defendant and wants to believe he is guilty – no matter what. They are not interested in wasting their time helping his defense team. This witness will tell me they don't want to say anything which might help a guilty man win his freedom.

I've repeated this phrase hundreds of times: "If he is guilty, there is nothing I can do to change that. I live out here too, I have no interest in helping a guilty person get out of prison. But if he didn't do it, he shouldn't be locked up. I'm just trying to find out *what happened*, and I was hoping you could tell me what you recall about that day."

Sometimes, that gets a witness to open up, adding their recall to my understanding of *what happened*.

And it should be no surprise that there are witnesses who claim to know more than they actually know ... way more. They are anxious to tell me everything about this person's guilt. Or maybe they have a lot to share about my client's innocence. They are anxious to share why they are positive he did it, or he didn't do it. But they can only tell me that they *know* these things, *not* why or how they know these things. The witness is reluctant to share specific details or sources. I will still patiently listen to their beliefs, without judgment. I list what they claim to "know."

At the end of the interview, I may find that everything they *know* about my client's innocence, or guilt, is really the sum total of what others told them.

I may still find it useful to go over every detail, every "fact" they claim to know, then identify their sources. It may help.

During the Interview: To Take Notes, or Not to Take Notes ... When and How

At the front door, the first 30 seconds went well. I've introduced myself and explained why I'm standing at her door. ("I'd like to ask you a few questions about that day...")

If I'm invited inside, or asked to sit outside on the porch, or I am given any signal she is willing to talk – I ask my first question.

> **Note to Reader**
>
> Remember, as a student or a novice starting out, I expect there will be two of you.

The witness may start talking while standing in her doorway and never invite me inside. She may or may not offer to step outside. If she just starts talking, I take that as a good sign – a sign she is willing to be interviewed. (I have never asked or expected to be invited inside for an interview.)

If she offers any of those outward signs, I feel it is ok to start taking notes. I never lose eye contact. I never interrupt her, so that I can set up my note-taking process. This is 100 percent her show, on her turf. And I remain hyper-sensitive to her body language. Is she comfortable discussing this incident with a stranger who represents the defendant?

I have asked a few questions, and gotten simple answers. Is she willing to engage in a candid conversation without further prodding from me? Is she willing to offer up everything she knows and remembers, or will there be some limits?

If I detect any apprehension, I wait for a clear signal that the witness is OK discussing this case with me, before I open my notebook to make written notes. If he is a "talker," I let him get very comfortable talking before I consider interrupting with a question or take notes.

But one question I will never (hardly ever) ask is: "Do you mind if I take notes?" That question suddenly makes this interview "official." He might say "Yes, yes I do mind."

If the witness invites me in, sits down with me, and starts talking (by my standards), she has just agreed to be interviewed and have her words documented in some way. (Remember, my introduction at the door explained why I was there and what I wished to do. This is the journalist in me.)

However, if the witness listens to my introduction, continues to stand at the open door, but his body language, or demeanor, says he is not entirely committed to cooperating – I start talking. I may ask a question which he does not answer. I don't wait for an awkward silence to take over. I just keep talking.

He may be asking himself a dozen questions about me, or this case, or who knows what? All I'm trying to do is keep his attention, while I continue a one-sided conversation to avoid him declaring he does not want to talk. Depending on the type of witness he is, I may begin offering what he told police, or offer general doubts about my client's guilt, or some concerns about the investigation. Did this witness know the victim? Did he testify? If he is a background witness, what is his connection to the crime?

At this point, I'm on the verge of tossing out my "Hail Mary question," but not yet. I'm still talking, and he is still standing at the door. This is definitely not a good time to begin taking notes.

I have conducted many 30-minute interviews standing at this partially open front door, with a witness who sends me the signal: "I'll talk to you, but I don't want to get involved." If I start taking notes before he is fully committed to this interview, that act may shut down our conversation.

Meanwhile, we may continue talking about the crime, or the witness. I am trying to get this witness engaged in conversation about whatever he may know.

One trick I've learned, if I'm not writing notes, is for me to verbally repeat any salient points a witness makes, as a way to clarify. By repeating his words, I'm creating a memory for me from which to make my notes later. (I've also learned that repeating his words – his salient observations – signals to him that his words and observations have value.)

If he keeps talking (too much for me to remember later), at some point, when he mentions a person's name, or location, something specific, some information I want to document (a person's age, an address, a phone number), I'll simply open my notebook to write down that specific fact. I *may* ask if he minds if I make a note of that name or some specific fact (because what he just shared with me is important). If I sense this witness is still hesitant (to become involved), I'll make my note, then close my notebook and let him continue.

(As a journalist the witness line: "Don't quote me ..." is not a cliché. It is a valid witness declaration that they will share their information, as long as their identity is not tied to that information. At the end of that interview, I'll ask again what they may be willing to say, "on the record." They might still say, "Nothing.")

If I detect this witness is accepting this interview process, after writing down a name, fact, date, or an address, while still listening to his answer, I start making additional shorthand notes – still maintaining eye contact, and without any interruption.

I have found that the longer a person talks, no matter how hesitant he was when he began, the more comfortable he becomes while talking with me.

The clue that I have crossed that threshold is whether or not this person sees me making notes and continues talking (good sign). If my open notebook causes no hesitation in his speech or thought process, I can then assume my interview request has been accepted.

My ability to make notes, while maintaining eye contact, while engaging in a conversation, while standing on the porch, has improved over time. I don't know if it is a gift or an acquired skill. But I believe those traits are necessary.

The simple reality is that most witnesses are not willing participants in a habeas investigation. These are not necessarily easy interviews with cooperating witnesses. Which is why I prepare the way I have described in the preceding chapters – as a way to engage the witness in the case.

Once I determine this witness is willing to be interviewed, once I see my note-taking won't interrupt her thought process, I'll take more detailed notes, as needed.

If I sense this witness needs to keep talking in order to "stay on task," I will abbreviate my note-taking and keep the conversation – and the questions – flowing. I make notes only when necessary for my retention. While maintaining eye contact, I am ready to write down a specific fact, or quote, or observation (i.e., "I remember her telling us that she had hung out earlier that day with the guys who robbed and killed Bruce").

Any confession or admission requires exact notes and always a follow-up question or simply repeating the admission – for clarification. This is an *active listening* technique.

A successful witness interview happens when I am cognitively engaged in this conversation. I am not just taking notes, listening to words. By actively listening to my witness, I can take fewer notes and retain more of what he is sharing with me.

I know the witness is engaged in this process when I realize he stops talking (a polite pause), waiting for my note-taking to catch up. That is another signal that this stranger has fully agreed to this interview.

When I hear a significant observation – but only after he completes his narrative – I calmly repeat what I thought I had just heard. I may repeat my handwritten notes and ask him to clarify.

"Is that what you heard?" ... or, "Is that what you think she said?" ... or, "Is that your best recollection of what she said?"

He may reply, "No, I remember that's *exactly* what she said. ... She said, she had '*hung out* with the guys who robbed and killed Bruce, earlier the same day.'"

Asking the witness to repeat a significant observation or conversation serves two (maybe three) important purposes. It ensures that I wrote the quote down accurately and I have a reliable, handwritten record. It helps create a better memory for this witness, who not only recalls the initial event but now will recall that he described that event, accurately, to me. And, third, if I have a recorder going in my pocket, and the recorder doesn't pick up the witness clearly, it will always pick up my voice more clearly. If I'm repeating what he said, and the recording picks up the confirmation, that's good. *(I discuss recording the interview later in this chapter.)*

Plenty of times, a witness shows no willingness to cooperate, but for some reason keeps talking. I remain standing at her front door, listening, worried that if I start taking notes, she might sense this contact has just shifted from an informal conversation to a formal interview.

She is undecided. I fear any indication that I'm doing more than just listening and she might stop talking. I still don't know all of what she knows. By concentrating on her words and staying ultra engaged, I can sit down somewhere immediately afterwards and make notes which cover most, if not all, of the observations she just made with her door slightly ajar. Again, using that technique of repeating a significant phrase works in this case – helping me recall the exact comment when I make my notes later.

Obviously, taking notes during an interview is always better. But not if my note-taking shuts down this witness before she has shared everything she knows.

Again, the reality is I am on a fact-finding mission. Gathering facts from reluctant witnesses is just as important as finding a witness willing to co-operate. Facts are facts. This reluctant witness can always be approached later for a more formal interview. Right now, gathering facts is paramount.

A Note-taking Tip

Many years ago, as a newspaper reporter, I learned that the mere exercise of scribbling notes created a good memory of the event, or the interview. I learned this by repeated instances of writing a story on deadline. I'd come in from a crime scene, or witness interview, pull out my reporter's notepad, and lay it next to the keyboard. I would write a 15-paragraph news story straight through without ever glancing at my notes. After writing and editing the draft, I'd check my notes for the accuracy of any quotes. Most of the quotes were accurate from sheer memory. Later, I learned that the brain works like that for many of us. The simple exercise of making notes is a cognitive act, creating an indelible memory.

I wish I had known that in college.

An Interview Tip

The ability to engage in a productive conversation with a witness I have just met, while evaluating that witness, while developing rapport, while recalling facts about the crime, while discerning relevant information, while gaining clarification, while taking notes, while maintaining eye contact ... may be a gift.

But I'm inclined to believe it is a skill which can be learned, over time. It will take practice and effort.

To Record an Interview ... Or Not ... When and How

Note to Reader

I suspect my thoughts here may cause some controversy. I expect my opinions to prompt a discussion. As always, the lead attorney, or the professor, or the legal director, has the final say.

My philosophy on recording interviews began as a reporter in Texas: a surreptitious audio recording is simply an accurate documentation of an interview I openly conducted. I always identified myself, whom I represented, and what information I was seeking. If allowed, I made handwritten notes. The audio recording would back up those notes.

Whenever I decided to use a recorder, I kept it in my pocket. I saw no need to wave a flag proclaiming a recorder was being used. I saw how some people would freeze or "go blank" when the television camera began recording. TV journalists were looking for sound bites – not necessarily the whole story of *what happened*.

I am aware that in some (12) states, it is illegal to record a conversation unless all parties are aware of, and agree to, the recording. Fine. Obey the law. In the other (38) states, where I am allowed to document my personal conversations with accuracy, I consider a recorder in my pocket, when interviewing a witness, to be a useful tool. Those states have so-called *One-Party Consent laws*, allowing any one party to a conversation (me) to make an audio recording of that conversation.

In Missouri – a One-Party Consent state – I am free to surreptitiously record a conversation I have with anyone who agrees to talk to me.

However, the Missouri State Bar Association has an ethics rule proclaiming that no attorney or their agent may secretly record any conversation without all parties' permission. All Missouri Bar attorneys I have worked with have required that I respect that ethics rule, since I work as their agent.

Why Not Ask the Witness for Permission to Record the Interview?

I personally do not think it is a good idea to walk up to a stranger, at their front door, pull out a recorder, and ask them if it's OK to record whatever they are about to say. I don't care how friendly they appear, that recorder will immediately chill the conversation.

That recorder will raise, not lower, the stress level for that witness, whom I am meeting for the first time. That recorder will undermine whatever trust I may have gained up to the point when I pull out that recorder and make that request. And, if the witness is somewhat hesitant about the idea of an interview, I believe that just the mention of that recorder will stop that interview before it starts.

Once a witness is confronted with a recorder and turns down that request, all she is thinking now is whether or not she can trust me. She is no longer thinking about the crime she witnessed 18 years earlier.

What if the Attorney Asks Me to Record the Interview?

Yes, I have conducted a few interviews with strangers while an audio recorder sat on the table, recording.

And each time an attorney made this request, it involved a so-called "friendly" witness.

However, each time I was asked to gain a recorded interview, I conducted the interview first – unrecorded – developing rapport, gaining trust, simply making handwritten notes. I gained his complete knowledge of the facts first, in a less stressful mode.

When it came time to "close the deal," I asked the witness if he would spend a few extra minutes going over what we had just discussed, with a recorder turned on. By then, the witness had shown a willingness to cooperate and was comfortable with the process. I felt he had "dumped all his memories" of the event and had candidly shared every relevant detail he could remember.

So, the recorder at that point was no different from gaining a written declaration or an affidavit – just a different medium.

And, in each of those scenarios, I perceived the witness' anxiety level increase, while they repeated their narrative with the recorder turned on. I sensed that their casual recall was affected, as was their overall candor.

As for *declarations* and *affidavits*, I have used both as written statements and find them much more useful than an audio recording, in court settings.

The written declaration (signed statement without a Notary's affirmation), or an affidavit (a witness statement signed and Notarized), is probably just as easily gained and more practical for the purposes of a habeas petition. Any signed witness statement – if well written – makes for a cleaner exhibit in a court filing than a recording, or its transcript.

Final Interview Tips

- Listening is a lot more important than talking.
- Maintain respect, sincerity, friendliness, and professionalism.
- Gain additional identifiers from this witness and about other witnesses.
- Whenever I am not sure what to ask, I always remember, each witness interview is essentially about: *what happened?*
- Close the deal – request future cooperation, assess their willingness to cooperate in the future (are they willing to testify, sign an affidavit, sign a declaration, speak to the attorney?)
- If they are reluctant, or they refuse to cooperate further, I remain willing to negotiate. I respect their desire to not come forward or their refusal to cooperate further (at this time). I understand they may have valid personal reasons or safety concerns. In that case, I ask for their help in finding others who might know what they know. I will ask, "Help me find another way to get from here to there ..." (Help me find another way to get this evidence before the courts.)
- Make a friend.

Chapter 11

My Work Completed – Now What?

When I was a journalist, at this stage, after my research, records review, and witness interviews, I had a few hours, maybe a few days, to write my story. The satisfaction of that completed – about to be published – story was always palpable. Occasionally, exhilarating.

As a fact finder in a habeas case, it doesn't work that way. The resolution is never immediate. The work, the legal process, and my involvement can drag on, and on, and on.

In Ricky Kidd's case, I was well into my investigation – on my own – before I was able to convince Defense Attorney Sean O'Brien to look at Ricky's claims. I already had a good reputation in the business and had developed a relationship with Sean. But it was my work product, I believe, which convinced Sean that Ricky may well be innocent. The lucky part came when Sean was able to find the time to formally sign on and take the legal case. Sean first presented Ricky's innocence claim in Federal Court (2009), then up the ladder to the U.S. Supreme Court, then back to State Court, then to the Missouri Supreme Court, and back to another State Court, before Sean and others helped Ricky gain relief and his first day of freedom on August 15, 2019.

Ricky has not so jokingly called his legal path, "the long, winding scenic route to freedom."

As mentioned in Chapter 1, I don't see an exoneration as proof that our system works. I had gathered all of the evidence needed to prove Kidd's innocence by 2009. Kidd's release came ten years later.

Looking over my other habeas cases, I see that most of those clients – their actual release from prison – took place four to nine years after I completed my fact-finding. The lone exception, Lamar Johnson, waited 12 years after my fact-finding concluded before he walked out of prison.

But I am not here to discuss the legal system, per se – only my role as the factfinder. In most of my habeas cases, I remained in regular contact with the attorney, working on that defendant's case long after my investigative role ended. She still needed to learn the case of innocence that I developed.

DOI: 10.4324/9781003543299-11

Sometimes the attorney saw a hole in my work, or an element in the state's conviction, which my work product did not address, or did not overcome.

In some habeas cases, we determined a witness I was not able to locate was too critical to ignore. The team agreed that contacting that witness was necessary. "We need to know what he would say, if asked." The attorney was anticipating the state's response to a plea of innocence. I liked that. Sometimes, it felt like completing the first 95 percent of a habeas investigation was relatively *easy*, compared with the final 5 percent of work to be done – the *last mile*.

With Erskine Johnson's wrongful conviction case out of Memphis, that *last mile* involved investigating the source for a palm print, which had been obtained by the St. Louis County Police ID Division and later passed on to the Memphis Police Department.

With Chris Dunn's wrongful conviction, we needed to identify a 12-year-old eyewitness with a common name, whom police reports had not fully identified. I later learned this witness had moved out of Missouri 13 years earlier, right after the crime. Identifying, then locating, then interviewing this witness in a county jail in California became part of that investigation's last mile.

In Ricky Kidd's case, finding and interviewing the background witness (Eugene) became part of the last mile. Eugene's interview represented a huge evidentiary bonus, as I had decided to dot all the "I's" and cross all the "T's" in wrapping up my investigation. Eugene had remained on my list of witnesses whom I thought might know something.

"Leave no stone unturned ..." I've heard so many good lawyers say this, I don't think it needs attribution, just adherence.

One last witness interview (and affidavit) in Faye Jacob's case in Little Rock pushed that investigation over the top. In Willard O'Neal's case, I tracked a key witness who had moved several states away. My unannounced visit and interview provided corroboration we could not find anywhere else. Obtaining documents – actually Brady Material – on our third or fourth formal request in Lamar Johnson's case completed our "last mile" effort. All of these *final steps* either tipped the scale, or greatly reassured the attorney that we had an innocence case that could now be proven in court.

In each of these habeas cases, my work product, my Murder Memo, my People List, sometimes an old To Do List, were critical in assisting me years (sometimes several years) after I had concluded my investigation. I knew I could push a case aside and pick it up on a moment's notice, without losing track of any elements.

So, what have I learned while developing cases of innocence for the wrongfully convicted and the falsely accused? That I have no magic wand. That there is no secretive or magical approach to proving innocence. But the simple steps I have described in these pages – I firmly believe – will work every time. Along with creativity, resourcefulness, objectivity, and tenacity.

Looking back over each of my successful habeas cases (whether they pled out for time served or gained their outright release), I realize every fact I used to develop an innocence claim could be somehow traced back to the original discovery. Everything.

I was recently asked to create a PowerPoint presentation for prosecutors, as a way to advise them on how to avoid wrongful convictions – on their end. I wrote the script and created the program. Fortunately, the presentation was cancelled. Because all I had to tell them was that they already had the answers. Every innocence case I developed grew out of the police and lab reports the prosecutors had originally provided the defense.

And, if all of my innocence cases grew out of the original discovery, that suggests the original defense team also had the answer – pre-trial.

In each case, reviewing the police reports in chronological order, line-by-line, revealed flaws in the state's case. Being objective while discussing the criminal charges with the defendant, and being willing to verify the defendant's narrative, always guided my investigative strategy.

If no flaws were evident in the original raw data (police and lab reports), then there might be missing reports to locate or witness statements to verify. Police reports often identified witnesses who had not been interviewed.

If the case contained bad science, or ambiguous science, normally that could have been resolved pre-trial (by the prosecution or the defense). Misidentifications can be discovered immediately (if an alibi exists). Often, that issue can be handled through additional witness interviews (by the prosecution or the defense). Police misconduct, prosecutorial misconduct, and any suspicions of misconduct could at least be recognized (or suspected) through a close review of the reports and then verified through witness contacts (before trial).

I believe I said this earlier: whenever the defense team takes the state's case at face value without any verification, the entire system breaks down. It has always frustrated me when I find, in my habeas cases, that the proof of innocence I developed was available back before the case ever went to trial.

As confirmation that the road map to proving innocence existed in the original Discovery, I looked at each of my jury acquittals and cases dismissed pre-trial. In each case, I identified elements during my detailed review, which could have easily been missed if I had conducted only a cursory review of the police reports. My raw data review allowed me to identify and interview certain witnesses or led me to verify certain witness interviews. Absent that effort, a wrongful conviction would certainly have occurred.

As important, conducting a candid and objective interview of the defendant always helped guide my investigation, ultimately avoiding another wrongful conviction.

For example: the dismissal of Capital Murder charges in a Kansas City case (*Missouri v. John G. Baker*) occurred in spite of the defendant's signed confession. The raw data supplied in Discovery confirmed that his confession had nothing in common with the crime scene or facts found at the autopsy. The Discovery identified all the critical witnesses needing to be interviewed. My candid interview of the defendant helped me track down and corroborate an alibi (which he had initially offered police), placing him far from the scene of the crime.

And then there is the matter of human error. When asked why the criminal justice system sometimes gets it wrong, I have suggested that the system is composed of humans, and humans make mistakes. But that answer may not be entirely fair to all of us humans.

For instance, I am aware of the protocols in place at hospitals. All, or most, hospitals have created protocols, most involving redundancies, designed to eliminate human error. The reason? My layman's guess is that they grew tired of being named in lawsuits for committing avoidable mistakes.

I do not know where one would begin creating the redundancies and protocols, which might help eliminate wrongful convictions in all of our courts, year after year. But I would love to be part of that conversation.

On the flip side, it also occurs to me that if doctors and nurses and hospitals had the same qualified immunity enjoyed by prosecutors and police, those protocols and redundancies in hospitals may have never been created.

More surprising, certainly more concerning, is the state's official reaction to each and every one of my habeas cases resulting in an exoneration or release. In not one case where the state's theory was proven wrong did the state reopen an investigation into the original crime. In not one case, in which the innocence case we developed included a likely alternate suspect, did the state attempt to investigate that alternate suspect.

I won't bother discussing here, how or why that matters. But it matters on several levels.

And my last lesson learned: every time I determined an individual was innocent of the charges or had been wrongfully convicted – that determination was often based on a specific issue or act, which I did not think could ever happen.

In my first case – *Texas v. Gary Graham* – I realized that a sincere eyewitness with a compelling story could be ignored. A year later, in *Texas v. Leroy P.*,[1] I learned it was possible for police to pressure a teenager into

1 A fictitious name.

lying to a Grand Jury, so they could gain the conviction they thought was correct.

Moving forward, in each case of proven innocence, I learned about a different element or human flaw, or systemic characteristic, which I saw firsthand, "was possible." Each of these elements was represented in what later became recognized as the *contributing factors* of wrongful convictions. I learned it was possible for a false ID to be both malicious and accidental. It was possible a false ID could be coerced, or a false ID could represent a wanton disregard for justice.

I learned that science can be mistaken, and medical reports can be so poorly worded as to be incriminating, rather than simply ambiguous. I learned that science (experts) can make mistakes, and that science (experts) can consciously misrepresent.

I learned it was possible that a police report could be fabricated in order to incriminate or fabricated in such a way as to imply criminal intent.

All along, remaining objective, I understood that these practices were likely the exceptions. Most police reports are accurate; most witness identifications are at least honest efforts; most scientific conclusions are professional and well intentioned; most sets of Discovery include *all* investigative material; most anonymous tips and confidential informants are honest efforts – at least until I learned they weren't.

It's hard for me to believe that what I found to be possible in the 1990s and 2000s was still possible in the 2020s. We have statistics now. We have loud headlines, sometimes weekly, proclaiming an exoneration after decades of incarceration. And we have body cams.

I recently reviewed Discovery from a 2021 criminal case filed in a large urban jurisdiction. This was an alleged assault case.

First I read the police report, which described an interview with an eyewitness. From the police report:

Two officers received this call for an "assault" at the (street location). Upon arrival, the officers encountered (witness) at those cross streets who was following the suspect on a nearby trail. "He just ran east on that trail," said (witness).

(Witness) provided a physical description of this man who was arrested minutes later without incident, while walking on that trail.

Later that afternoon, Officer #2 interviewed (witness), "who stated while walking his dog (in the area) he heard someone screaming from the marsh area (to his south). (Witness) let his dog off the leash and (the dog) ran toward the screaming. (Witness) stated he chased after (his dog) and observed (his dog) jumping on a black male, who fits the description (of the defendant). The male was on top of a white female (later ID'd as the victim), who was screaming, 'Oh God, Oh God, help me he's trying to rape me.' (Witness) observed (suspect) punching (victim) in the face and grabbing her breasts and vagina area."

"(Witness) stated he ran toward (victim) and observed (suspect) grab victim's (cellphone) out of her left front coat pocket and began to run east (on the path). (Witness) stated (suspect) took about ten steps and then dropped the (cellphone) and continued running east ..."

This eyewitness apparently witnessed the assault and identified the assailant.

Months later, the defense received, and I reviewed, the body cam video in Discovery. The recorded video and audio portions were unedited and lengthy.

More than an hour into the audio/video on Officer #2, I listened to a telephone conversation between Officer #2 and (witness). This conversation constituted the witness interview contained in Officer #2's written report described above. The officer was in his patrol car, talking to the witness on speaker phone.

Officer #2 thanks (witness) for his help and assistance and advises the witness that the man he saw has been arrested and placed in jail. The officer asks, "What did you see?"

Witness: So I was uh ... so I got – I got out of my car, I parked on that (road) a little bit down from where you guys – ya know where we – where you guys found her so when I got out of my car, I could hear this weird noise from down in that area – I didn't know what the hell it was. It sounded – it sounded like a bunch of kids screaming or something it was really kind of odd. I'm like, "what the hell would be going on in this sh**y ass weather." So, I'm walking my dogs, I leave them off the leash and I didn't think much of it, and I didn't hear anything and as I'm walking down that path – my dogs running – and she just runs all over the place and she just ran into them. And the next thing I hear – I heard the noise – I heard someone said, "Oh God, Oh God" and then ... which usually to me – I've walked my dogs there a million times and that – it usually means someone is pissed off that my dogs have – you know what I mean?

#2: Yeah.

Witness: So – so then I see the guy walking and she's – I looked back, and I didn't think much of it and she's like "Help me," you know, "He's raping me," or he's assault ... – I think she said he's raping me; I don't know for sure. Umm I'm like "Oh my god, are you serious?" I started walking back and then I saw her you know she had a black eye and a bloody mouth I'm like Holy F**k. So ... then as I call 9-1-1 he – he started walking the opposite direction – he started walking over towards the (building). Just walking – just – just – just like you saw him walking – you know what I mean ....

#2: Yeah.

Witness: ... like there was just nothing going on. And then so I'm like okay I needed – I got her over to the intersection where the street and then I pulled over that woman I don't know if you met her, I just wanted to get her in a warm car.

#2: Yeah.

The witness never saw this "suspect" anywhere near the "victim." The witness never saw the "suspect" touch the "victim" in any way. The witness only saw a black male walking away from the victim.

So, I guess it is still possible that a police report may be grossly inaccurate (implying guilt). And therefore, witness interview reports continue to need verification. Just for starters.

I know when I start my next habeas case, and I am asked to assess an innocence claim, I will approach this new case the same way I approached Ricky Kidd's case, and the dozens that came after. I know it will be necessary to commit an open mind and a great deal of attention to detail.

Case Names and Citations

Missouri v. John G. Baker [Case# CR1996-72069, filed in Jackson Co.] (*)
Defense Attorney: Charles W. Gordon Jr.

Texas v. Odell Barnes Jr. [876 S.W.2d 316 (*Odell Barnes v. Texas*, filed 1994 in Ct of Crim Appeals)]

Missouri v. James W. Boyd III [Case# 7CR199004228 originally filed in 1999 in Clay Co. Sentenced to LWOP.]
[Case# 7CR199004228, re-filed (Alford Plea) October 4, 2004 in Clay Co. Sentenced to ten years.]
Defense Attorney: Cynthia L. Short

Missouri v. Gregory W. Breeden [Case# CR0196-051536F, filed in Boone Co. in change of venue.] (*)
Defense Attorney: Patrick J. Berrigan

Missouri v. Chris Dunn [Original Case# (unknown), filed (1990) in City of St Louis.] (*)
[889 S.W. 2d 65 (1994) Missouri Court of Appeals affirmed Dunn's conviction.]
[17TE-CC00059, Habeas Petition filed (2017) in Texas Co. Judge ruled that despite Dunn's proven innocence, the Judge was legally constrained from granting relief (in 2020).]

[Case# 2422-CC00222, a motion to vacate filed (2024) in the City of St. Louis, Granted.]
[Incl. National Registry of Exonerations.]
Defense Attorney: Booker Thomas Shaw

Oklahoma v. Karl Fontenot [Case# CRF-1984-00183, filed in 1984 in Pontotoc Co.]
[Case# S-2024-205, filed in Oklahoma Ct of Crim. Appeals]
Defense Attorneys: Tiffany R. Murphy, Andrea D. Miller

Texas v. Gary Graham [671 S.W.2d 529 (*Graham v. Texas Crim Appeal*, filed 1984)]
[Case# 03-95-00050-CV (*Gary Graham v. Tx Bd of Pardons & Parole*)]

Arkansas v. Laquanda Jacobs [Case# 60CR-92-682, filed 3/18/1992 in Pulaski Co.]

Missouri v. Lamar A. Johnson [Original Case# 941-3706A, filed in St Louis City.] (*)
[654 S.W. 3d 883 (Mo 2022)]
[Case# 2222-CC09375, motion to vacate filed in City of St Louis.]
[Incl. National Registry of Exonerations.]
Defense Attorney: More than ten lawyers have represented Lamar since I developed his case in 2010.

Tennessee v. Erskine Johnson [762 S.W. 2d 110 (Tenn 1988) (*State v. Johnson* affirmed conviction)]
[Habeas Appeal Case# C.C.A. # 0201-9707-CR-00292, filed in 1997 in the Tenn. Court of Criminal Appeals. Case remanded for resentencing.]
Defense Attorneys: Jonathan I. Blackman, David E. Brodsky (Cleary, Gottlieb, Steen, & Hamilton)

Missouri v. Ricky L. Kidd (& Marcus Merrill)

[Original Case# CF96-2137A, filed in Jackson Co.] (*)

[75 S.W.3d 804 (2002) – Missouri Court of Appeals upholds Kidd's conviction in 2002.]

[Case# 03-00079-CV-W-SOW – Failed Habeas Petition filed (2009) in U.S. District Court, Western Dist. of Mo.]

[Case# 18DK-CC00017, Final Habeas Petition filed in DeKalb County in 2018.]

[Incl. National Registry of Exonerations.]

Defense Attorneys: Cynthia Marie Dodge, Sean D. O'Brian

Oklahoma v. Willard E. O'Neal Jr.

[Case# CR-2002-5639, filed in 2002 in Tulsa Co.]

[Case# 06-CV-0610-CVE-PJC, Failed Appeal to Okl Ct of Cr Appeals]

Defense Attorneys: Tiffany R. Murphy, Andrea D. Miller, Vicki Z. Behenna

Missouri v. Lloyd E. Schlup

Schlup v. Delo, 513 U.S. 298,329 (1995)

[Related Case# CR382-810FX, filed in 1982 in Cole Co.]

[Case# 11R0185000927, filed 1985 in St Charles Co.]

[Case# 25R05970325F, filed 1997 in Pulaski Co. (Change of venue)]

Defense Attorneys: Sean O'Brien, Cynthia L. Short, Christopher E. McGraugh, Joseph L. Green

Missouri v. Leamon White

[Case# 16CR87003928-01, filed 1988 in Jackson Co. Sentenced to Death.]

[Case# 16CR87003928-02, filed March 31, 2006 in Jackson Co. Sentenced to Time served.]

Defense Attorney: Charles W Gordon Jr.

Missouri v. Theodore W. White [Original Case# (unknown), filed in Jackson Co.] (*)

[81 S.W.3d 561 (2002) The Missouri Court of Appeals remands this case to the trial court for a new trial.]

[Incl. National Registry of Exonerations.]

Defense Lawyers: Sean D. O'Brien and others.

Note: (*) In Missouri, court and police records are to be purged and/or sealed following the dismissal of charges or, an acquittal at trial, per the Missouri Sunshine Law (aka: Public Records Laws). I believe this is unique to Missouri and I have always questioned the constitutional logic of automatically purging/sealing court records from public court hearings.

Index

Page numbers in *italics* denote figures.

D

E

K

L

M